DORIS DAY

Sentimental Journey

Garry McGee

McFarland & Company, Inc., Publishers

Jefferson, North Carolina, and London

The present work is a reprint of the illustrated case bound edition of Doris Day: Sentimental Journey, *first published in 2005 by McFarland.*

LIBRARY OF CONGRESS CATALOGUING-IN-PUBLICATION DATA

McGee, Garry, 1966–
Doris Day : sentimental journey / by Garry McGee.
p.   cm.
Filmography: p.
Includes bibliographical references and index.

ISBN 978-0-7864-6107-3

softcover : 50# alkaline paper ∞

1. Day, Doris, 1924–   I. Title.
PN2287.D324M38   2011   791.43'028'092—dc22   2004025789

British Library cataloguing data are available

Front cover: Doris Day, 1968 (*The Movie Market*)

Manufactured in the United States of America

Reprint with corrections

McFarland & Company, Inc., Publishers
Box 611, Jefferson, North Carolina 28640
www.mcfarlandpub.com

DORIS DAY

Table of Contents

I never had the ambition to "be somebody."
I worked because I enjoyed it. There's a big difference, I think.
It wasn't a matter of becoming a "star."
That's nice when it happens; it's kind of the frosting on the cake.
—Doris Day

Preface

❧

DORIS DAY IS NOT my favorite actress, nor is she my favorite singer. But she is one of my favorite entertainers. In the words of actor George Clooney, "There was something about her that was so cool."

My earliest memory of her was when I was very young. I saw her on television—with approximately twenty million other viewers—on *The Doris Day Show* on CBS. She would run down a spiral staircase in the opening and get into all sorts of situations, such as auditioning to be a Go-Go dancer and attending to a full service gas station. She seemed down-to-earth, the type you wanted to have as your neighbor if not in your family, a pretty, funny, smart blonde with a nice figure. Little did I know then that she was pushing 50.

Later, with cable television and video, I saw her films, primarily the comedies that made her the biggest box office actress of all time. I also was able to view Alfred Hitchcock's *The Man Who Knew Too Much*. After seeing her in comedies, I questioned Doris Day in a Hitchcock thriller. She was excellent. As odd as Day in a Hitchcock film may seem, even more so was the fact that this film introduced Day's signature song "Whatever Will Be, Will Be (Qué Será, Será)." In addition, it won an Academy Award.

Day was light years away from arguably her most recognized film, the comedy *Pillow Talk*. The same can be said with her dramas *Love Me or Leave Me* and *Midnight Lace*. She possessed this balance in which she could believably play both dramatic and comedic roles. Then I discovered musicals from early in her film career in which she not only starred, but danced and sang.

Unlike other actresses who, at times, hide true performances under a guise

1

of make-up, wardrobe, and accents, Day's interpretation of each film character she played was different from others. To her credit, Day made more of the material by reaching further in her approach rather than simply reading her lines. Jack Lemmon once remarked Day was an Actors Studio all unto herself. While Day accepted the compliment, she denied there was no method to her acting. She worked on instinct in her acting, much like in her music.

Since the films of Doris Day lifted her to the upper level of success, many have forgotten her work as a singer, where her list of accomplishments rival those she achieved as an actress. Day has had 56 U.S. Top Forty hits and seven million-selling hits including "Sentimental Journey," "Secret Love," and "Everybody Loves a Lover." Day's *Love Me or Leave Me* film soundtrack album sat on the top of album charts for seventeen weeks in 1955. Half a century later, it continues to rank as one of the most successful charting albums of all time.

Through researching, I found practically every medium Doris Day worked in turned to gold: movies, television, recordings, and radio. Few entertainers in the course of the past century achieved the successes Day has: 39 motion pictures, more than 150 television shows, over 500 recordings, countless radio shows, and performing tours of the United States. The wealth of material this one person produced is impressive, especially considering that for the few singer/actors today, one movie a year, one tour every two years, and an album every three is considered exhausting.

I admire how Day handled things that came her way, directly and indirectly: fame as a band singer and then as an actress; personal disappointments with four marriages; near bankruptcy due to negligent handling of her funds by her lawyer and her fight to bring her case to justice; and the devotion to animal rights, which she began in the early 1970s, a time when few noted people campaigned for the welfare of animals. It is a crusade she continues to this day. She wasn't a person easily swayed but remained true to herself and determinedly did what she wanted without taking advantage of others.

The Hollywood Foreign Press gave her its Cecil B. DeMille Award for lifetime achievement in 1989, and in 2004, President George W. Bush awarded Day the Presidential Medal of Freedom, the United States' highest civilian honor. Cited for her cultural contributions and distinguished service to the United States, Bush remarked, "She captured the hearts of Americans while enriching our culture.... Doris Day is one of the greats, and America will always love its sweetheart." He also praised Day for her work on behalf of animals: "It was a good day for our fellow creatures when she gave her good heart to the cause of animal welfare."

Although Day did not attend the White House ceremony, because of her fear of flying, she was surprised at being named a recipient: "My first reaction was 'For what?' I'm not being coy or looking for a laugh. I have never thought about awards, whatever I do." She expressed her appreciation for the citation, however, and added: "I am deeply grateful [to] my country."

Save for the Cecil B. DeMille Award and the Medal of Freedom, Doris Day has not been widely honored for her contributions to the entertainment communities. There is no honorary Grammy Award for her music, no honorary Academy Award for her acting, and no Kennedy Center Honor for her offerings to American culture. The last requires its recipients to attend in person; Day has been offered the honor several times but declined each invitation because of her dislike of travel. The result was that her name was removed from the Kennedy Center Honors list. The same has been said in regard to the American Film Institute.

With the Academy Award, the academy's Board of Governors decides the recipients. Whether Day has been considered for an honorary Oscar is a matter of debate. As for the Grammy Awards, those artists

In the 1940s, Day was labeled "an American beauty with a voice of liquid gold."

chosen for honorary awards are invited to appear by the National Academy of Recording Arts and Sciences, but are not required to attend the ceremony.

Fans are quite angered by these oversights, as are such news media personalities as Liz Smith, Rex Reed, and Roger Ebert. While Doris Day entertained millions from the 1930s through the 1980s, she continues to do so today through the memories of yesterday's film and music—perhaps that in itself is reward enough. The lack of recognition apparently does not bother Day. Working in the entertainment fields was a lifetime ago, and she does not live in the past.

Though Day is no longer an entertainer, this does not mean she is not productive. To the contrary, she says she has been busier in the past several years than when she worked in the entertainment industry. With the establishing of the Doris Day Animal League and the Doris Day Animal Foundation, as well as the maintenance of her large acreage spread in Carmel, California, and the Cyprus Inn Hotel there, which she co-owns, Day jokes that she should make a movie just to have a rest.

This book is divided into four sections: an overview of Doris Day's life and career, followed by specifics on her careers in film, music, and television. It is a compilation meant to pay homage and to bring awareness to the wealth of entertaining one person has provided to people around the world for four generations—and counting.

Recently, MPI Home Video announced *The Doris Day Show* television series will make its DVD debut beginning in spring 2005. The series, which ended its network run in 1973, later aired on the US cable channel CBN in the 1980s, and has appeared only sporadically on local stations since then, has never been released to the mass home market. The series' episodes will be released in chronological order with five sets planned for each season of *The Doris Day Show*.

Complete, uncut versions of all 128 episodes, along with bonus material including interviews with cast members and footage of Day in other programs, will be featured in each set. In addition, Day's television specials, which have not been televised since the 1970s, are also planned for release to the home market. For more information, visit www.MPIHomevideo.com, as well as Doris Day's official website, www.DorisDay.com.

There is also a stage version of Day's 1953 Oscar-winning musical *Calamity Jane* currently in the works. Tony Award–nominated director Randy Skinner will adapt the film to the stage; it is planned to play on Broadway by the end of 2005. While there is a continuing public renaissance celebrating her work, Doris Day recently suffered her greatest private loss with the death of her only child, Terry Melcher.

Melcher, who was close to and worked with Day on several projects, including her television shows and animal organizations, as well as in music such as the album *Love Him!*, found his greatest successes apart from his mother. As a record producer, musician, composer, and singer, he helped form the "California Sound" of the 1960s. Melcher produced The Byrds' number one hits "Turn, Turn, Turn" and "Mr. Tambourine Man," as well as Paul Revere and the Raiders' top-ten songs "Hungry" and "Kicks." He also worked with The Mamas and the Papas, Glen Campbell, Bobby Darin, Randy Newman and Ry Cooder, among many others, and co-wrote and sang background vocals on The Beach Boys' last number one song "Kokomo." Melcher died at the age of 62 on November 19, 2004, after a long battle with cancer.

Doris Day: Sentimental Journey is the result of the work of not one, but several individuals who helped with research, personal collections, and support. These include Pauline Smith, Matt Tunia, Linda L'Heureux, Kathy Martin, the staff at the Margaret Herrick Library in Beverly Hills, Jean Russell-Larson, Joan Kufrin, Jim Suddeth, Pierre Patrick, my parents Gerald and Marian McGee, and the rest of my family and friends.

My thanks to all of you for seeing this book realized.

Garry McGee
Fall 2004

Yesterday and Today:
A Biography

⌁

BANDLEADER BARNEY RAPP heard a distinctive female singer on a Cincinnati radio station one day in 1940. He thought that voice was what he needed to make his band not only stand apart from the countless other big bands of the era, but make it a huge success. He learned the voice belonged to a Doris Kappelhoff and he telephoned her, inviting her to audition with his band. When Doris arrived, Rapp had mixed emotions. She was pretty—"a looker," as they said in those days—but she was younger than he expected. Sixteen years old, in fact.

The audition went well and he hired her. Doris had stage presence, and she could sing. The age issue could be resolved by saying she was really 18. But after a few days of playing with the band, Rapp approached Doris.

"Now about this name...."

"Means something like churchyard," the teenager offered.

"And that's where it belongs."

Rapp explained to Doris she needed a name that would be remembered, one that fit on the marquee, and one that suited her personality. He added that his name was Rappaport before shortening it. Doris Kapps? No. "What's your mother's maiden name?" Rapp asked the teenager. "Doris Welz? Not bad, but not good. Doris Kappel? Definitely not!"

Rapp then thought about song titles. Everyone enjoyed Doris' rendition of "Day After Day" so he suggested Day. "Not crazy about it," she replied. Rapp suggested she think about it because he felt it was just right. "Has a nice fresh sound to it—like the dawn of a new day."

"I'm glad you didn't catch me singing 'Gotterdammerung,'" she joked. But Doris was not terribly fond about the name, feeling it rang artificial. "It sounds like the headliner at the Gaiety Burlesque House," she told her mother. "It sounds like a stripper at a burlesque house—'Doris Day and her Dove Dance' or something like that." But she finally agreed to the new name when she could not think of another and Rapp wanted one immediately. Although Doris Kappelhoff never completely grew to love the name, it was, as Barney Rapp predicted, the dawn of a new day—and one of the most successful entertainment careers of the twentieth century.

"I think that people like 'Doris Day' because she wasn't the typical glamour girl.... I was called 'the girl next door' by people in the industry,'" Doris Day once remarked. "The ladies looked at the screen and thought, 'Ah! If she can make, so can I.' ...And they probably could."

Not quite. Not all of the girls next door can act, dance, sing and possess a seemingly endless supply of optimism. But Doris Day is one of the few successful performers who never gave herself full credit for the talents she possessed and the things she achieved.

To most people, the name Doris Day is synonymous with sunshine and daisies, the quintessential American girl, the girl next door, Miss Goody Two Shoes, the virginal Doris Day. To those who look at the other side of the public persona, Doris Day is a woman of conviction, one who, despite four marriages, personal despair and near-bankruptcy, leads the life she more or less wanted: a quiet existence, keeping house, spending time with her family and close friends, and fighting for causes in which she believes. She ended a still-thriving career in the spotlight to live the life she wanted.

Born to German descendent parents Alma Sophia and Frederick Wilhelm von Kappelhoff, Doris Mary Anne von Kappelhoff arrived on April 3, 1924, in the Cincinnati, Ohio, suburb of Evanston. Doris was the first daughter for the von Kappelhoffs as they had a son, Paul, who was born three years earlier, and another son, Richard, who died at age two, before Doris was born. Doris' father was known as William, and the "von" was eliminated from their surname shortly after Doris' birth, perhaps an attempt to Americanize themselves.

William was a professional teacher of music, including piano, violin and theorizing classical music. While William was an introvert, his wife was quite the opposite. Alma loved parties and preferred popular music, mainly hillbilly music and country-Western songs. She also enjoyed the arts, primarily the theater and movies—so much, in fact, that she named her only daughter after her favorite movie star, Doris Kenyon. Coincidentally, the adult Doris Day later lived a few houses away from her namesake in Beverly Hills, whom she saw on occasion and described as a "beautiful, vibrant, chic lady."

As a child, Doris spent much time playing by herself, inventing games with her dolls and playing house. She was definitely a "mama's girl" although she yearned to gain total acceptance from her father. As a young child, Doris often awoke crying in the middle of the night from nightmares. She ran into her parents' bedroom for reassurance, but William sent her back. "You go back to bed," he'd tell her. "And let's not have no more of this nonsense." Doris would stand in the hall, shaking until her mother quietly went out to comfort her.

The Kappelhoff family lived in a two-family, red brick house at Jonathon and Greenlawn streets, and they attended St. Mark's Catholic Church where William was the parish organist and choir director. The neighborhood was largely German, and festive gatherings were common with beer gardens, music, food, conversation and games.

During a party the Kappelhoffs hosted in their home, Doris overheard her father and her mother's closest friend making love in the room next to her bedroom. She was around eight at the time, and Doris kept her knowledge of the act secret for more than 40 years. She did not denounce her father, but hoped the family would remain intact. In the following weeks, however, the affair became public. Alma was humiliated and William was forced to leave his position in the church. Doris' parents separated.

"He seemed to have very little warmth or affection to Doris, but she seemed … devoted to him," Doris Day biographer A.E. Hotchner said. "On the morning that her father left, Doris hid behind a drape and looked out on the driveway and watched as her father said goodbye to Paul. [He] didn't say goodbye to her and there, with the drape wrapped around her, tears ran down her face."

"It is my nature to forgive," Doris later conveyed, "to try to accentuate what is good, and not to pass judgment. I am often made sorrowful by the disappointments and disillusionments I have suffered in people, but hate or condemnation is not a part of it."

The Kappelhoffs eventually divorced in 1936, despite their Catholic beliefs. Alma and the children moved to nearby suburb College Hill, and she secured a job at Evanston Bakery to support the children. Doris and her brother saw their father on Wednesdays when he took them to his sister's home for dinner. William Kappelhoff remarried soon after the divorce, but his second wife had cancer and died shortly after.

Doris loved performing, and it was clear to her neighbors that she was going to be famous someday. In fact, Doris concentrated so much on studying that an early boyfriend nicknamed her Priscilla Preoccupied. Doris' mother had plans for her daughter to develop herself in the arts. Although some critics would label her a stage mother, Alma Kappelhoff was more supportive of her daughter's talents, rather than a woman driven by greed, pushing her daughter into show business.

"I always felt that she was vicariously having this thrill through me," Doris later admitted. "My mother was an adorable lady and I think that she would have liked performing. When I mentioned this to her, she'd say 'Oh, no. I didn't want you to do it for that reason.' And I'd say, 'Oh, I don't know about that. I think so.' But she never admitted to that." Alma remained her daughter's biggest source of support the remainder of her life, through good times and bad. She was not judgmental, never pushed her daughter into things she personally wanted, and never attempted to focus the spotlight on herself.

After Doris expressed her dislike for piano lessons to her mother, Alma enrolled her in Pep Golden's Dance School when Doris was in kindergarten. Young Doris' debut performance in front of an audience was memorable, but disastrous.

She was set to perform in a minstrel show, and her costume included a red satin skirt. It had been a long evening and by the time she went on stage, Doris had wet her pants. She started reciting amid the barely contained laughter from the audience, then saw her mother in the audience and apologized to her as the tears flowed. "It was devastating, but it stayed with me," Doris said years later and believes that experience may have caused her resistance to perform live. A professional at that young age, she did remember to curtsey to the audience before fleeing the stage.

Alma was not pleased with Doris' progress at the dance school, so she enrolled her at Shuster Martin's to study ballet, elocution, singing and acrobatic dancing. After standing on her hands longer than any other student, Doris won first prize — 25 free lessons at the school. Between school homework, dance lessons and appearing in amateur contests, Doris had little time to develop lasting friendships with children her own age. This was furthered when Alma moved her family from Evanston to College Hill, where Doris enrolled in Our Lady of Angels School.

During one dance competition, Doris noticed a boy tap-dancing on stage. She mentioned to a woman that she thought the boy was "awfully cute." The woman happened to be the boy's mother. She introduced her son, Jerry Dougherty, to Doris, and the two got along so well they decided to try dancing together. In costumes made by Alma, the pair developed a song and dance routine entitled "Clouds" which became such a crowd pleaser that the duo found themselves performing all over Cincinnati at charity and church functions.

Shortly after, in the fall of 1937, the Alms and Doepke department store held a contest for the best dance team in Cincinnati. Doris and Dougherty entered it and, after several months of competing on weekends in a local radio studio against hundreds of other contestants, the pair danced away with the $500 grand prize for their comedy and dance routine "The Funny Little Bird on Nellie's Hat."

That evening, the two families gathered at Alma's home and decided that the youngsters should use the money to go to Hollywood. The mothers would accompany them and the children would study tap dancing under Louis De Pron at the famous Fanchon & Marco dance school. Mr. Dougherty agreed to the idea. While he was finalizing his dairy business, Doris and Jerry continued performing through the winter and spring to earn more money for the trip west.

In July 1937, Alma Kappelhoff drove Doris, Jerry Dougherty and his mother to California. There they rented a small apartment for a month, taking turns as to who slept in the bedroom and who slept in the less comfortable Murphy bed in the living room. The lessons with Louis De Pron were positive, and the instructor sent the promising duo to perform at events in the area.

Alma Kappelhoff remarked in the mid–1950s that Doris almost began her film career while studying at Fanchon & Marco. A person affiliated with Paramount apparently saw Doris and felt she possessed the talent to be in films. The studio was excited with the potential of the teenager, deeming her a "natural." Paramount, however, was not interested in Jerry Dougherty and Doris would not dissolve their partnership. She declined Paramount's offer. "Don't you want to be an actress?" the studio asked her. "Not that much," she replied. "Not if it might hurt someone else."

While Doris dreamed that perhaps someday she would return to Hollywood as another Betty Grable, the realities of the film capital surfaced. The four did not see any movie stars during their month-long stay, although they believed they saw Ginger Rogers' house. At least that is what the map of the movie stars' homes said.

As a result of the encouragement Doris and Jerry received in Hollywood, Alma and Mrs. Dougherty decided to make a permanent move to Hollywood. They returned to Ohio to make arrangements and say their goodbyes. By October, an apartment was rented in Los Angeles and the families were packed for the move.

On Friday, October 13, Doris was at a farewell party given for her and her mother in Hamilton, 25 miles outside of Cincinnati. At the party, Doris received a phone call from her boyfriend Larry Dougherty, Jerry's brother. He was with a couple of mutual friends who wanted to see her before leaving. Larry and Doris, along with Albert Schroeder and Marion Bonehamp, went to a cafe for a short time before returning to the party.

Since it was a cold, rainy night, the windows had fogged over inside the car. Albert was driving slowly with Marion next to him in the front seat. Doris sat behind Albert with Larry in the back seat. Suddenly, they saw a flash of light and were hit twice by a train. There were no lights or signs on the road warning of the railroad crossing. Albert and Marion were pushed into the windshield, but the second impact freed Albert, causing his seat to crash back into Doris, who had already sustained injuries.

There were no fatalities, but Doris was taken to Mercy Hospital and treated for a double compound fracture and shattered bone fragments in her right leg. Doris wondered about her dancing career—when would she dance again? She did not know at the time that the doctors were concerned whether she would ever walk again.

After surgery in which a steel pin was inserted and the fractures corrected, a large cast extending from her thigh to her toes. Doctors were optimistic of a full recovery, but that did not include the ability to dance. The dance team of Doris and Jerry came to an abrupt end, as did Jerry Dougherty's dream of a professional career. He returned to school, as did Doris. She soon quit after the difficulty she entailed in taking three streetcars on crutches, as well as the problems of going through the school to classes and the threat of someone tripping her. Alma stressed that she was to return to school once the leg healed.

While convalescing, Doris slipped on a throw rug and broke her leg again, injuring it more than after the accident. Instead of the initial four-month recovery period, Doris was now required to spend a total of 14 months in a leg cast. The doctors told Alma to keep her daughter busy despite the confinement. Alma brought a ukulele, but Doris' interest in it lasted, as she recalled, about a week.

While confined to her bed, Doris began singing along to songs on the radio. Her favorite singer was Ella Fitzgerald. "There was a quality to her voice that fascinated me," Doris recalled, "and I'd sing along with her, trying to catch the subtle ways she shaded her voice, the casual yet clear way she sang the words." Alma Kappelhoff felt her daughter possessed a beautiful voice and allowed Doris to take voice lessons. She first went to a classical voice teacher—which Doris disliked. Then Alma discovered Grace Raine, a gifted music teacher. To pay for the lessons, Alma took in sewing.

Although Grace Raine was not a singer, she taught Doris the importance of feeling each song's lyrics, and conveying their meaning in an intimate, personal manner. Raine told Doris, "When you sing, don't think of a big audience. Sing into someone's ear—a person. You're acting."

Raine also knew that Doris' family income was limited. But she was so impressed with the potential of her young pupil that she decided to give Doris three lessons for the price of one. "That training helped me immeasurably years later when I became an actress," Doris admitted. Although still in need of her crutches, Doris secured a job earning five dollars a night singing at Charlie Yee's Shanghai Inn, a Chinese restaurant. Through Grace Raine's influence, Doris appeared as a non-paying singing vocalist on *Carlin's Carnival* on Cincinnati's WLW radio.

While her leg mended and she appeared on the radio show, the time spent at home became more tolerable with the company of Tiny, a small black and tan dog who was the family pet. While the family had pets before, this was the first time Doris realized the unfaltering dedication a dog can give its caretaker. For months, Tiny remained by Doris' side, and twice a day she took him outdoors for a walk. Since Tiny was trained and remained by her while she hobbled on her crutches, he went outdoors without a leash (not to mention that a leash could become entangled causing Doris injury). But one day Tiny fled from Doris and into the street. She shouted for him to come back to her but the dog was hit by a vehicle and killed. Doris went into the street and picked her friend up, weeping uncontrollably. "I cried for days," Doris recalled. "My loneliness was intolerable. And so was my guilt."

In 1939, bandleader Barney Rapp was set to open his own nightclub in Cincinnati and needed a girl singer. Rapp heard Doris sing "Day After Day" on *Carlin's Carnival* and felt she would be ideal to sing with his band. Doris auditioned for Rapp (through his suggestion) with "Jeepers Creepers," and was selected over 200 vocalists. She earned a salary of $25 a week, but later learned her salary was actually $50 a week, with the manager pocketing the difference for himself.

Although she was a minor, those who asked were told Doris was 18, in order to legally work in nightclubs. Shortly after, Rapp and his New Englanders were given the opportunity of live radio broadcasts from his club, the Sign of the Drum. Rapp also rechristened Doris (from Kappelhoff to Day) at this time.

Alma drove Doris to Rapp's club for shows and told Doris she'd have to change her clothes at the club so that her dress wouldn't wrinkle. Doris argued there was no place to dress. Alma said she could dress in the ladies room. "So there I'd be in the john," Doris recalled, "and my mother would be saying, 'Do you have your bra?' I'd be so embarrassed."

Rather than have her mother drive her to Rapp's club every night, Doris asked Al Jorden, a trombonist in the band, for rides. Twenty-three at the time, Jorden lived near Doris and he reluctantly agreed to drive her. Although the pair tolerated one another, several weeks passed before Doris found herself in love with the slender musician, and soon after, the two began dating. It was while they were dating that Doris witnessed Jorden's jealousy over her, but she simply shrugged off his developing obsession.

One incident occurred while Doris and Jorden, along with the band's drummer Wilbur Shook and his wife Virginia, were boating on the Ohio River. Jorden gunned the boat maniacally, zooming it past the *Island Queen*, a tourist steamboat that carried 1500 people. Jorden's speedboat capsized, throwing everyone into the river. The group was rescued by Jerry Hurter, who happened to be a Cincinnati *Times Star* reporter. The boating accident became a front page story in the next day's newspaper.

Barney Rapp's nightclub was not a success, so he took his group on a series of one-night gigs. Doris disliked the grueling job, often working until two in the morning. The situation worsened when Rapp took his band on the road playing four one-nighters a week, up to 100 miles from Cincinnati for an appearance. Unlike stars today who travel in comfort, the band rode in an old bus to their dates, sang for six or seven hours, then returned to Cincinnati.

While Al Jorden quit Rapp's band to play for Gene Krupa in New York, Doris learned that Bob Crosby was in need of a female vocalist for his band. Doris cut a recording of "The Wind and the Rain in Your Hair," and a disc of the song was sent to Crosby. Grace Raine and her husband then drove Doris to Chicago for an audition. In front of an audience of teenagers, Doris sang three songs and got the job at $75 a week. Bob Crosby and his Bobcats went on the road and also played New York's Strand Theater on Broadway.

Doris stayed with Crosby for only three months. Shortly after the Strand engagement, Crosby told Doris he could only keep the other girl singer, Bonnie King, who was returning to the group. While Doris performed with Fred Waring for a few weeks, Crosby told band leader Les Brown about Doris. Brown was in the need of a new girl singer for his band, which was about to go on tour. Doris joined Brown in 1940. She kept her same $75 weekly salary, and first appeared with the Les Brown band on the same bill with Gypsy Rose Lee at Mike Todd's Theater Café in Chicago. In 1940 and 1941, Day and Brown recorded several single records; however, none were successful.

Shortly after her seventeenth birthday, Doris informed Brown she was leaving the group. Al Jorden had called and asked Doris to marry him. "It was the happiest time that I could ever have," Doris recalled. "But that's when I stopped my career."

"I'm going to go home to Cincinnati and get married," she told Les Brown.

"You're going to do what?" Brown replied. "You're just getting started!"

"Well, I'm in love. I think."

Brown told her he thought she was making a mistake in marrying Jorden, as did her mother and almost everyone else. Jorden's mother had also voiced her disapproval, telling Doris that her son was not the marrying kind. But their opinions fell on deaf ears.

Jorden was playing with Jimmy Dorsey's band at the Martin Beck Theater in New York, so Alma and Doris drove there. Between shows, Doris and Al Jorden got married at City Hall. Since Jorden's engagement with Dorsey entailed a lengthy period of time in New York, the newlyweds leased an apartment in a run-down building, the Whitby.

"We had a correspondence courtship and it was not good," Doris later said. "I do not recommend it. We got married and we really didn't know each other." When Doris recalled the marriage in 1976 on *The Mike Douglas Show*, guest Steve Allen commented that marriages at 17 years of age are statistically very risky. "Marriages at 40 are risky!" Doris joked. "Had we been together more, I wouldn't have married him."

The marriage took a turn for the worse when she discovered Jorden's unnatural jealousy bordered on pathological. Many times in private and in public, he became hysterical, screaming at her, berating her and becoming physically abusive. One incident occurred two days after the wedding when Doris went to the Strand to meet her husband. There the Dorsey band gave the newlyweds a gift, but something triggered inside Jorden. When the couple returned to their apartment, he beat Doris and falsely accused her of being unfaithful. Jorden calmed down and begged his wife for her forgiveness. Doris did, believing that his outburst was a single incident. But in the next months, she realized this was not the case.

Planning to leave him, Doris discovered she was pregnant. Having no money and too proud to borrow from friends, she decided to wait until her child was born before returning to Cincinnati. At first, her relationship with Jorden appeared to improve, but it returned to more abuse. One day Jorden threatened her and their unborn child's lives while driving a car by holding a loaded gun against Doris. On another occasion, Jorden suggested she have an abortion but Doris refused. He later attempted to perform an abortion himself on her.

When Dorsey booked an engagement in Chicago, Doris and Jorden decided to stop over in Cincinnati to visit family and friends. Although Jorden forbade Doris to mention her pregnancy, Alma could tell her daughter was expecting. Doris confided in her mother, but later in the evening, Jorden accused her of telling everyone. Doris denied it, but it set her husband into a rage. Later that evening while staying at Jorden's parents, Doris was once again beaten until her in-laws demanded that he stop. Mrs. Jorden confronted Doris, who revealed the beatings since their wedding. Mrs. Jorden said that it did not look as if her son hit her very hard. Doris pushed her mother-in-law out of the room and locked the door. Early the next morning, she fled to Alma's. Doris confessed the problems, and while Alma begged her to leave Jorden, Doris instead made a pact that she would return to Cincinnati after the child was born.

While Jorden was playing in Buffalo, Alma traveled to New York to be with Doris, who was close to her due date. Alma tried to telephone Jorden to tell him Doris was in labor, but was unable to make contact. On February 8, 1942, Doris gave birth to a healthy son whom she named Terry after her favorite comic strip, "Terry and the Pirates." When Jorden returned from the gig, Alma discovered a note from a woman enthusing about what fun she had over the previous three days, but wondering what will transpire if she is pregnant. "No wonder I hadn't been able to locate him," Alma thought. She kept the note from Doris, feeling it would only upset her.

The marriage did not improve with Terry's arrival. Jorden did not care for his son and he did not allow Doris to keep him in their bedroom. He continued to rage at her, and again threatened to shoot her. While Alma found a house in Cincinnati for Doris, Jorden decided to return there with her. One final tantrum there prompted Doris to lock her husband out of the house and out of her life. Soon after, she obtained a divorce. "One beautiful thing came out of that marriage, and that was my son," Doris later said. "And if I hadn't married this bird, I wouldn't have my terrific son, Terry. So you see, out of these awful experiences comes something terrific."

In the years that followed, she saw Jorden only once, in a public place where he was with another woman, presumably his wife, Doris thought. In July 1967, Doris read in a newspaper that Jorden died, an apparent suicide.

After performing with Les Brown and Bob Crosby, Doris was in a position to choose any band she wanted to sing with, but did not want to tour or play one-nighters on the road. To help pay expenses, Doris landed a job at Cincinnati's WLW radio station with the short MGM variety show "The Lion's Roar." For 15 minutes five times a week, Doris chatted with the announcer about the latest MGM movies, then sang a song or two with the studio band. She also did a beer-sponsored show on the weekends.

While singing on the radio show "Moon River," a nightly half-hour music program that aired at midnight and broadcast throughout the Midwest, Doris met and became friends with the Williams Brothers, who were also featured on the program. One of the brothers, Andy, went on to a long and distinguished career in music and television.

It was also during a broadcast of "Moon River" that Les Brown heard, quite by accident, Doris singing. He located her and offered Doris a larger salary to rejoin his band. She left Terry in her mother's care and went back on the road singing one-night stands that she despised. But it was a job, it paid better than the radio station, and she liked Brown and got along well with the band members.

The group literally lived out of suitcases, slept on buses while being driven to their next gig, and ate at greasy diners. But this way of life did not affect Doris' appearance, much to the surprise of the band members. "Doris would always come out of the wings, walk to the microphone and look million-dollar gorgeous," says Ted Nash, "and sound just as good as she looked."

Although Doris's appearance was more than acceptable, as was her singing, Brown was concerned about her slightly Southern accent. Doris did not know she had an accent, even though Cincinnati is in the lower part of Ohio. "Les said, 'Doris, you don't sing 'I,' you sing 'Ah,'" Doris recalled. "'I don't!' 'You do.' 'I'm not from the south, why would I say "Ah"?'" Brown played Doris a recording of her singing to prove his point. She was shocked and immediately changed her enunciation.

Les Brown and His Band of Renown appeared in soundies (a precursor to the music video), which were recorded performances of bands playing their songs. While these and the first Day/Brown single recordings were not successful, that soon changed.

"Sentimental Journey"

In late 1944, arranger Ben Homer went to Les Brown with part of a song he was working on. Brown added a bridge to the piece and brought in Bud Greene (who had written "Flat Foot Floogie") to write the lyrics. The result was "Sentimental Journey."

"'Sentimental Journey' was just incredible," Doris recalled. "I remember at the rehearsal ... [Les] gave me the sheet music, and I said 'That's a lovely title.' And he said, 'Wait until you hear it.'" The first time Doris and the band played the song was during a late night rehearsal at the Pennsylvania Hotel in Newark, New Jersey. Doris recalled she felt a "distinct rise in my scalp" at that moment. "I *always* feel a rise in my scalp or on the back of my wrists when something is special," she later explained. The band performed the song to an audience the next night. Shortly after Doris began singing her part, the couples stopped dancing to listen to her and the song. The audience applauded wildly and requested "Sentimental Journey" many times that evening.

The song was recorded and released in January 1945. At that time, the war in Europe was largely finished and victory appeared to be around the corner. "It almost makes me cry because the servicemen, there they were overseas, and they were about to come home," Doris later said. "And the letters starting coming in. That song said so much." (One of the servicemen affected by the song was a young seaman shipping out of San Francisco who later became actor Rock Hudson.)

"I got sick and tired of having to sing the song but I never tired of reading the mail from the servicemen."

"Sentimental Journey" became a huge success, selling more than one million copies and staying at number one on the charts for nine weeks in 1945. Shortly after, the group's "My Dream Are Getting Better All the Time" shot to number one where it stayed for seven weeks, making the Brown-Day combination the most successful music act of 1945. More songs were recorded and subsequently released with a dozen cracking the Top 20.

While with Les Brown's band, Doris noticed one of the group's saxophonists, George Weidler, the younger brother of actress Virginia Weidler. He had replaced the first sax in the band after that musician left to fight in World War II, but found himself relegated to third sax when the musician returned. Weidler quit the group soon after and when he left, Doris went with him. The couple married in Mount Vernon, New York, on March 30, 1946, and moved to Los Angeles where there were more job opportunities. There the newlyweds found themselves living in a trailer on Sepulveda Boulevard due to the housing shortage that occurred in Los Angeles after the War.

Weidler found a job playing in Los Angeles while Doris got a job singing on Bob Sweeny and Hal March's CBS radio show. She earned $89 a week for 13 weeks, but the network dropped her, believing she had no future. Doris also signed as a solo artist with Columbia Records. The company tried to make the ingénue comfortable, and during her first solo session with the label in February 1947, the sextet which backed her included two former musicians from Bob Crosby's band. In June she returned to the recording studio with Frank Comstock, a friend from her tenure with Les Brown. But the releases were not huge sellers.

Doris decided to sign with agent Al Levy for representation. Levy had seen her perform with Les Brown and asked her then to let him represent her, believing she was going to become a star. Doris dismissed the idea and the need for an agent then, but now agreed to allow Levy find her work. This decision led to another plateau in her life.

Levy co-owned the management agency Century Artists with Dick Dorso. Dorso founded Century Artists with a loan from Lew Levy (no relation to Al Levy), manager of the singing group, the Andrews Sisters. As part of the deal, Lew Levy stipulated that Century Artists could represent the Andrews Sisters so that he could get Marty Melcher, the husband of Patty Andrews, "out from under his feet." Lew Levy disliked Marty and felt it was easier to part with the Andrews Sisters than to deal with Marty. Through this deal, Marty Melcher become a second partner in the agency with Dorso.

Al Levy secured a job for Doris singing at Billy Reed's Little Club in New York for two weeks at $150 a week. The gig was a success with Doris singing songs like "Buttermilk Sky," "I Only Have Eyes for You," "Best Man" and "Glocca Morra." *Variety* reviewed her show and noted" ... she'll need a little more zing and change of pace to give her special distinction that really counts for above-par values. Right now she's a shade too 'sweet.' On the other hand, she's more than the adequate ex–band singer." Although Reed wanted to sign Doris for another four weeks, she had a change of heart when she received a call from her husband.

Over the telephone, Weidler said he wanted a divorce because he could see Doris was on her way to stardom, and he did not want to stand in her way. Doris returned to California in an attempt to assure and reconcile with her husband, but Weidler could not be swayed as he did not want to be known as "Mr. Doris Day." Doris took the breakdown of their marriage very hard as she had no warning it was in trouble. The separation took place on April 10, 1947, but Doris did not file for divorce until June 16, 1948. The final decree did not occur until the spring of 1949 when she and her attorney, Jerome Rosenthal, appeared in court and asked for the divorce on grounds of desertion.

After Weidler first confronted Doris regarding divorce, she planned to leave Los Angeles and return to Cincinnati, to her mother and son. While preparing for the move, Al Levy invited her to a party at composer Jule Styne's home in Beverly Hills. Although Doris was in no mood to go to a party, she went. She noticed everyone was invited to sing a song, and Doris hoped she would not be asked. Perhaps this was a bit naive since she was a well-known vocalist. When Doris was asked, she grudgingly sang "Embraceable You."

Styne and his partner Sammy Cahn had just written the songs for an upcoming Warner Bros. movie called *Romance in High C* (which was changed to *Romance on the High Seas*). Both Betty Hutton and Judy Garland were considered for the lead role, but Hutton was pregnant, and Garland was with MGM and the studio wouldn't loan her out to Warner Bros.. Also considered were Lauren Bacall, who turned down the role, and Betty Hutton's sister Marion, a singer with bandleader Glenn Miller. Cahn, however, felt Doris Day, with no acting experience, could work in the role.

An interview was set with the director of the film, Michael Curtiz, who had directed such classics as *Casablanca* and *Mildred Pierce*. Prior to the meeting, Doris and Al Levy met with Sammy Cahn in Curtiz's office for a rehearsal. Doris did not care if she was chosen for the film as she was still upset over the break-up of her marriage and the still-pending plans to return to Ohio weighed on her mind.

She appeared simply dressed, and sang the chorus of "Embraceable You." The combination of the song's lyrics coupled with thoughts of her personal life overcame her, and she began to cry. Levy explained to Cahn about the breakup of Doris' marriage while she left the room to compose herself.

Cahn suggested she sing the happier, peppier tune "Rainy Night in Rio." Doris sang well, but simply stood, unmoving, as she had during her radio and live performances. "Look, Doris, you gotta move

With Les Brown, with whom Day catapulted to the top of the music charts with "Sentimental Journey" and "My Dreams Are Getting Better All the Time," 1947.

around," Cahn remarked, saying Curtiz was looking for someone in the mode of Betty Hutton. Doris allegedly replied, "Betty Hutton moves around because she doesn't sing!" Doris denied she made the remark and attributed it to Al Levy, as she did not speak ill of other performers.

The three then went to see Curtiz. When Doris sang "Embraceable You," Curtiz remarked to Cahn, "This is very good," but when she followed with "Rainy Day in Rio," Doris moved very little. Curtiz walked over, put his hands on her hips and told her to move. After the song, Curtiz was impressed enough to order a screen test. Doris recalls not feeling one way or another about making the test. She went into the makeup department at Warner's the day of the test and eventually fell asleep in the chair while the personnel worked on her. She awoke and disliked what she saw. They had molded her into a Betty Hutton type, with thick makeup to hide her freckles. Doris later referred to the Warner makeup personnel as "embalmers."

For the test, Doris had to sing two songs and memorized three scenes. Again, she had a problem with "Embraceable You" and fell apart. But through the patience of Curtiz, Doris managed to complete the screen test. Curtiz saw she was sensitive, and he felt it was those types who always became the better actresses.

Three tests were later shown to Cahn and Curtiz. In addition to Doris, there were those of Marion Hutton and actress Janis Paige, who eventually played a prominent role in *Romance on the High Seas*. Doris's was the last of the three shown, and Cahn recalled that when Doris' test appeared, "the screen just exploded. There was absolutely no question. A great star was born." Doris was not only offered the role, but a seven-year contract with Warner Bros.. Doris had reservations even when she signed the agreements. She knew nothing about acting and told Curtiz that.

"You're taking a singer and putting her into a top spot in your film—the leading lady," she said to Curtiz. "I haven't studied. I want to study." "I don't want you to study. No, no, no, no, no, no, dahling," Curtiz ordered.

"And I didn't [take acting lessons] because he was the boss and he said no," Doris recalled. "I sometimes think I should have." Doris' lack of both film technique and knowledge of filmmaking was evident on the first day when she appeared at the studio with her luggage packed, believing they were going on a cruise since most of the action in the film takes place on the ocean.

Al Levy moved Doris into a room at the Plaza Hotel, across from the famed Brown Derby restaurant. Every day he took her to the studio for filming *Romance on the High Seas*. Levy's appearances on the set alarmed director Curtiz. At the time, Doris had begun dating co-star Jack Carson but she assured Curtiz that her agent knew about the dating. Curtiz confided to Doris he felt Levy was spying on her. "Al's like a father to me," she told Curtiz. "Maybe you should keep the eyes open," Curtiz suggested.

From then on, Doris began seeing Levy in the hotel lobby hiding behind a newspaper, watching her. Doris did not confront him as it could prove embarrassing to both if her suspicions were false.

After production was completed on the film, Levy secured a job for Doris singing on "Your Hit Parade" with Frank Sinatra. She moved to New York and did the shows for several weeks; however, the American Tobacco Company, who sponsored the show, felt her singing style was too similar to Sinatra's, and she was dropped. She learned Bob Hope was looking for a replacement for Frances Langford, who was leaving Hope's NBC radio show. Les Brown suggested Doris, but Hope was not sure Doris could be a suitable replacement for the popular Langford. Hope waited and contemplated. By the time he decided he wanted Doris, her asking price multiplied ten-fold to $1250 a week when Hope could have gotten her for considerably less.

Hope's concert and radio group required flying from city to city to perform, and with him, Doris was involved in two 15,000–mile tours. Doris developed a lifelong dislike of flying during this tour because of too many close calls in bad weather. But Doris and Hope got along well, with Hope teasing Doris about her full figure. He nicknamed her J.B.—short for "jutt butt"—and would call her J.B. during their set, but the audience never knew about the joke.

After her tenure with Hope, Doris once again felt like going back to Cincinnati. But she had a contract with Warner Bros., and after viewing dailies from *Romance on the High Seas*, the studio decided to groom her for stardom. They weren't the only ones who thought Doris was destined for success. *Film Comment* wrote: "Day is going to be spelled Dough at the box office, from here on out."

Warners put her in the musical *My Dream Is Yours*, again with Jack Carson and director Michael

Publicity shot, 1947 (the Movie Market).

Curtiz. The movie's dream sequence, "Freddie Get Ready," features a dance routine with Doris, Jack Carson and Bugs Bunny with an appearance by Tweety Bird. This scene was almost eliminated before filming occurred due to studio economics, but director Curtiz insisted to Warner Bros. executives that it be included as he felt the film already had a very weak story.

It's a Great Feeling featured cameos by many of Warner Bros.' stars. The film was originally called *Two Guys From Hollywood*, then *Two Guys and a Gal* to follow on the Jack Carson–Dennis Morgan hit films *Two Guys from Milwaukee* and *Two Guys from Texas*. This was the third—and last—Doris Day–Jack Carson film.

Doris appreciated the consideration and patience Michael Curtiz and Jack Carson gave her while she was learning the techniques of film acting. She was also extremely grateful to Al Levy for helping her with the opportunities in Hollywood. Doris asked her lawyer to draw up a new contract with Levy which contained an escalator clause giving Levy up to 25 percent of her earnings as they increased. Levy informed Doris that a new contract was not necessary, but Doris insisted he sign it as it was an expression of gratitude for his believing in her and securing the jobs. Levy signed the agreement.

Shortly after, however, Doris and Al Levy went out together for dinner. She returned to the hotel to pick up a bag in her room as Levy was going to drop her off at a friend's house. But Levy followed Doris into her room. According to Doris,

Levy attempted to rape her, confessing his love. She managed to break free and made it clear she was not romantically interested in him. The attempt ruined their friendship and working relationship.

In 1950, Levy was transferred to New York. He married, had a family and had nothing to do with Doris Day until several years later when Century Artists was sold to MCA. Apparently, the contract Doris made with Levy needed to be closed. While the lawyers told Levy the contract did not "mean anything," they insisted on a signed release from him. Levy countered that if the contract was not valid, the matter should be dropped entirely without his signature. The lawyers insisted that he sign the release.

"All right," Levy said. "I've never asked Doris Day for anything in my life. Fact is, I put more money into her than I ever took out in commissions. So if you give me a check for $3000 signed by Doris—it'll buy a mink coat for my wife." Levy received the check but his wife put the money into their bank account.

Warner Bros.' publicity department attempted to dub Doris "The Golden Tonsil" and "The Tomboy with a Voice" to take advantage of her successful recording career. Her duet "Love Somebody" with Buddy Clark in 1948 was #1 in the U.S. for five weeks, and her rendition of "Bewitched" in 1950 was a huge hit.

When Doris was under contract to Warners, she felt the studio was initially trying to turn her into "the stereotyped blonde bombshell, the very glamorous blonde. I had very little to say about it because in these days you didn't. You were in the stable and you did what you were told and you wore what they designed for you."

Doris' Warner films consisted mainly of musicals, and most of them were healthy moneymakers. *Young Man with a Horn* in 1950 was based on the life of legendary trumpet player Bix Beiderbecke. Dorothy Baker fictionalized Beiderbecke's life story, which was purchased by Warner Bros. in 1945 as a possible vehicle for John Garfield. Five years later the film version was made with Kirk Douglas in the lead. Since co-star Lauren Bacall and Douglas had dated earlier and reacquainted themselves during the production, Doris recalled she had no way to get to know the two actors. The making of the film so reminded Doris of her own experiences with her first husband that many nights after filming she went home depressed.

This was followed by the musical *Tea for Two*, which marked the first of five films Doris made with Gordon MacRae. It also introduced her to Billy DeWolfe, who became a lifelong friend, and later played her nemesis on *The Doris Day Show* on television.

Doris had doubts about the dance routines in the film as she felt rusty, and had not danced since her accident. Miriam Nelson worked with Doris for several hours, days on end until she was satisfied with Doris's dancing. Doris remarked she never worked harder at anything than the dance routines in her films, and *Tea for Two* was the first.

The West Point Story, also in 1950 and another musical, featured Doris in a secondary role. Surprisingly, the film was one of co-star James Cagney's favorite films. "Cornball as hell," he said, "but don't let anyone tell me those songs by Jule Styne and Sammy Cahn aren't worth listening to. They were sure worth dancing to." If nothing else, the film allowed her to work with Cagney, who was one of her favorite actors.

Doris also acted alongside another childhood favorite, Ginger Rogers, in 1951's dramatic film *Storm Warning*. It was daring in its depiction of the Ku Klux Klan, and a departure for Doris Day in her first non-singing role. While Rogers played Doris' older sister, the part was originally slated for Lauren Bacall and it was also offered to Joan Crawford. "Jack Warner asked me to play her sister," Crawford recalled. "I said, 'Come *on*, Jack. No one could ever believe that I would have Doris Day for a sister.'"

Although placed in the Deep South, the film was shot 60 miles north of Los Angeles in the small community of Corona, California. Filming started when the town had its Christmas decorations up for the holidays. Rather than ask the town to remove them, director Stuart Heisler incorporated them into the story, making the setting more eerie.

Doris had already met *Storm Warning* co-star Ronald Reagan through mutual friends; he had been recently divorced from Jane Wyman. Doris and Reagan liked each other and began dating. Two things attracted Reagan to Doris: how much he liked to dance and how much he liked to talk. Doris wrote that Reagan was a very aggressive liberal Democrat at the time, and although he was not political at the time, he had what she called a "political personality—engaging, strong, and very voluble."

She also liked the view from his apartment in the Hollywood Hills, where she was able to see the lights of Los Angeles spread below to the Pacific Ocean. When Reagan later became the President of the United States, Doris was invited to the White House many times. Although she declined because of the traveling distance, she did speak with Reagan on the telephone at times in regard to certain laws and issues concerning animal rights.

Doris followed with 1951's *Lullaby of Broadway*, which contained the most difficult dance routine she was required to perform on film, consisting of a routine up and down a flight of stairs with co-star Gene Nelson. Although it was difficult to turn and spin on the steps, it was made that much more dangerous when Doris was required to wear a full-length, gold lamè dress in the scene. For her efforts, Doris won *Photoplay* magazine's Best Actress of the Year award for this film, and her hometown mayor declared March 28, 1951, as Doris Day's Day when *Lullaby of Broadway* opened in Cincinnati. Doris was also named one of the ten top box office attractions that year—a scant 30-some months since her screen debut.

The period musical piece *On Moonlight Bay* was Warner Bros.' answer to MGM's film *Meet Me in St. Louis*. Not quite on a par with the latter, the film featured Doris, Gordon MacRae, Rosemary DeCamp, Leon Ames, Billy Gray and Mary Wickes and was based on stories by Booth Tarkington. It was a big hit with audiences and was Doris' biggest box office grosser up to that point. Her next film, *Starlift*, in which she played a minor role, was a flop despite featuring some of the biggest names in the Warner stable.

With Al Levy out of Doris' careers, Century Artists agent Marty Melcher was assigned to represent her. Marty was separated from his wife Patty Andrews, and he and Doris began dating. After he obtained a divorce from Andrews, Marty and Doris were married on her twenty-seventh birthday on April 3, 1951, at Burbank City Hall. The newlyweds honeymooned at the Grand Canyon, then Phoenix, and then Palm Springs for a week. After their return to Los Angeles, they moved into a Toluca Lake house they purchased from Martha Raye for $42,000.

"He was her Svengali," a friend remarked. "He divorced [Doris] from the world of business, which she disliked. He loved money. Money was the Big Scoreboard, the way to judge success or failure." Doris concentrated on her careers while giving her husband power of attorney.

In 1952, Marty legally adopted Doris' son, Terry, who was then ten years old. Their relationship was ideal in the beginning. "Terry knew Marty was all right the minute he laid eyes on him," Doris said in 1955. "Kids seem to have an instinct for that sort of thing. Marty is a wonderful father to Terry—and a wonderful husband to me."

Although Doris had been raised a Roman Catholic, she was dismayed with the religious practicing, especially when years earlier she had gone to a priest for guidance and counseling. The priest implied that Terry was illegitimate since she had never married in the church. The priest also insinuated that anyone whose marriage was not blessed in the Catholic Church was living in sin. It was through her second husband George Weidler that Doris had been introduced to Christian Science. When she discussed the religion and its beliefs with Marty (who was an Orthodox Jew), he began reading the works of founder Mary Baker Eddy. Doris and Marty became Christian Scientists and gave up excessive drinking and smoking (Doris was smoking up to three and a half packs of cigarettes a day).

By the end of the year, Doris was earning $2500 a week at Warners and was starring in her own radio show, *The Doris Day Show*. She also had another #1 song on the music charts with "A Guy Is a Guy." She and Marty founded their film company Arwin Productions and the music-related companies Daywin and Artists Music, Inc., which published several of Doris' songs and later songs by several artists including the Beach Boys and Paul Revere and the Raiders. The company held the rights to incidental music from Doris' later films, some of which were later reused in her television series.

In a poll conducted by Armed Forces Radio during the Korean War, Doris was not only named the servicemen's favorite singer, but also "the girl we would like to take a slow boat back to the States with."

Within six years of her first film, Doris had become not only one of Warner Bros. highest earning stars, but the film industry's as well. Her recording career continued to blossom, as did her venture into radio.*

I'll See You in My Dreams (1952) with Danny Thomas as songwriter Gus Kahn was one of the year's top-grossing films, and Doris received the best reviews of her film career to date as the encouraging, driving wife. The next film, *The Winning Team*, based on the life of St. Louis Cardinals baseball pitcher Grover Cleveland Alexander, reunited Doris with Ronald Reagan in the lead role.

Warners then put her in the substandard *April in Paris*. Doris was unhappy with the script and with the choreography in the film. The dance routines were not fresh, well-planned numbers and Doris requested that Miriam and Gene Nelson choreograph the film. Jack Warner turned her down. "The choreography was as banal as the script," Doris said of the finished film.

After reuniting with most of the original cast of *On Moonlight Bay* for its successful sequel, *By the Light of the Silvery Moon*, Doris followed with a musical written especially for her. *Calamity Jane* began when, in 1950, Doris asked the studio to loan her out to MGM which was planning to film *Annie Get Your Gun*. Warner was not about to let their star work for another studio, and so the film was begun with Judy Garland in the lead; due to her inability to perform, Betty Hutton was next given the role. To keep their new star happy, Warner's 1953 production *Calamity Jane* was tailor-made for Doris. It turned out to be a huge hit, Doris' favorite role, and one of her favorite films.

Doris lowered her voice for the part in both her acting and singing because the dailies revealed that when she spoke in her normal voice and yelled at Wild Bill, it sounded "strange, so they asked me to lower my voice."

The song "Secret Love" from the film was released as a single, and it turned out to be a bigger hit than the film.

"Secret Love"

Sammy Fain and Paul Webster were hired to write the songs for *Calamity Jane*. After writing "Secret Love," Fain went to Doris Day's house in Toluca Lake and played the piece for her. "I just about fell apart," Doris recalled after hearing the song for the first time. "I loved the whole score so much I was just dancing around the house."

The arrangement for "Secret Love" was written by Frank Comstock. When

*She had appeared on several programs including One Night Stand *from 1944 to 1945,* Your Hit Parade *in 1947 and* The Bob Hope Show *from 1948 through 1950, and later as an occasional guest. This was followed by* The Doris Day Show, *a radio series which debuted in 1952 as a 25 minute weekly format over the CBS network.*

it came time to do the prerecording, Ray Heindorf, the musical director at Warner Bros., told Doris he would have the musicians rehearsed before she arrived at 1 P.M. That morning Doris did her vocal warm-up at home, then jumped on her bicycle and rode over to Warners since the home in Toluca Lake was only a few minutes from the studio.

When Doris arrived, she was told the orchestra was ready to rehearse with her. Doris suggested they record a take on the first attempt, just to try it. "When I got there, I sang the song with the orchestra for the first time. When I'd finished, Ray called me into the sound booth, grinning from ear to ear, and said, 'That's it. You're never going to do it better.' That was the first and only take we did."

"Secret Love" was another number one million seller for Doris, and won the Academy Award for Best Song. The song cemented her popularity in Great Britain where the single was number one for nine consecutive weeks, a record for a female recording artist that lasted for almost four decades.

At Warner Bros. standing before a backdrop for *Calamity Jane*, 1953.

When Doris was asked to sing the song at the Academy Awards, Doris politely declined. She had sung "It's Magic" at the 1948 Oscar ceremony when it was nominated for Best Song, but in the six years that followed, Doris had experienced a huge change in her life and her career. She was no longer a starlet, but part of the industry. Singing publicly to her industry colleagues— on the industry's most important evening—was too much for her. She did not feel she could sing the song well under the circumstances. "I know I've been accused of being overly sensitive," Doris later said. "When they asked me to sing 'Secret Love' on Academy Awards night, I told them I couldn't—not in front of those people."

As a result, Doris was given the 1953 Sour Apple Award for the most uncooperative actress of the year by the Hollywood Women's Press Club. She was hurt by the "honor," which contributed in part to her experiencing trouble breathing. For weeks, Doris kept to her home, believing she was either dying or experiencing a breakdown. Paranoia set in after she received a prank telephone call from a man who threatened her (in shades of Doris' film *Midnight Lace* a few years later). Doris continued resorting to her Christian Science beliefs and readings in an attempt to heal herself, but the illness had progressed that she finally saw a medical doctor. The doctor concluded she was hyperventilating, caused by overwork and stress. Through a combination of her faith and medical help, Doris was able to overcome her problems.

Publicity shot, 1953 (Jerry Ohlinger's Movie Material Store, Inc.).

When Doris learned she was assigned to appear in 1954's *Lucky Me*, she was dismayed with the script. "There were times when I didn't like scripts that I had to do. But a deal was a deal," she later said. "I felt that it was wrong to go on suspension. My working in a film and being good in a film didn't depend on Jack Warner. [It was] someone much higher. And I just put my trust where it was supposed to be. And I just said, 'I know that nothing's going to hurt me. I will give a hundred percent.'"

Doris, just recovered from a mental breakdown and now contending with a weak script, found it difficult to find energy and enthusiasm in the project although she gave all she could and did not merely walk through her performance. *Lucky Me* was the first musical filmed in CinemaScope, but it was not a hit film, as Doris predicted. The song "I Speak to the Stars" from the film was released as a single and hit the Top 20 on the music charts.

She followed *Lucky Me* with *Young at Heart*, a remake of Warner Bros. 1938 film *Four Daughters*. Doris played Laurie (portrayed by Priscilla Lane in the original), with Frank Sinatra taking the role John Garfield originally played.

"[Frank] had a few problems on the [film]," Doris recalled. "He had something in his head that made him not like Marty, and he did not want Marty on the set. He also had a problem with our director of photography, Charles Lang, and he threw him off the set as a matter of fact. And that sort of caused a lot of friction, although not with me."

In a very unprofessional manner, Sinatra regularly appeared late on the set, hours late sometimes. He refused to allow his character to die at the end of the film, as in the original. He demanded and received a script rewrite in which his character Barney Sloan survived. "We all thought that this was hilarious and he didn't," Doris recalled. "For some reason, he always gets his way."

By 1954, Doris had a yearly income of $500,000. She recorded an average of 12 singles a year, and her annual record sales were approaching the $5,000,000 mark, thanks to such hits as "Secret Love," "I Speak to the Stars" and "If I Give My Heart to You," another number one song.

After 17 films in seven years with Warner Bros., Doris became a free agent in 1955 when her Warners contract expired and she chose not to negotiate a new agreement. In addition, she had not forgotten a business meeting she had with studio head Jack Warner in which she wanted to decline a movie role because the script was subpar. Rather than listen to her reasons, Warner literally tore into Doris, demeaning her for acting as if she knew how to run a studio. Doris left Warner's office humiliated, and promised she would never put herself in that position again; every time she encountered Jack Warner, she would walk away rather than be ridiculed again.

No longer confined to one studio, Doris was given the freedom to choose films she wanted to act in. Her first film as a free agent was *Love Me or Leave Me* at MGM with James Cagney. Doris became the only co-star to have billing above Cagney since he became a star in the 1930s, a testament to her box office power. Doris was paid $150,000 for the film and a guaranteed ten percent of the gross after costs.

It was rumored that MGM had not considered Doris, but it was Cagney who told studio executives to sign her in the role of torch singer Ruth Etting. Doris was thrilled to work with one of her favorite actors again. "There aren't enough accolades for Jimmy Cagney," she said years later. "He was the most professional actor I ever met." Cagney returned the compliment: "Doris Day illustrates my definition of good acting: plant yourself, look the other actor in the eye, and tell him the truth."

Producer Joe Pasternak watched Doris's acting during the film and while on the set. "For all her effervescence and apparent *joie de vivre*, I sometimes have the feeling Doris is busting inside," Pasternak said. "Sure, Doris is a wonderful, wholesome girl, but she *is* complex and she *does* have uncertainties about herself. That's what makes her such a great performer. Simple girls can't act. If she were as uncomplicated as her publicity would lead you to believe, she wouldn't be the tremendous box office draw that she is."

"There was apparently something in [*Love Me or Leave Me*] that reminded her of something she didn't want to be reminded of," Pasternak added. "We could never figure out what it was. But she did it and gave the finest performance of her career."

The film was an all-around success, from critical reviews to box office receipts. It broke several records, including grossing more than $114,000 over one weekend at New York's Radio City Music Hall. After the success of *Love Me or Leave Me*, Doris signed a five-picture contract with MGM for $900,000.

The film was nominated for six Academy Awards, including one for James Cagney as Best Actor. Doris Day, in the pivotal and more demanding role, was not cited. Forty years later, the lack of an Oscar nomination for Doris caused film critic Robert Osbourne to label it "one of Oscar's greatest mysteries."

In her home with third husband Marty Melcher, 1954 (Jerry Ohlinger's Movie Material Store, Inc.).

Music-wise, the *Love Me or Leave Me* soundtrack album was a success story all its own that belonged to Doris. The song "I'll Never Stop Loving You" became a Top 20 hit, and the soundtrack album itself sat at number one for more than four months in the U.S., a record for a female vocalist that stood for almost 40 years.

Billboard magazine reported Doris was voted the most popular singer by radio disc jockeys in a nationwide poll in 1955. She retained the title again the following year, which provoked Charlton Brown to write in *Redbook* magazine that this was "a reassuring verdict in a period when the fads of rock-and-roll and progressive jazz have produced a greater volume of strained and affected vocalizing than could be found in the whole preceding half-century of recorded music."

Even though she was Columbia's biggest female singer, recording sessions tended to be low-key. Doris frequently arrived with doughnuts, and the coffee was always on. This kept the atmosphere calm and helped keep the creative ideas open during recording. Doris liked doing a song in one take because she felt that the first usually sounded spontaneous and fresh.

Doris followed *Love Me or Leave Me* with 1956's *The Man Who Knew Too Much* co-starring James Stewart and directed by the master of suspense, Alfred Hitchcock. Doris had met the director at a party in 1951. Hitchcock complimented her on her acting, specifically in *Storm Warning*. "You can act," he said and added that he hoped to use her in one of his films. Doris was too flabbergasted to say anything more than a thank you to the prestigious director whose films *Notorious*, *Suspicion* and *Rebecca* had firmly established him as a leading director in Hollywood. Five years later, the two were working together.

Filming *The Man Who Knew Too Much* did not start well. For one thing, filming took place on location in Morocco and England rather than Hollywood. Since Doris disliked traveling by air, she, Marty and Terry arrived in New York via train (the Santa Fe Super Chief). They then took the *Queen Elizabeth* across the Atlantic to London. This was followed by a trip to Paris, then to Cannes when the film festival was occurring. Doris felt out of place there with the city swamped with a mixture of American tourists, European and Hollywood film industry personnel, and starlets running around in bikinis looking for photographers (and vice versa).

Doris, Marty and Terry were then driven to Marseilles and took a small boat to Morocco, where she witnessed much poverty and starvation of the people and animals of Tangiers. To her dismay, the situation was worse when she arrived in Marrakech.

Doris did not like North Africa and its local cuisine which she found inedible. She

Publicity shot, 1954 (Jerry Ohlinger's Movie Material Store, Inc.).

also could not bear the mistreatment and malnutrition of animals in the area. In one of the few times in her career, Doris used her clout to have the animals used in the film taken care of and fed. Despite the poor living conditions of the area, the locals who appeared in the film as extras were also properly fed.

The filming was not smooth, unlike most of the director's previous films. Pages from the script were constantly being rewritten. The climate of Morocco contrasted greatly with London, affecting the cast and crew. "It was extremely, and I mean extremely, hot in Marrakech and we were just about fainting every day," Doris recalled. "And it was extremely cold in London and we were just about freezing every day."

The production fell several weeks behind schedule, and Doris felt it was she who was not pleasing Hitchcock. The director called for many takes—up to 30 of a scene—when Doris was used to two or three takes. James Stewart told Doris that was simply Hitchcock's method of working, but she was not assured.

Doris also felt Hitchcock wanted another actress in the role. She privately suggested to Marty that the director should replace her with Grace Kelly, who had starred in Hitchcock's *Dial M for Murder*, *Rear Window* and *To Catch a Thief*. Doris's insecurity continued to manifest as Hitchcock said nothing to her in regard to her acting. Back in Hollywood to film interior scenes, Doris arranged a meeting with Hitchcock. To her surprise, he said everything was fine, just as James Stewart had told her. "I don't direct if you don't need it, my dear."

"Whatever Will Be, Will Be (Qué Será, Será)"

Composer Jay Livingston saw the film *The Barefoot Contessa* and noticed (on a castle wall) a motto cut into the stone: "Che Sarà, Sarà," which means "what will be, will be." He wrote the words down thinking it may make a good song title. With Ray Evans, the two wrote a song.

Shortly after, while Alfred Hitchcock was preparing to film *The Man Who Knew Too Much*, he met with the composers and told the team he wanted Doris Day to sing in the film. Hitchcock explained the storyline and that he wanted a piece that Doris could sing to her little boy.

After the composers left, they immediately knew "Che Sarà, Sarà" would work in the film. They waited a couple weeks before returning to the director with the composition. After playing it to Hitchcock, he replied, "*That's* the kind of song I want."

Livingston and Evans changed the Italian in the title to the very similar Spanish "Qué Será, Será," feeling there would be a wider appeal since there are more Spanish-speaking people in the world. "However, the legal department wouldn't let us use that title," Livingston later said. "So we had to call it 'Whatever Will Be, Will Be,' with 'Qué Será, Será' in parentheses."

Doris, however, did not like the song. She felt it was fine for the film where it was needed, but that it had limited appeal. Everyone else felt it would be a big hit, and Columbia Records asked her to record the song for the record-buying public. She reluctantly recorded it in one take and remarked to a person at the session, "That's the last time you'll ever hear that song." Livingston said that Doris' remark was no reflection on her. "We've all been wrong in picking hits."

"I thought it would make a good record—for children. But I wouldn't buy it," Doris said 40 years later. "I ate those words. Everybody bought it!" Doris eventually learned to love the song and it later appeared in the Day films *Please Don't Eat the Daisies* and *The Glass Bottom Boat*, and as the theme song for *The Doris Day Show*; Doris re-recorded the song in 1964 for her *With a Smile and a Song* album.

The song peaked at number one in Britain and number two in the U.S. where it was another million seller. It also won the Academy Award for Best Song.

While *The Man Who Knew Too Much* was Hitchcock's only remake of a film he previously made (in 1934), the director preferred this 1956 version. "Let's just say that the first version was the work of a talented amateur," Hitchcock said, "and the second was made by a professional."

Despite the remake being another top moneymaker, several critics preferred the original, and dismissed Doris in the new version. *The Man Who Knew Too Much* was later pulled from circulation for several years, along with Hitchcock's *Rear Window*, *The Trouble with Harry*, *Rope* and *Vertigo* because the rights to these films reverted back to the director. After Hitchcock's death, his estate allowed the film's theatrical re-release in the early 1980s before their appearance on videotape. Many critics and feminists reevaluated Doris's performance, with several saying the film was her best.

In 1956, Doris and Marty purchased and moved into a Beverly Hills house on North Crescent Drive. Although small not only by Beverly Hills standards, but by Doris' standing in the film industry, she loved the one-story dwelling and made the house into a home.

Doris also signed a new contract with Columbia Records the same year. It was one of the biggest deals at the time, for $1,050,000. Doris' records become more stylish with each year and her LP records became concept albums. Doris was never a problem. "It was her husband who was sometimes a problem," Mitch Miller recalled. Marty Melcher had a taste for classical music and opera; his knowledge of popular music was nonexistent.

After the financial and critical successes of *Love Me or Leave Me* and *The Man Who Knew Too Much*, Marty signed Doris to star in her third straight dramatic role as the title character in *Julie*. While filming in Carmel, California, she began to hemorrhage heavily. But Marty did not want her to see a doctor, and insisted she overcome her illness through Christian Science. Although she studied intently, the bleeding continued. The day after *Julie* wrapped, Doris decided to forego her religious beliefs and see a gynecologist about the condition. She was immediately admitted to the Glendale Memorial Hospital where a tumor the size of a grapefruit was removed from her intestines. Although the growth was benign, the damage the tumor caused resulted in Doris enduring a full hysterectomy. At age 32, she discovered she wouldn't have another child.

Since *Julie* was an Arwin production, it was decided to hold the film's premiere in Doris' hometown. Doris and Marty took a train to Cincinnati for the festivities, with Governor Frank Lausche proclaiming "Doris Day Week." When the couple arrived, they were met by a mob of friends and fans. In the crowd was Doris' father, whom she had not seen or heard from in many years. She invited him to her hotel suite for a reunion, then later joined him at a bar and grill he purchased and ran in a lower-middle-class neighborhood. William arranged a party for her, and during the course of the fun-filled evening, he introduced his daughter to Luvenia Bennett, a black woman who worked at the bar—and who would soon become Doris' stepmother. "He was very happy, and I met her," Doris said at the time. "She was lovely. What difference does it make [that she was black]?"

Doris saw her father once more a few years later when she was visiting her aunt and uncle. She telephoned her father and invited him over, but the relationship between her relatives and her father were strained, so the visit did not last very long. Luvenia, not invited inside, stayed in the car. Doris stepped outside and waved, regretting she did not invite her inside the house. Although it was not her home to do so, she disliked the racism that was evident among some of her relatives. When her father died a few years later, Doris sent flowers as she never attends funerals, disliking public displays of grief and preferring to keep her emotions and thoughts private.

For the 1957 musical *The Pajama Game*, Doris returned to Warner Bros. for the first time since leaving that studio. Based on the Broadway musical of the same name, it was rumored the film version was to star Frank Sinatra and Patti Page in the leads. Stanley Donen said he had never heard of that combination and thought the original Broadway cast would reprise their roles in the film version.

All but one appeared in the film. The lead female role played on stage by Janis Paige (who was in *Romance on the High Seas*) was played by Doris in the film because the studio felt the musical needed a box office name. As a consolation, Paige later played a Broadway actress in Doris' movie *Please Don't Eat the Daisies*.

"I wanted the original cast to do it," remarked director Donen. "[But] Doris was wonderful: energetic and lovable. It's the best thing she's ever did. I also liked Janis, who was something quite different. She was made of iron in that part. Had you been able to see her in a movie up-close, she would have been so tough that you wouldn't have been able to love her, to think she was vulnerable."

Although unsure of herself joining the already established performers, Doris fit into the role and enjoyed the filming. Unfortunately, during one of the dance scenes, co-star John Raitt accidentally injured one of Doris' ribs.

As with her other musicals, Doris was at times allowed to sing live while the song was being recorded, a procedure she preferred. But it was not done very often as there were difficulties in obtaining a perfect take. For one, there had to be complete silence on the stage while Doris sang so that the hidden microphone wouldn't pick up extraneous sounds. Also, Doris had to wear a concealed microphone as she was being filmed. The microphone could easily rub against her clothing, resulting in a muffled or scratchy sound on the recording.

More often, however, Doris sang along or lip-synched to a previously recorded song. "In the films we used to pre-record and then sing to playback, so as a recording star, I had never done that. But that came easy to me. They used to always call me 'the one-take girl' because I could lip-synch very easily. I'm not bragging, but I usually did [it in one take] because it was easy for me. The main difference that I noticed between recording and the studios was that in the studios they take so much time and I just never felt that I wanted to take all that time, you know? I didn't want it to take three or four hours to do one song."

In *The Pajama Game*, Doris sang "Hey There" live because she felt the recording did not correctly capture the requirements of the scene. She reasoned it would look ridiculous if she were playing the heartbreaking scene while lip-synching to an upbeat recording. This song, however, replaced a scene of Doris singing "The Man Who Invented Love," which was cut from the final film. In 1999, the deleted and rarely viewed scene was released when *The Pajama Game* was reissued on videotape.

On April 8, 1957, Doris's brother Paul died at age 34 of a cerebral hemorrhage. Paul had suffered from a baseball injury from his youth that resulted in several years of medication to ward off seizures. Employed by Doris' publishing company as a record promotion manager, he was well-liked and respected in the industry as a person, not because he was Doris Day's brother. In fact, Sam Weiss said that Paul had done more for Doris' career than Marty Melcher had, and that Marty had continually berated his brother-in-law for not doing enough work. Weiss also claimed that Paul was paid very little for his job but did not complain, and the entire situation was kept from Doris as she adored her brother and probably would have removed Marty from her life had she known.

Paul's death dealt another severe blow to Doris, who would have preferred to take time to recover from her brother's passing, but she was committed to began filming *Teacher's Pet* with Clark Gable. Of the many people Doris Day acted with, all got along well with her—if not on a personal, then on a professional level. Strangely, *Teacher's Pet* co-star Mamie Van Doren was a fan of Doris Day the singer and the actress, but not Doris the person. In her 1987 memoir *Playing the Field*, Van Doren recalls that Doris ignored her when they were introduced and acted like "a spoiled star." She also claimed that both director George Seaton and co-star Gable had to "stoically bear [Doris'] tantrums and disagreeable attitude. Doris' cold attitude toward me never improved, and mercifully we saw little of each other."

Doris learned of Van Doren's claims through her houseman when the book was published. She adamantly denied there were any problems on the set. "She is really not well," Doris said in a taped interview when posed to respond to Van Doren's claims. "This lady is making that up, and that's too bad. I feel sorry for her to say something like that. That is not true. I don't behave like that."

"Everybody Loves a Lover"

While the title song from *Teacher's Pet* became a minor Top 40 hit, Doris' last Top Ten hit on the U.S. music charts was heard during the summer of 1958, "Everybody Loves a Lover." Mitch Miller, who by 1957 was overseeing album projects for Columbia Records, commented that Doris could sing anything on request and that she was "a wonderful artist, a hell of a singer." Miller recalled to writer Ted Fox that he was more concerned with the Columbia artists having their own, singular hits, not just remaking hit songs made popular by other singers.

"The sales department would come and say, 'So-and-so has this hit. Why don't you make it with Doris Day?'" Miller recalled. "I'd say, 'Wait a minute. Let's make something with Doris Day where she'll have the hit, not be chasing somebody.'"

After working on *The Pajama Game* with Richard Adler, Doris told Adler she was looking for a novelty song to record. After Adler returned to New York, he remembered a line his lawyer told him once in conversation: "You know what Shakespeare said. All the world loves a lover." Adler took the line, reworked the wording, and came up with lyrics that became "Everybody Loves a Lover." He met with composer Bob Allen and in a short time the two had a completed song, which they felt was a hit.

Allen took "Everybody Loves a Lover" to Doris, Marty Melcher and Mitch Miller when he went to the West Coast. The trio agreed it was a song Doris should record, but Marty wanted the publishing rights for his and Doris' Artists Music company. Allen would not give up the rights, so Marty turned down the offer. After a few days of thinking it over, Marty gave in and phoned Allen, telling him Doris would record it. The song became one of the first recordings to include a double-track of the lead singer's vocals, in which the listener heard two Doris Days singing on the same recording. "Everybody Loves a Lover" became a solid top ten hit, spending more than three months on the U.S. charts. Doris was also nominated for a Grammy Award for the song.

Also in 1957, Day collaborated on two successful albums with Paul Weston, who had become an A&R man and musical director at Columbia Records. Weston was no stranger to the music scene. He had previously worked at Capitol Records and produced songs for Ella Fitzgerald and Rosemary Clooney, and married singer Jo Stafford in 1952. His first experience with Doris Day dated back to 1951 when she recorded the hit song "(Why Did I Tell You I Was Going To) Shanghai." Weston recalled he truly enjoyed working with Doris and felt she was a better singer than she thought she was.

Weston noted how Doris' voice stood out when she sang. He deliberately styled her songs so that the accompanying instruments never competed with her voice or were too high to prevent her style from coming through. For Doris' recording sessions, Weston usually had a rhythm section, five woodwinds, a dozen strings and eight brass players. When necessary, there were up to eight singers to provide backing vocals.

The long play record, known as LPs or albums, came into popularity in the early 1950s. The record companies divided their singers into singles artists and album artists. The former were labeled as vocalists with immediate appeal, while the latter were regarded to have a broader and lasting allure. Although Doris enjoyed much success with her singles, Columbia considered her an album artist.

Publicity shot, 1958.

The Day-Weston collaboration resulted in two of Doris' most popular and appealing albums, *Day By Day*, which included a compromise of songs requested by Columbia and those Doris wished to record, and *Day By Night*, made up of songs primarily from the 1930s. Both Doris and Weston feel these two albums were the best collections they did, and Weston reported that the ever self-critical Doris was completely satisfied with her performances on *Day By Night*.

The following year Doris released the two-disc set *Hooray for Hollywood*, a 24 song collection comprised of some of the more popular film music tunes. Also in 1958 came the film *The Tunnel of Love*, which marked the first time Gene Kelly directed a film he did not star in. Featuring Doris, Richard Widmark and Gig Young, and based on the play of the same name, *The Tunnel of Love* was not profitable and was partially responsible for Doris Day falling off the list of top film moneymakers.

The comedy *It Happened to Jane* followed in the summer of 1959, teaming Doris with Jack Lemmon. The film began as *That Jane From Maine*, and Doris recorded a song with the same title for use as the film's theme song. At another time, the film was known as *Miss Casy Jones*. In the end, the film was released as *It Happened to Jane* and Doris recorded a different song for the new title. Lemmon hated the new title, and the film became an inexplicable flop in the U.S. In Britain, however, it caught the public's interest and resulted in, according to columnist Hedda Hopper, the "biggest grosser in five years in London with the exception of *Around the World in 80 Days*." The film was later re-released as *Twinkle and Shine* with yet another new theme song. It didn't help, and the film sank into obscurity in the U.S.

By 1959 the film industry concluded that the "Doris Day movie" had lost interest with the U.S. moviegoing public. While the Warner Bros. years consisted mainly of light musicals, the post–Warners years were made up of a mixture of dramas, musicals and light comedies. By the late 1950s, Doris not only dropped from the top box office personalities, but her last five films were not as profitable as previous ones. Then came *Pillow Talk* and what followed were a succession of sophisticated comedies, and a rebirth in Doris' film career. She became the number box office attraction in the United States and for several years was voted the most popular movie star in the world by many Hollywood organizations.

Doris Day went into *Pillow Talk* not in attempt to change her image as has been reported, but because she loved the script. Producer Ross Hunter, however, molded Doris into his vision of interior decorator Jan Morrow. He told Doris, "You have the wildest ass in Hollywood and you've got to show it. Guys want to see it. Girls want to be like you and if you change your image, maybe they will." Hunter hired Jean Louis to design the clothes, Bud Westmore for make up and Larry Germain for hairstyles. "We've got to change this gal," he told the trio. "She is gorgeous. She is stunning. She is something special and the audience doesn't know about it yet."

Rock Hudson, who had previously acted in dramatic films including *Giant* and *Written on the Wind*, had apprehensions of playing comedy. Director Gordon and Doris herself convinced Hudson to sign on. "You don't have to worry about it," Doris told him. "The script is funny. When you have funny lines, you're funny."

"Shooting *Pillow Talk* was like going to a party," Rock Hudson later revealed. "It was a day's work of fun; it wasn't work at all."

The film (co-starring Tony Randall) was a huge hit and Doris was nominated for the Best Actress Academy Award for the first and only time in her career. It was a time when few nominations were given out for comedy performances, especially in the lead actor and actress categories. Although some critics today question why she was nominated for *Pillow Talk*, the reasoning possibly stems from how she had evolved into an actress in the 11 years since her film debut. There is a growth in her performances, and after establishing herself in musicals and dramas, she had now conquered sophisticated comedies, and thus she was honored.

Marty Melcher tried to convince Ross Hunter to change the film's title to *Anyway the Wind Blows*, which happened to be the title of a song Doris had recorded. Hunter was not swayed, but the song was later released and also heard in Doris' next film *Please Don't Eat the Daisies*. The comedy, co-starring David Niven and Janis Paige, was another hit with Doris juggling her Broadway critic husband, their four sons and the sniping of the people around her while redecorating her family's house in the country. The film, based on the best-selling book of the same name by Jean Kerr, allowed Doris to smoothly move from the sophistication of the single working woman in *Pillow Talk* to a domestic, harried housewife, a contrast of versatility mainly overlooked due to the film's comedy genre.

In this stage of her career, all of the films she made were comedies with the exception of one musical (*Jumbo*) and a psychological thriller (*Midnight Lace*).

The role of the paranoid wife in the stylish *Midnight Lace* was perhaps the most difficult for Doris to play in her career. "I wasn't sleeping at night," Doris recalled. "It was very difficult to sustain that because I had to just break down every day, and one dries up. You just don't cry that much. You can't." At one point, production was shut down so that Doris could recover from one of the many hysterical scenes she was required to perform. Cast and crew reproached director David Miller for making Doris stay in a hysterical state for hours, days on end, throughout the filming.

"But thank God, being very positive I decided that I had everything I needed," she later said. She also refused to ever play as intense a role ever again, and Marty Melcher decided Doris would act in only comedic roles from this point on in her career.

Although the Academy bypassed Doris for all of her dramatic film roles in the past, her performance in *Midnight Lace* almost ensured her an Oscar nomination. When the nominees were announced, she was not on the list, nor was another considered shoo-in, Jean Simmons for her evangelist role in *Elmer Gantry*.

"Of course I'm disappointed," Doris told columnist Sidney Skolsky at the time, "but it's not the end of the world." While Elizabeth Taylor walked to the podium to accept the Best Actress Academy Award for the soap opera-like *BUtterfield 8* (an honor which many critics have since considered unworthy in comparison to her other screen performances), Doris was at home with Marty enjoying homemade concoctions from their soda fountain. "It's a rotten shame she didn't even get a nomination," gossip columnist Louella Parsons lamented.

The year 1960 had also been a busy one for Doris in terms of recording. Three albums were released including *Listen to Day*, a Top 30 compilation album which included songs from *Pillow Talk*, *Please Don't Eat the Daisies* and the title song from *Tunnel of Love*. *What Every Girl Should Know* and *Show Time*, featuring her Grammy award-nominated rendition of "The Sound of Music," were followed by two studio albums the following year.

Bright & Shiny, consisting of "happy" songs like "Singin' in the Rain" and "On the Sunny Side of the Street," and *I Have Dreamed* were both issued in 1961. *I Have Dreamed* was comprised of dream-related songs. The title track was from the musical *The King and I*, written by Rodgers and Hammerstein. Composer Richard Rodgers was notorious for being very critical of renditions of his songs. But when he heard the track, he wrote a note to Doris and producer James Harbert telling them he thought it was the most beautiful version of the song he had ever heard.

Nineteen sixty-two saw Doris reteaming with Rock Hudson

With mother Alma, circa 1961 (Jerry Ohlinger's Movie Material Store, Inc.).

and Tony Randall in the comedy film *Lover Come Back*, whose story was in a similar vein as *Pillow Talk*, but added a battle of the sexes in the advertising world. The film resulted in a bigger financial hit than its predecessor. Working on the film was "like a picnic," Rock Hudson recalled. Scenes that should have taken two hours to shoot lasted for two days, including the beach scene in which Doris was to take the lead sexually. "We were lying there in our bathing suits when a stagehand pointed out that my swimsuit wasn't covering all of me. No one laughed harder than Doris," Hudson recalled.

Lover Come Back director Delbert Mann felt that both *Pillow Talk* and this film were not intended to be taken as a serious comedy, nor stories of morality, "but to poke fun at social mores. The assault on Doris' fiercely guarded virginity was where the humor came from."

Doris agreed with Mann's assessment in regard to the social mores remark,

On the set with *Lover Come Back* co-star Rock Hudson.

but did not feel she was playing a virgin. For example, she played a businesswoman who planned to sleep with Hudson without the blessing of marriage. The only reason she didn't succumb to relations was due to the discovery that Hudson's characters in the films had lied to her. "The audience—*you* thought I was a virgin," Day said decades later. "*You* thought when I went off with him, 'Oh, she'll think of some way to wiggle out.'"

Years later, Doris was asked if she noticed the homosexual innuendoes in *Lover Come Back*. She said she had, but thought they were more prominent in *Pillow Talk*. When asked if Hudson was affected by them, she replied, "I don't think so. I didn't see it as such. Nothing was ever talked about, as far as private life. And many, many people would ask me 'Is Rock Hudson really gay?' and I'd say, 'It's something I will not discuss. First of all, I know nothing about his private life, and if I did I wouldn't discuss it.'"

That Touch of Mink (1962) coupled Doris with Cary Grant. Delbert Mann, who had also directed Doris in *Lover Come Back*, noticed a change in the actress. "The toughness I saw in Doris was expressed in her extreme attention to show how she looked, which led to that sort of overgauzed, soft-focus sort of close-up," Mann said. "She was aware of the fact that lines were starting to show, and one can understand that concern, but beyond that she was marvelously witty and gay and fun, and highly professional. I would say she was more popular with the crew than Cary was ... he didn't bring the kind of totally relaxed fun that Rock [Hudson] brought to the set."

Although Doris did not experience the same camaraderie with Grant as she had with most of her leading men, she regarded him as her second favorite actor after James Cagney. She recalled that because of her and the crew's interest in baseball, Grant became a devoted baseball fan after the film.

That Touch of Mink was another blockbuster and set an all-time record for being the first

Publicity shot, circa 1963 (the Movie Market).

film to gross $1 million at a single theater, Radio Music Hall in New York City, where it earned $2 million in its ten-week run.

Doris returned to the musical genre with MGM's big budget *Jumbo* with Jimmy Durante, Stephen Boyd and Martha Raye. This was Doris' first musical film in five years (and the last of her career), and she did some of the circus stunts required by the role. The film received decent reviews, but was a box office flop. Perhaps one reason for its lackluster performance can be the audience expectations of a Doris Day film. *Jumbo* was not only a musical but a period piece. It had been several years since Doris had done both genres and it was a far cry from the contemporary films she has been making.

Although *Jumbo*'s disappointment was not directly aimed at Doris, there were professional repercussions. MGM decided against casting Doris in the musical *The Unsinkable Mollie Brown*, giving the role to Debbie Reynolds, and it allegedly cost Doris the coveted role of Maria in Twentieth Century-Fox's film version of *The Sound of Music*.

Her recording career was just as full as her film career in 1962. Four albums were released including the soundtrack to *Jumbo* which also featured the film's cast; the inspirational *You'll Never Walk Alone*, comprised entirely of hymns; the belated *Doris Day's Greatest Hits*; and *Duet*, which successfully teamed Doris with André Previn and the André Previn Trio for a minimal jazz album that surprised critics who had not thought Doris would attempt this genre.

In regard to *Duet*, James Harbert was instrumental in bringing the two talents together. He knew Doris was beginning to dislike working with a full orchestra. He also knew Previn admired Doris. With only a piano, a bass, drums and Doris' voice, the simplicity and intimacy of the collection resulted in it becoming one of Doris's personal favorites. Years later when a track from the set was played on the radio, Tony Randall heard the song and rushed out to purchase the *Duet* album. When he couldn't locate one, he contacted Doris for a copy, and told her, "I didn't know you could sing such great jazz!"

The pairing of the versatile vocalist with the classical pianist brought another idea to Harbert. He proposed to make an album of Doris singing opera, but the heads at Columbia vetoed the idea. Harbert wished they had at least made a preliminary recording. "She sang Mozart like a dream," he recalled years later. "Absolutely charming!"

The Day-Melcher combination was a leading force in Hollywood, and the couple was perceived as one of the town's wealthiest couples. But they did not flaunt their wealth. They lived modestly by Hollywood standards, and rather than be seen at the "in" restaurants (Chasen's, the Bistro, etc.), Doris and Marty favored such places as the kosher Nate-N-Al Delicatessen.

As Doris' business partner, Marty commanded a co-producer title on several of her films, as well as a $50,000 to $150,000 fee per film for himself. Many of Doris' film producers stated that Marty simply took his fee and never did any work. In addition, the duo held music publishing and film production companies, and a merchandising firm to market Doris Day dresses and cosmetics. The relationship evolved from a marriage into a business partnership. Doris was the president, Marty the treasurer.

While her film and music careers continued to spiral upward, her personal life was becoming more and more unstable. Marty and Terry's relationship was changing. "When I was younger we had a kind of an easy, fun relationship," Terry recalls. "As I got older things appeared to become more complicated. I don't know exactly why. I think his life became more complicated."

In a heated argument, Marty struck Terry. Doris ordered her husband out of the house, and on November 30, 1962, Marty and Doris separated. At the time, Doris was starring in and Marty was co-producing *The Thrill of It All*. Despite the personal problems between the couple, business continued and filming went uninterrupted.

Since their wedding, Marty was continually involved in Doris' projects, which led several gossips saying he took advantage of her fame to make a name for himself. Of course, both he and Doris heard the whispers, but while Doris ignored them, Marty became angry.

During the separation, Marty decided to venture out *sans* Doris with a play he produced called *The Perfect Set-Up*. It folded after one performance on Broadway. Did he realize he could not professionally succeed without his wife? Or had he tried too hard, too quickly, to establish himself, only to be disappointed? Whatever private reasons he may have had at the time were only known to Marty.

Jerome Rosenthal informed Marty that the dissolution of the Melcher-Day marriage and businesses would lead to financial ruin. Marty returned to California in hopes for a reconciliation. He explained to Doris that they could not divorce because of the complicated investments that he and Rosenthal had made.

Although Doris did not involve herself in business matters, there was a recent episode that alerted her there may be something wrong. "She wanted to buy a $600 painting," Edie Adams, who co-starred in *Lover Come Back*, recalled. "Now this woman was one of the top money earners, and she went to this business manager, and he said, oh no, she couldn't afford it. I think that was the first clue that she had that there was something wrong with her business dealings." Doris earned $3 million in 1962 alone.

Doris somewhat understood the dilemma to which Marty referred, regarding their finances. Their money was heavily invested in different areas including oil, cattle and land, and there were complexities involving their production and music publishing ventures, as well as tax shelters. Dissolving the marriage would result in a massive loss on the fortune they built.

After meeting with Rosenthal, Doris told Marty she'd agree to a reconciliation, but on her terms. They were to remain married in name only, with the understanding each would be discreet with other people. Although Marty did have affairs (including, allegedly, Angie Dickinson and Raquel Welch), it has been rumored that Doris did the same with Lakers player Elgin Baylor, Dodgers shortstop Maury Wills, Glen Campbell, Jerry West, Pancho Gonzales, Frank Sinatra "and would you believe it—Jimmy Hoffa!" Doris later said. "Some of the best fiction of the '60s was written about my amorous adventures with an assortment of lovers who could have only been chosen by a berserk random sampler. I was Lady Bountiful of the Sheets."

One alleged affair was with singer Sly Stone and the rumor was reported in *Time* magazine. The truth was Stone knew Terry Melcher and heard that he or Doris had an old car. Stone wanted to see it, so one afternoon he went to Doris'. When they were introduced, Stone told Doris how much he liked her song "Whatever Will Be, Will Be." "The two sat down together at the piano and sang it," recalls Steve Paley, Stone's friend and his A&R man at Epic Records, which was owned by Columbia. "And that was it. [The item] was just grist for the rumor mills, and the rumor spread just like a poison ivy. I also heard that Doris Day was not amused by the rumor, by the way."

During one of her films, Doris fended off a romantic pass by a married actor. She turned off her subtle sexuality and began acting and talking like a little girl. The actor wasn't amused or interested in her after that.

Marty and Doris lived a comfortable existence together but without the physical love they had in the early years of their marriage. They regularly attended Los Angeles Dodgers baseball games and Lakers basketball games together, and continued to entertain small groups of friends, but only on occasion. "You're invited to dinner at their house," designer Irene recalled, "and generally there's another couple there—maybe Audrey Hepburn and Mel Ferrer. There are no cocktails. It's carrot juice at 5:45, dinner at 6, dessert from Doris' soda fountain—where the bar used to be—at 6:45, a movie shown on their living room screen at 7, and home to bed at 9."

The Thrill of It All almost became the third Hudson-Day film, but Rock Hudson turned down the role. James Garner was cast instead, and he became one of Doris' favorite leading men. Thirty years later, Doris said if she made another film, she would like to make it with Garner.

"She didn't try to play sexy, but she is. She turns me on, or she couldn't have

Publicity shot, 1963.

been the star she was if she didn't turn men on," Garner believes. "And I don't think she was quite aware of it all." Garner felt Doris simply thought of herself as a freckle-faced, pretty blond who could sing.

Her next film that year was also with James Garner. *Move Over, Darling* was a remake of the 1940 Leo McCarey film *My Favorite Wife*, that had starred Cary Grant and Irene Dunne. The remake was originally in production in 1962 with Marilyn Monroe and Dean Martin under the title *Something's Got to Give*. Difficulties between director George Cukor, Monroe and the Fox head office resulted in the firing of Monroe and the film was shut down. Shortly after, Monroe died.

A new director and cast was assembled, and the *Something's Got to Give* script was rewritten to suit the talents of Doris Day and James Garner. Despite the previous difficulties with getting *My Favorite Wife* remade, the final result was another box office hit. The Day-Garner version, however, did not proceed without a few problems in production.

While shooting the confrontation scene in the bedroom with Garner, Doris suffered a couple cracked ribs when the 200-lb. Garner picked up the 125-lb. co-star a little too enthusiastically. Doris didn't say anything about the incident to Garner, and made the rest of the film with her ribs wrapped in adhesive tape. Garner later learned what happened and although it was an accident, he felt terrible. He still does to this day.

The title song from the film was sung by Doris and released as a single. It hit the Top Ten in the U.K., despite being banned there because of its "suggestive" lyrics. "Move Over, Darling" was co-written and produced by Terry Melcher. By this time Terry was a successful songwriter and record producer, with hits by the Beach Boys and the Byrds. He also produced his mother's 1964 charting album *Love Him!* which is perhaps the first time a son produced his mother's music. The *Love Him!* album included cover versions of Brenda Lee's "Losing You" and Elvis Presley's "Can't Help Falling in Love," and also included a song entitled "Night Life," which is one of the first pop recordings of a Willie Nelson song.

Doris fulfilled a personal goal with the album *Doris Day and Robert Goulet Sing "Annie Get Your Gun."* The recordings were made under strange circumstances with both Doris and Goulet singing the score with piano accompaniment in California. The tracks were then sent to New York where orchestration was added. Although not uncommon today, in the early '60s unions were only beginning to allow such a practice. The main reason this was allowed in regard to *Doris Day and Robert Goulet Sing "Annie Get Your Gun"* was because Doris was then very busy with her film career.

Under Marty's guidance as her film career rose, Doris granted fewer and fewer interviews. Marty established what he called "areas of sensitivity" into which no reporter was allowed to ask. It was a mutual agreement with the couple. "The press makes me sound foolish," Doris said.

The press, however, largely refused to play this game and called Doris a "Goody-Two-Shoes," and ridiculed her for playing the "professional virgin" in her films. Doris reacted, asking how could she be playing a virgin when many of the characters she played on-screen were married?

"I'm not anti-press, but I'm just like anybody being exposed. You get nervous exposing yourself in print," Doris said at the time. "I just got so tired talking about my broken leg, you know, the same old questions, and my religion, and things like that. They're just personal questions because people are prying and nosy, and trying to make something out of nothing."

Tabloid magazines sniped at her for "hiding" her adult son in order to keep herself looking younger. This was one of many untruths printed about her, and Terry came forward and said it was his choice to remain private. Terry explained that when he was younger, studio photographers had come to their home to take pictures of Doris out of the workplace. "I'd be out playing baseball and my mother would come and get me [for the pictures]. I wasn't crazy about leaving an exciting game of baseball, but I thought if it was important to my mother and her work for me to be there, I'd better go."

Terry complied, but once when photographers were taking longer than he wanted, he asked Doris if he had to stay. "Don't you want to, Terry?" she asked. "Not unless you really and truly want me to, Mom. I hate standing around all afternoon and posing like some nut," he confessed. "I'd rather be with my friends."

Doris told Terry he did not have to pose for pictures any longer, and that he should be playing and having fun. From then on, whenever a writer or photographer requested a picture of Terry, Doris turned them down without any explanation. "It wasn't anybody's business but hers and mine," Terry said.

But in 1964 Doris was voted for the second time in ten years the most unco-operative actress of the year by the Hollywood Women's Press Club. This time, however, Doris was not nearly as upset as she was disgusted. "Isn't that a dreadful thing?" Doris remarked. "Those poor, suffering, sick ladies who do that—still playing little kid's games with apples. Can you *imagine*? With all the things going on in the world and there they are at the Beverly Hills Hotel, giving out *apples*!"

A decade later Rock Hudson stated, "I think the press was very unkind to her. And I never understood why. So she had a soda fountain in her home instead of a bar. She didn't live in a protective cocoon. When Doris offered me a milkshake, I told her I'd have a chocolate malted with Scotch. No big deal. When I first met her she didn't drink whiskey. Later she did. Doris took up smoking for awhile and quit. ...I never thought of her as a goody-two-shoes."

Send Me No Flowers in 1964 reunited the Hudson–Day–Randall team for a third and final time, with Doris named the top box office draw that year. Garson Kanin, in his book *Together Again: The Story of the Great Hollywood Teams*, ranked the Day-Hudson team right up there with Katharine Hepburn and Spencer Tracy. The comedies were, he wrote, "intelligently crafted, sophistically conceived and brilliantly produced.... Neither [Hudson nor Day] ever achieved again the charm or personality or interplay or magnetism they created when they played so beautifully together."

The frothy comedy had the pair married (with Randall as their next door neighbor) and a series of misunderstandings that almost lead to divorce. "The [films] were purely entertainment and there's nothing wrong with that," *Flowers* director Norman Jewison, who later became an acclaimed film director with Oscar-winning films like *Moonstruck*, said years later. "I was just getting started in Hollywood and under contract. I was assigned to the film and had no control over them."

Since Doris had only one film released in 1964 as well as in 1965, her recording career took precedence. In addition to the Terry Melcher–produced *Love Him!*, *The Doris Day Christmas Album* arrived in time for the 1964 holidays. In 1965, three distinctive and well-constructed albums were issued, showcasing her versatility as a singer. *With a Smile and a Song* contained lushly produced children songs accompanied by Jimmy Joyce and His Children's Chorus; *Latin for Lovers*, which expanded upon the then-current bossa nova craze and included Doris singing some parts in Spanish; and *Doris Day's Sentimental Journey*, a collection of standards from the 1940s era including a few reworkings of cuts she originally recorded with Les Brown.

"I didn't choose [the] songs because 'they're not writing songs like they used to,'" Doris recalled in 1965 upon the album's release. "I picked songs I like, but not just because of their age." Among the songs she re-recorded for the album was "Come to Baby, Do!" because she disliked her first interpretation of it and felt it deserved better treatment.

Publicity shot, 1965 (the Movie Market).

With *Doris Day's Sentimental Journey*, Doris had come full circle in her recording career. Throughout the previous 20 years, she had recorded with the cream of the crop of new and standard songs in the company of musicians, conductors and orchestrations including Harry James, Frank DeVol, André Previn, Alex Stordahl, Les Brown and Percy Faith. But by 1965, Columbia apparently had lost interest in Doris Day. While Capitol Records resurrected the career of Frank Sinatra in the 1960s (arguably his best decade in terms of material and voice), Columbia unfortunately did not do the same with Doris. Instead, the label had a new female singer who became the label's main priority: Barbra Streisand.

In an interview with *The New York Times* in 1968, Doris was asked about Streisand, whose music career was already established and whose film career was only beginning, and whose vocal style was arguably at the opposite end of the spectrum from Doris'. "Streisand is great with the big orchestra. She can really belt," Doris offered. "I'm not like that. I like the *simplest* form of music. I would prefer singing with just a guitar or piano. See, *I have to sing into somebody's ear.*"

Doris' last charting album was 1964's *Love Him!* and, although her records continued to sell well overseas, the United States was another matter. For instance, the *Latin for Lovers* album presented Doris in another departure in that she sang some songs in a Latin flavor that was in vogue at the time. But despite the critical attention it received, the set sold quietly. An example of the label's ignorance of Day in later years concerns this album. When the album was reissued under Columbia's budget-line Harmony label, the company printed the album's title incorrectly as *Latin Is for Lovers* on the record label, as well as on the cover's spine.

Her recording career was not given the priority her film career was given, and the selections given the most promotion were the film themes she recorded. Although six songs Doris recorded for her films were nominated for Academy Awards, she disliked many of the later title tunes she was asked to record. Doris suggested Henry Mancini or someone of Mancini's stature to compose the title songs, but Marty Melcher did not feel it was important. "So we never had a decent song," Doris later said. "All those pictures and nothing but mediocre, lackluster music."

"She felt that what she loved to do was not terribly relevant as far as recording for Columbia Records," explains Terry Melcher in reference to his mother's retirement from recording. "She just felt around '67 or '68 that the ballads and the Broadway-type tunes were not relevant. She wasn't bitter about it. She really loved the new music. She loved Motown records. She thought, 'Well, that's terrific. Now this is going to happen and I had a wonderful time.'"

After her million dollar-plus contract with Columbia expired in 1967, Doris independently booked studio time and hired Don Genson to prepare arrangements for her personal favorite songs. The songs were recorded in two days, then forgotten for several years.

While it was unknown at the time, both Doris' music and film careers were coming to an end at roughly the same time.

After her first comedy flop of the decade with 1965's *Do Not Disturb*, she rebounded the following year with the hit spy farce *The Glass Bottom Boat*. Both films teamed her with actor Rod Taylor, and the success of *The Glass Bottom Boat* aided in Doris' plac-

Publicity shot, circa 1964 (the Movie Market).

ing among the top box office money earners in 1966. But after ten non-consecu-
tive years on the list, it was the last time she appeared in the Top Ten.

The conservative Eisenhower era had changed into the swinging '60s style,
and the Doris Day "image" looked out of place in the late 1960s, an era of hippies,
war protest and sexual revolution. Doris appeared in three subsequent critical and
financially unsatisfactory movies, due to Marty and their business manager's signing Doris to make them without her approval.

Doris' 1967 movie *Caprice*, with Richard Harris, Ray Walston and Michael
J. Pollard, and directed by *The Glass Bottom Boat*'s Frank Tashlin, had the earmarks
of another spy spoof success like its predecessor, but something was lost. Whether
it was in the script (as Doris claimed), the actors themselves could not be blamed
as there were several humorous scenes. The title song, backed with the ironically
titled "Sorry," was Doris' last original single released by Columbia Records.

Caprice was followed by the Western-comedy *The Ballad of Josie*, which was
light years from *Calamity Jane*. With a cast including Peter Graves, George Kennedy and David Hartman, the actors themselves were not at fault with its failure.

Where Were You When the Lights Went Out? (1968) was the third film in a row
that was not considered a hit by Doris Day's box office standards, although MGM
considered it a strong ticket seller. Co-starring with Robert Morse, Terry-Thomas
and Patrick O'Neal, Doris was enjoyable in the role of an actress appearing on
Broadway in *The Constant Virgin*, an undeniable joke in reference to the news
media's label of Doris.

During rehearsals for the film, Patrick O'Neal picked Doris up in a wrong
way and she suffered a severely pinched nerve in her back. The pain was excruci-
ating and one doctor told her she should remain immobile for several weeks. But
Marty Melcher found a specialist who allowed Doris to continue working. She
stayed in traction between scenes, and when it was time to film her, Doris was
helped to the set, shot her scene then returned to traction for the remainder of
production.

With Six You Get Eggroll (1968) with Brian Keith provided Doris a vehicle
which enabled her to play a more realistic, contemporary, single-working-mom
character. Critics applauded the "new" Doris Day. Interestingly, and perhaps as a
comment to naysayers about the Doris Day film "image," one assumes Abby and
Jake were intimate before their elopement. When he leaves her house during a
downpour, she goes out to him then leads him back indoors.

Marty Melcher produced the film. "I wanted [Marty] to do things on his own
for many years," Doris later recalled. Marty usually was a co-producer on Doris's
films rather than completely taking them over. "He was always afraid."

Variety remarked that when the film was shown at a New York sneak preview
"at a large suburban theater, the capacity-filled crowd greeted Miss Day's name
on the screen with heavy applause and audibly enjoyed the film throughout."
Unknown at the time, *With Six You Get Eggroll* was destined to be Doris' last film.

With Brian Keith in her last film, *With Six You Get Eggroll*, **1968.**

Shortly after production wrapped, Marty became ill with chronic diarrhea. He eventually became bedridden and Doris never left his side. Although she urged him to allow a doctor to see him, Marty refused because of his Christian Science belief. Three months passed before Marty finally agreed to go, after the urging of family friend Dick Dorso. He entered Mount Sinai Hospital where doctors discovered Marty was suffering from an infected, enlarged heart. Surgery was performed, but at four A.M. on April 19, 1968, Marty was dead at age 52.

"Our marriage wasn't perfect—whose is?" Doris later said. "But there were many good things and suddenly there was a big black aching void. All I wanted to do was sit in my backyard looking at the trees. Nothing could compensate for the void, not even religion. I was a Christian Scientist. I *still* believe life is eternal. But Marty's death threw me completely, and for awhile I didn't believe in anything."

There was no funeral for Marty, and his remains were cremated. Less than a month after Marty's death, Doris found a script in her home for a television series entitled *The Doris Day Show*. She had regularly told Marty she did not want to do a television series because it was difficult, time-consuming, and she would be required to play the same role week after week. But he not only went against her wishes, but committed her to a five-year run with CBS-TV.

The oddity with this is that a year earlier an article appeared in the trade newspapers announcing the series. But Doris knew nothing about it.

Mounting a television show using a film star was a risky venture. Several film actors and actresses tried but flopped in television: Jean Arthur, Lana Turner, Henry Fonda, Bing Crosby and Jimmy Stewart all failed to create a hit television series. But the deal provided ready cash for the Day-Melcher empire (*Variety* called the CBS-Day coup "one of the industry's all-time plush talent deals") and included Doris owning outright the negatives to the show and controlling all rerun rights, with lucrative side provisions to make movies for CBS.

"The picture business was in a state of revolution. Ideas were changing. While Doris could still pack 'em in at the Music Hall, the Doris Day-type … of picture wasn't bringing the kids out," Marty said not long before his death. "They would rather see Rosemary impregnated by the devil."

Doris went to Palm Springs to recover after Marty's death, trying to regain her strength and composure, and to come to terms that her husband had gone against her professional wishes. Terry went to visit his mother to convince her that *The Doris Day Show* could not only be a good series, but a positive experience and a whole new career for her. Terry also reminded her that the deal was made and that she would need to honor it, and that the series wasn't just about her, but that many people were employed in the production. Although she had not personally agreed to it, Doris could have finagled her way out of the contract through legal maneuvers. But she felt that she must honor the agreement. In 1968, however, it was not publicly known why Doris Day ventured into a television series. Insiders said she didn't need the money, but according to one of Doris' film producers, it was Marty Melcher who saw television as an outlet for his wife to make more money. He had accepted a $500,000 advance from CBS for pre-production costs. Doris soon learned, however, that money was long gone.

Although most of Hollywood cheered Doris for honoring the contract with CBS and going to work despite the recent death of her husband, not everyone applauded. Shelley Winters criticized Doris for "doing television" in what she saw was a choice of purely financial reasons over the art of acting. "She must have zillions of dollars," Winters told *The New York Times*, "and yet she gets up every morning and does that cockamamie TV show. What else *would* she do? But me, I came to New York at the end of my seven-year contract at Universal and enrolled at the Actor's Studio."

The first year of the show was filmed at Golden West Studios in Hollywood. To accommodate her, CBS gave Doris a huge trailer, complete with a white picket fence, trees and grass, and enveloped with daisies—on the table, on the plates, even on Doris' canvas director-style chair. It was reported that in all of Hollywood, only Barbra Streisand had a larger trailer (on the set of *Hello, Dolly!*).

Doris was cast as a widow with two young boys who return to live on her father's farm in California. It was not the setting she would have chosen for her series, but she accepted it and tried to look at the positive aspects of the project. "I really like these stories," Doris told *Look* in late 1968. "I like the ranch life; I like the idea that I come back to my father. The way I care for my father on the show is really what I feel about Denver [Pyle]. I really like Denver. In fact, I probably love him!"

Doris confessed that it was more difficult for her to have those same feelings for the children on her show. A selection of 140 young boys were narrowed down to 30 during the casting process. Those 30 read with Doris, but she did not feel any of them would work well enough in the series. Finally, Philip Brown and Tod Starke were cast in the roles as Billy and Toby Martin, respectively. Doris admitted she was not one to "gush" over children, but she grew to love the two boys who played her sons. Tod Starke innocently thought Doris Day was one word, so he greeted his television mother with "Good morning, Dorisday!" That always broke Doris up.

"We had eight weeks to basically mount the show, and pick a location and to film it and to post-production and score it," Terry Melcher remarked. "And we delivered."

But many times throughout the filming of the first season, Doris broke down between scenes. She had also lost 18 pounds. "I still don't know how I was able to do [the series so soon after Marty's death]," she reflected in 1971. "I was just lucky to get my lines studied and my makeup put on."

To help her widowed—and now busier—daughter, Alma moved into Doris' home. Doris' brother-in-law, Jack Melcher and her Aunt "Rocky" also moved in to be with her during the first months after Marty's death.

With one of her favorite best friends, Biggest, while working on an episode of *The Doris Day Show* (Jerry Ohlinger's Movie Material Store, Inc.).

After Marty's death, Rosenthal sent a check to Terry to endorse since he was named executor of Marty's estate. The check was a film residual in the amount of $60,000 and Terry was reluctant to sign it over to him. "Son, sign it," Rosenthal said. "I need to have it right away. Your father trusted me, your mother trusted me." With trepidation, Terry signed the check and gave it to Rosenthal, but he felt something was very wrong.

In the weeks that followed, Terry confronted Rosenthal in several meetings that led to a shocking discovery: Doris Day was not only bankrupt, but deeply in debt. At age 25, Terry had the responsibility of telling his mother the unfortunate news of the mismanagement of her career by her former husband and, more considerably, by their business associate and legal advisor, Rosenthal. It seemed unthinkable that Rosenthal would have done anything wrong. As far back as 1949, Rosenthal was Doris's attorney and had represented her in her divorce from George Weidler. Since 1956 he advised the Melchers and made many investments for them. Rosenthal had an impressive clientele which included Van Johnson, Ross Hunter, Ava Gardner, Gordon MacRae, Kirk Douglas and Dorothy Dandridge.

Soon after Marty's death, Rosenthal also claimed 50 percent of the future Day earnings, another act Doris found unacceptable. Doris decided to take legal action not only to recoup her losses and expose the man who she felt mismanaged her finances, but to prevent him from benefiting from any of her future earnings.

Terry went to Marty's office to get his stepfather's files, but found the office cleaned out. He returned to Doris and asked her where she kept the duplicate copies of the papers, including deeds, film and music contracts. She knew nothing about the copies—or the originals—and came up empty-handed. "I was so angry with myself," she recalled a few years later. "You know, like where had I been all those years? I thought now is the time to take a good, long, hard look at myself."

Since Terry was named executor of Marty Melcher's estate, he took charge to find out what happened to his mother's money—as well as his own since he invested money with Rosenthal as well. In order to untangle the legal red tape, Terry had to sue Doris in a purely legal maneuver to formally remove her from the proceeding so that he could obtain a proper accounting of her income. It would take several years before a full dossier of Rosenthal's actions could be assembled.

Meanwhile, Doris had to give full attention to her television show. Doris said working on the show helped her get on with her life; however, the loss of Marty and the trouble with money did not resolve itself overnight. She consented to a few interviews to promote the show, and in one, despite the cheery, positive outlook she tried to convey, there was a underlying sadness that lingered: "I never had a lot of friends," "I'm really a square" and "I'm pretty dull, I guess," she revealed in one interview in late 1968.

Doris got through the first year of her television series remarkably well. On-screen, one could not tell of the terrible blows she had endured; off-screen, however, she had a very hard time coming to grips with all that had been handed to her. She spent almost a year mourning Marty Melcher's death. Doris asked herself, "Why can't I handle this?" She asked her son, "Will I ever get over this? I somehow feel that I will never be ... joyful."

During the first season of *The Doris Day Show*, Doris sensed the show's concept was all wrong. She felt the viewers did not want her living in the country, but rather in the city, "wearing pretty clothes and getting involved with sophisticated people." For the 1969-70 season, the locale shifted from the farm to nearby San Francisco. She also replaced two of the show's producers and moved the filming to the modernized CBS Studio City facilities. Additions to the cast included Rose Marie and McLean Stevenson.

The change succeeded and the series saw an increase in viewers placing in the yearly Top Ten. As a result, CBS raised the show's budget for its third season, arguably the best of the series' five years. Without setting out to do so, Doris Day conquered television. Conversely, however, Doris' private life was unsettling.

In August 1969, the world learned of the brutal murder of actress Sharon Tate and four others at 10500 Cielo Drive in Bel Air. The house where the murders occurred had been rented by Terry Melcher and his then-girlfriend, actress Candice Bergen. They lived there until December 1968 when Terry moved to Doris' Malibu beach house to keep it from being vandalized.

Publicity shot, 1971 (the Movie Market).

Terry had been approached by Charles Manson, who had written several songs he hoped to have recorded. Terry met with Manson and had visited him and his family of followers in the desert. However, Manson's songs were not quite what Terry was interested in, and he considered the matter closed.

But when it was discovered that Charles Manson was the mastermind behind the murders, it was suspected that Terry may have been the intended victim. Manson follower and murderer Susan Atkins confirmed this to police. It is believed that Manson may have held a grudge against Terry for not producing his songs. There were rumors that Manson and his followers were planning to murder some famous celebrities, including Doris Day. The police could not provide protection for Doris or Terry, so they hired round-the-clock bodyguards until Manson and those responsible were jailed for the crimes.

"Terry didn't plan on recording Charlie Manson," Doris later said. "It was not his decision [not to record], it was the record company that had made the final decision. [The murderers] were not after Terry.

"The house was not Terry's; it was a rental house," she elaborated. "Charles Manson knew he was living in Malibu because I had bought my husband a telescope, and it was on the veranda at the beach house. And Charlie Manson stole that telescope."

The demands on Terry were more than he could bear. Battling to recover some of his and Doris's lost money, in addition to helping with *The Doris Day Show* and dealing with the Manson murders, all contributed to him breaking up with Candice Bergen and delve into drugs. In the summer of 1971, Terry had a motorcycle accident that nearly cost him his life. Though he survived, doctors did not think he would ever walk again.

"She'd [drive] all the way to the hospital—90 miles away, [then] come back and go to work," *Doris Day Show* co-star Jackie Joseph recalled. "But she'd never go 'I'm tired.' She didn't share her grief, she'd never say, 'Why me, why is this happening?'" Terry regained the use of his legs, and after his release from the hospital, he moved into Doris' home and convalesced there. After several months he recovered and returned to his own house.

Professionally, her life was on a high. Her first variety special, *The Doris Mary Anne Kappelhoff Special*, was aired in 1971 as part of her contract with CBS. Appearing with Perry Como and including a short reunion with Rock Hudson, the special was well-received.

"The TV special was one of most rewarding things that ever happened to me. I don't mean as far as my career is concerned or the money—although who likes to be in debt? It was the joy I received doing it, and finding out the joy it brought to others," Doris recalled in 1973 to *Ladies Home Journal*. The salary from the special was used to pay the IRS $450,000 in back taxes she owed—another realization after the investigation into her lawyer's mismanagement. To raise additional money, she appeared in a margarine commercial for British television directed by Nicolas Roeg.

The 1971-72 season of *The Doris Day Show* focused more on Doris Martin as a career woman. When Ed Feldman moved into the producer's chair for the series' fourth season, he revamped the format. Gone were the boys and the staff at *Today's World* magazine where Doris Martin worked. John Dehner was hired to portray the city editor of the magazine and Doris Martin's boss. "When we promoted Doris from a secretary to an associate editor, we needed a strong, dynamic character as the boss to cope with her," Feldman said. "I don't know anyone stronger and more dynamic than John Dehner."

Shortly before his death in 1996, McLean Stevenson wrote a letter to Doris. Although he was in the show for two seasons, he asked to leave so that he could do other work. The letter was flattering and expressed his gratitude to her and the chance of working with her on *The Doris Day Show*.

"I couldn't believe it," she said. "I didn't know he felt that way about me. He was very good and very funny. I don't know why they didn't keep him [on the show]. I think the word was that he was too goofy. And he couldn't run a big magazine like *Today's World* and be like he was, I guess, in *M*A*S*H*, with his style of comedy." After Stevenson left, his biggest professional success came immediately after *The Doris Day Show* when he starred in *M*A*S*H* and was nominated for an Emmy award.

Doris assumed the executive producer role in her show's final season. In 1973, when Doris learned she had fulfilled the television series contract with CBS, she decided to end *The Doris Day Show*. "I'm tired," she explained at the time. "Doing a film series is extremely hard work and I feel that five years is enough. There are so many other things to be done and said, and doing a situation comedy week after week is no longer fulfilling for me. It's time to go on to something else.

Publicity shot, 1971 (the Movie Market).

"There is really no reason why prime-time TV must devote so much time to pure entertainment. TV is the most powerful medium in the world; and Hollywood, its prime source of material, has used it almost entirely as an outlet for entertainment. It has provided me with a good living for many years. But it is not the alpha and omega of the world.

"...I just don't think another season of *The Doris Day Show* in its present form is going to lead anybody anywhere, except maybe to the bank." She also regarded the rigors of doing a television series was more difficult than anything she had experienced while fulfilling her seven-year contract at Warner Bros. in the beginning of her film career.

Without the commitment

of the series, Doris concentrated on resolving her financial matters and her suit against Jerome Rosenthal. "[T]he small print in a contract was just that—small print," Doris said. "I didn't read it; I felt that I didn't have to—and nobody told me otherwise. As a result I got a few surprises." Doris didn't even know when she signed to do the film *That Touch of Mink* that her co-star was going to be Cary Grant until a friend told her after reading about it.

"'Nobody told me' became my pet phrase," Doris told *Ladies Home Journal*. "Well, my 'nobody told me' days are over. [If] I've changed as a person, the answer is no. But I do feel I have matured. [As a result] my outlook is much healthier. Like anyone else, I've made mistakes ... [but] each mistake was a lesson—so I've learned a few good lessons along the way." As a working businesswoman, Doris admitted she had changed primarily because when Marty died, "I knew that I had to take a more active part in my business affairs than I had before."

At one point Doris was spending $40,000 a month in legal fees trying to get her fortune back, using her salary from *The Doris Day Show* to pay lawyers. By the spring of 1974, Doris and her team of attorneys headed by lawyer Robert Winslow brought Jerome Rosenthal to court. The preceding years were spent trying to locate records of Rosenthal's handling of Doris' money. Few files existed, and it took the force of sheriff's deputies to get possession of whatever files Rosenthal still retained. Doris forged ahead, but did not allow the case to devastate her.

"Having all your money taken from you is no joke," she told the press during the trial, "but you have to put it all in its proper place. I told my son I have so much to be joyful about. That man is not going to take my joy for any minute of any day. I'll do what I have to do, but I'll do it in my way. No matter what comes of it, it's for a reason."

Thirteen suits were filed against Rosenthal, and 67 witnesses took the stand during the 100-day court battle. Doris testified that she had given Marty power of attorney because she was busy working. "My husband trusted Rosenthal, and I trusted my husband," she said.

Publicity shot, circa 1974 (Jerry Ohlinger's Movie Material Store, Inc.).

Forbes reported that Rosenthal "made a habit of commingling his funds with his clients, taking kickbacks on deals he engineered, getting clients into bogus transactions and then charging the victims exorbitant fees in face-saving rescue efforts."

In September 1974, the judge ruled in favor of Doris, awarding her $22,835,646. The judge ruled that Rosenthal had committed "the grossest of negligence" with the handling of Doris' business and financial dealings. The judge also criticized Doris for being "too busy making movies to pay attention to her own affairs." The trial cost taxpayers $250,000 and several people blamed Doris for not keeping her business affairs in order. But in her defense, Doris had easily paid much, much more than that amount in federal and state taxes throughout her career.

"It's been my own little Watergate and I'm glad it's over," Doris said after the ruling. "I really don't know how much I will actually realize from this. People think you walk out of the courtroom with a check in hand, but that isn't what happens at all." Although the amount that Doris lost through Rosenthal was closer to $28 million, it was reported she eventually settled for around $6 million from Rosenthal's insurance company. Rosenthal, however, continued to attempt to reverse the court's decision until 1986 when the appeals were exhausted. Doris, however, continued to fight Rosenthal on another level, eventually seeing him disbarred.

She blamed Rosenthal entirely, but not her husband. "I think Marty just trusted the wrong person. Completely," Doris said in retrospect. "And found himself really in trouble."

After the battle with Rosenthal came to a close, *People* magazine reported that Doris would record a new album, do two television specials and make a film in 1975. Of these plans, she only made one television special for CBS in 1975, the well-received *Doris Day toDay*. Doris had guested on *The John Denver Show* in December 1974 on ABC-TV, and Denver returned the favor by appearing in Doris' second special. Also joining her were Rich Little and Tim Conway. While *Doris Day toDay* was a ratings winner and applauded by critics, including those who had forgotten Doris the singer, it was her last prime time special and it fulfilled her contract with CBS.

With all of her business obligations met, Doris had one more item she wished to publicly address. She wanted to primarily lay to rest the rumors and misconceptions the public had of her. In 1975, she wrote her memoirs with the help of A.E. Hotchner, who had received acclaim for *Papa Hemingway*, his book on Ernest Hemingway.

"Jacqueline Susann was very instrumental in the writing of this book," Doris told Barbara Walters. "I told her about my life, and she said I should write a book. She said, 'You've had so many sharp experiences that you should share with people, and you could be a good influence perhaps because [you] had the strength to overcome and become a very happy lady.' God gave me the strength. We all have it." At the time, Doris had no intention of writing her story, but Susann not only convinced her, but suggested Hotchner should write it. Hotchner met with Doris but told her he wasn't terribly willing to write her story.

"I really don't think there is a book. Look at you—you're very successful, you made great movies, a number one recording artist in the world," Hotchner recalled. "And she said, 'I've had a perfectly rotten life.' She started talking about events in her life, talking about her father. I think that was the most painful part of her life."

Hotchner listened and concluded the Doris Day on screen was not the Doris Day in private, and the public had no idea who the real Doris Day was. Hotchner wrote the book with Doris and the result was an immediate number one bestseller with millions of copies sold.

The public was shocked with her frankness and the terrible blows she had endured in what they believed was a happy life. *The Los Angeles Times* applauded the effort, reviewing it with, "Miss goody two-shoes kicks back!" Oddly, in 1982 an Alabama censor had the book removed because it conflicted with Doris' "image of the typical American" woman.

Although Doris primarily shunned doing promotional tours at the height of her career, she agreed to do so to promote her book. On the talk show circuit, Doris answered the same recurring questions and replied with the same comments. The most repeated comment was that she was the girl-next-door virgin. "I don't know where the label came from. Maybe it's the way I look—do I look like a virgin?" she asked Barbara Walters, which caused the *Today Show* crew to break up laughing. "What does a virgin look like?"

Author Hotchner had composed *Doris Day: Her Own Story* in three parts that were mixed throughout the work. The main was Doris speaking in her own voice; the second was Hotchner adding his thoughts and tying events together; the third was first-person comments by Doris's family, co-stars and friends.

Many comments by the latter surprised Doris, especially the sometimes brutal attacks against Marty Melcher. She had no idea so many of them disliked her husband as none of them (except Frank Sinatra) had shown any signs to prove otherwise. The book provided more than a few shocks to its readers, especially when Doris said, "I really think people should live together before they're married. It may be shocking, but it really isn't. I think it's important."

"People should live together before they sign that contract," she told Merv Griffin, "to really get to know each other and you don't know each other until you live with each other. I know a lot of people wouldn't agree with that. To each his own."

Doris said her first three marriages had all been unhappy "and I vowed that, should there be a fourth, I would live with the man first." She did not, however, think she would ever marry again. "I never say 'never,' but I don't see [marriage] happening."

At a book signing for her autobiography *Doris Day: Her Own Story* **in 1976 (Jerry Ohlinger's Movie Material Store, Inc.).**

In 1975, Doris met Barry Comden through her dentist, Dr. Robert Franks, who was investing in a restaurant business with Comden. Dr. Franks asked Doris for her opinion of his Old World Eatery restaurant in Beverly Hills. She visited it with A.E. Hotchner, who recalled Comden was gushing over Doris and "practically threw himself on her lap." Comden was helping manage three Old World Eatery restaurants at the time, including the one Doris visited. The two spoke at length for months, then one day Comden asked her for a date. She agreed and the two began to date regularly. Comden accompanied Doris on a book tour to promote *Doris Day: Her Own Story*, and while in New York, Hotchner saw Doris was becoming seriously involved with Comden. "I knew that this was ill-fated," Hotchner later said.

In April 1976, Barry Comden became Doris Day's fourth husband when the couple married at a friend's home in Carmel, California. Comden was ten years his wife's junior.

"I just think he's a beautiful person," Doris said of her new husband, "and we have a marvelous relationship, really better than any relationship I've ever had before. With Barry, I am romantically fulfilled. We're so happy with each other! I am now a contented, happy, outgoing person."

In the mid–1970s, Doris' mother suffered a series of mini-strokes which obliterated her memory, but did not affect her physically. Doris spent much of her time caring for Alma, but as time passed, Alma's conditioned worsened. She needed medical care and was moved to a nursing home where she later died of pneumonia.

After Alma's death, Doris and Comden purchased an acreage in Carmel and over the course of three years built her dream house. Doris kept house while Comden did the cooking. The couple enjoyed living quietly, entertaining small groups of friends and rarely going to big parties they were invited to in the community. Doris also decided to increase more time working for animal rights. Comden suggested she begin her own foundation, an idea she had been toying with. The Doris Day Pet Foundation began operation in 1978.

Comden also had big plans for a chain of pet care centers bearing Doris' name. In the end, Doris disassociated herself from Comden's plans and was embarrassed by them, although she declined to go into detail. "That wasn't my venture at all. [Comden] dealt with that at the beginning of our marriage, but I don't want to discuss it. I should have known better than to get involved, but I was gullible."

It was rumored that the couple had invested in a pet store business in California, and although Doris did not want to do it, Comden convinced her. The store was a disaster in that there was alleged stealing occurring and the store lost money.

In addition to business problems, there were personal problems in the marriage. One time Doris and Comden went to the Los Angeles International Airport to pick up some friends who had flown in. They had an argument and Comden angrily drove off, deserting Doris at the airport to greet her friends alone. The final straw came when Comden allegedly struck her in the course of an argument. Doris telephoned Terry, who went to the house and suggested to Comden that he leave.

"I said once before that I would never get married again, and I did. And we do some very foolish things, and I did a very foolish thing. I like being single, but I really don't know what's in store." Doris filed for divorce in January 1981 and invited some friends to her home, including Frank Comstock. As he walked to the house, Comstock realized Doris was going to survive the breakup. Hanging from a tree, Comstock saw a stuffed dummy with "Barry" written on it.

The divorce became final in February 1982. It was not a pleasant parting. Comden received a private financial settlement from his ex-wife and they went their separate ways. Doris resigned herself to being a single woman and focused on enjoying her life and home in Carmel. Overlooking a golf course with the Pacific Ocean in the distance, the estate is secluded by tall, ancient oak trees, manicured lawns and gardens, and a security fence. The 11-acre property includes several redwood "cottages" to house Doris' pets, and a building separate from the

From the 1975 variety special *Doris day toDay* (from the collection of Matt Tunia).

main house which contains Doris' bedroom. It is a huge room with a cathedral ceiling, a large canopy bed and a stone fireplace.

Inside the main house are country antiques, china, crystal and silver, overstuffed chairs and sofas. Huge rock fireplaces give the house a warm feel. After years of being unable to pamper herself with pretty things for her house while working, Doris is content in the first true home she has been able to call her own.

While Doris retained her house in Beverly Hills, she was calling Carmel home. The complete move to Carmel resulted in many in the movie capitol feeling that Doris was turning her back on the industry that made her famous beyond her—or anyone's, for that matter—wildest dreams.

Rather than accept the course she had chosen in this phase of her life, the tabloids once again began attacking Doris. "Doris Day now a bitter recluse..." began most stories. Alleged friends gave the tabloid writers accounts of how Doris had changed for the worse. "She's closed the door on the world. She's very bitter and paranoid, and shuns close friends ... she has become a vitamin-popping hypochondriac who lives in terror with being stricken with cancer and sits at home playing records for her pets."

A neighbor claimed Doris' new house "looks like a concentration camp," and a Beverly Hills hairdresser offered that she wears disguises and that her hair had gone completely gray. "The once beautiful actress, who was America's sweetheart, often looks like a ragged and disgusting old lady," one article reported. "She's a lonely, pathetic figure who's certainly become weird and eccentric."

The articles concerned A.E. Hotchner, who had last seen Doris only a few years earlier. He telephoned her and the two arranged to meet in Carmel. Hotchner was relieved to find she was well, and that she had not changed—the articles were purely fiction. "You can't imagine what mail I received after those articles

With fourth husband Barry Comden, 1976 (from the collection of Matt Tunia).

began to appear. Thousands of letters from people asking if I was all right, how they could help, genuinely concerned." Doris replied to all of the letters, assuring them she was fine, but Doris confided to Hotchner she was convinced the constant tabloid press stories about her had contributed to her mother's demise.

In May 1983, Doris became a grandmother when Terry and Jacqueline (Melcher's second wife) became parents of a baby boy they named Ryan. She was thrilled with the new addition to her family. "I just can't believe it. It's incredible," Doris said. "That baby is really part of my father, my mother, my brother, an extension of all us."

A decade had passed since Doris Day last appeared performing on television, although she did occasional interviews, including a week-long stint on *Good Morning, America* in 1983. In early 1985, the Christian Broadcasting Network (CBN) network approached Terry Melcher with an original program idea for his mother. The cable network, which combined religious programs with Westerns and sitcoms of the past, believed they could lure Doris Day back to television. Although Doris was content with staying in Carmel with her family and disliked traveling, she agreed to host a weekly program about animals, to be produced in and near her home. The network hired Terry as co-executive producer, and the company was allowed to air *The Doris Day Show* as part of its regular programming.

"First of all, it's great fun to be working again," Doris told reporters at the press conference announcing the series. "I'm looking forward to that. The show is called *Doris Day's Best Friends*. My best friends are people and animals—not necessarily in that order. That's a terrible thing to say. It's a chance to really work with the animals, to [make] musical videos, which I am loving, and it's great fun.

"We have a man-in-the-field doing all kinds of film on animals at the zoo. We want to raise money for all the humane societies all over the country. We want to make people more aware of the animal kingdom, and what it means to have a pet, how wonderful it is for the elderly to have pets. We're just going to do all kinds of things and have some funny things, we hope. It's going to give me a chance to see some of my old friends, which is really neat."

Doris herself hosted *Doris Day's Best Friends* and most episodes featured celebrity guests. Some of them worked with Doris in films or music, and each reminisced about their projects of years past. The conversations then moved on to the matter at hand— an animal.

Publicity shot, 1978.

The first guest selected was a natural: Rock Hudson. Although he was in the final stages of AIDS, Hudson agreed to appear with Doris because she was a good friend. Hudson never told Doris he was dying or had the disease. She knew he was ill from his gaunt appearance, and Doris begged him to see a doctor. Hudson simply said he had a bad case of the flu, but Doris knew it was worse than that.

In *Rock Hudson: His Story* by Hudson as told to Sara Davidson, Doris recalled, "When we were walking around out there together, it crossed my mind it might be the last time. But I didn't really know. I hoped and prayed it wouldn't be. I didn't know what was wrong with him, but I knew he was determined to do that show if it took his last breath. It was his final thing and I really cherish that." After taping the show, Hudson returned to Los Angeles, then decided to go to Paris to see an AIDS specialist. "Doris is mad at me," Hudson remarked to a friend. "There's a doctor in Paris I've got to see because I guess there's something wrong with me. I don't like it that Doris is mad at me."

Hudson died shortly after on October 2, 1985. In an appropriate gesture of sympathy and tact, it was decided that the Hudson-Day episode would be the second show broadcast of *Doris Day's Best Friends*. In perhaps one of her bravest and most eloquent performances, Doris spoke from her heart as she opened the show with a special memorial to one of her best friends. Doris explained how she had to have Hudson as her first guest on the show:

> So I called him and he said ... "I'll be there. You can count on me." And that was the truth. All his friends, and there were many, could always count on Rock Hudson. Not only was he a very talented dramatic actor, as we all know, his favorite thing was comedy. And he always said to me, "The best time I've ever had was making comedies with you." And I felt the same way. We had a ball.
>
> As I reflect on his arrival in Carmel, I can only tell you, my friends, that it was a heartbreaking time for me to see him. He didn't talk about his illness, not one time, He just said, "Eunice, I've had the flu and I can't gain weight." And I said, "You've come to the right place, my darling, because I'm going to put weight on you. I'm going to force feed you." And we laughed. And he said, "I just can't gain weight and I have no appetite."
>
> And, of course, I felt that he wasn't feeling well enough to work. And I told him, I said, "You know, nothing is as important as your health. You don't have to do this show, and I don't want you to. I want you to forget it. I want you to just stay in Carmel for a while and relax and enjoy it." And he said, "Forget it. I came here to do your show and that's exactly what I'm going to do." And he did. That's what he did, and he was wonderful.
>
> And I feel that without my deep faith I would be a lot sadder than I am today. I know that life is eternal and that something good is going to come from this experience.

By the end of the tribute, Doris had visible tears and her voice was choking with emotion, barely able to speak the words. Rock Hudson's biographers, Jack

Vitek and Jerry Oppenheimer, described Doris's homage as "one of the most heart-rending sequences ever broadcast" on television.

The series also contained uplifting stories and allowed the audience to see Doris interact with her guests. She reminisced with Les Brown and his Band of Renown, talking about playing at the Café Rouge, which she said was her favorite place that they performed.

In another episode, actress Joan Fontaine joked that she had a hand in Doris' film career in that she continually played Doris' records when working on a film, and everyone who came into her dressing room heard Doris singing.

"Everybody knew Doris Day before most people did," Fontaine said.

When Fontaine asked, "What are your plans?" Doris replied, "I never make them." "Who makes them for you?" Fontaine asked quizzically. Doris laughed and explained that she simply takes one day at a time.

The series lasted for only 26 episodes. CBN was unable to get big ratings, pitting the show against the top-rated CBS program *60 Minutes*. In addition, a large portion of the public expected to see more of Doris Day herself in the series. Despite the huge following Doris had in Britain, *Doris Day's Best Friends* was not televised there. "[T]he quality of production did not warrant [a] purchase," according to Leslie Halliwell, who was then responsible for selecting shows for British television.

After the CBN series ended, Doris introduced and narrated a three-part series on animals in films for *Entertainment Tonight* entitled "Hollywood's Wildest Stars." She continued with other endeavors including the Cypress Inn, which she co-owns with her son and Dennis Le Vett. A 15-minute drive from her home, the Cypress Inn has operated as an inn since 1929 and is a 34-room establishment which admits dogs and cats. Pets are welcomed with a dog biscuit and special beds, and the inn has pet sitters available as it is forbidden for owners to leave their pets alone in their rooms.

The Cypress Inn was restored to its original splendor with recognizable white Mediterranean facade and red tiled roof. Each room in the inn differs with its own distinctive character that includes exposed rafters, overstuffed couches and a small library bar. Continental breakfasts are served every morning in either the garden courtyard or the bar, where Doris Day movie posters decorate the walls.

To many people, Doris Day the humanitarian involves herself solely with the well-being of animals and animal rights. Although she has been most vocal on this subject, her efforts have extended to other areas, but she has chosen to do so quietly. She does not care to be part of any organization unless she can play an active role, thereby declining the use of only her name on a piece of paper along with other "supporters" of a cause.

"Who cares what I give to what?" she asked. "My feeling is, do it quietly. Why is it so necessary to raise hell about 'I'm doing a benefit!' They're always saying that Bob Hope does all the benefits, that Jerry Lewis does all the benefits …

does that make you nice, or good, or what? I mean, who knows what anybody is doing it for, deep down? I feel charity should be done quietly, and you can give where you want to give, and do what you want, but just don't blow your horn about it."

The well-being of animals was instilled in Doris at a young age. When she was a girl living in Cincinnati, the next door neighbor had a dog she played with on occasion. One weekend the neighbor left the dog home alone, outside in the cold weather. Doris took the dog into her house to give it food and water, then took it to her uncle's place where it lived a long and happy life. The neighbors never learned the fate of their dog, and Doris was never found out. She also never spoke to her neighbors again after that.

The importance of animals, however, came later in her adult life when she learned the hard truth regarding animal shelters, medical and cosmetic testings on animals, and the treatment of numerous confined animals. In 1971, Doris co-founded Actors and Others for Animals. The organization was established to find protection for animals and to educate the public and control overpopulation. Doris also organized Holiday Human, a San Fernando Valley kennel which housed more than 300 dogs.

"Her spotlight carried over," recalls actress Jackie Joseph who also belonged to Actors and Others for Animals. "And she spoke from her heart. It was the only time I saw her cry. Her personal life, she could put on the back shelf and handle it in her own internal way. But if an animal was abused, it was intolerable." Doris recalled the most shattering experience of her life occurred in the early 1970s when she and others removed approximately 100 dogs from a dirt and diseased-infested Burbank home.

Doris used her celebrity to make public the treatment of animals in certain areas. One day she berated the owner of a local pound on television. When later asked what it was like there, Doris replied, "Can you say Nazi in print?" When asked to describe other local pounds, she answered they were "concentration camps. And Los Angeles is supposed to be the best. It must be hell everywhere else. So think what it is for the animals. That's what it is!"

Doris viewed animal pounds as moneymaking businesses rather than welfare organizations for neglected or homeless animals. "Money is at the bottom of all the trouble with the pounds," she said in 1972. "Throw them in the decompression chamber. Make fertilizer out of them. Get the money for the fertilizer. Get the money, get the money, get the money."

While living in Beverly Hills, Doris cared for 11 dogs and cats in her home. Arguably, her favorite was an abandoned dog originally named Tiger. Doris placed him in a home, but the owners preferred a smaller dog. The second place was with her secretary at the time, but the landlord wouldn't allow it. The third home for the dog was with the cousin of her stand-in on *The Doris Day Show*.

"She loved him, but he didn't want to be there," Doris recalled, "so he spent one night and the following morning. Something told me that he should stay with me. She called and said, 'Doris, Big Tiger wants to be with you.' Doris picked him up the next day. Since Doris already had a dog named Tiger, the new addition was named Big Tiger, then eventually Biggest.

While Doris' main concern for the rights of dogs evolved to include cats and other pets, it has extended to all animals. She once berated a fellow actor for not leaving his dog in the care of a competent caretaker, and also a man who had beat a shark to death on a California beach. At an "Animals Have Rights, Too" rally in the early 1970s at the Beverly Hills Hotel, Doris shared the stage with actor Gardner McKay and a seven-foot cheetah. "Will he bite?" she asked McKay. "Not if you don't irritate him," he replied. Doris didn't. Her shaming owners in public for delinquency of their pets became legendary in Beverly Hills.

One of Doris' most publicized appearances for animal rights occurred in the early 1970s when she wore a fake fur coat and posed alongside Mary Tyler Moore, Angie Dickinson, Jayne Meadows and Amanda Blake. It was an advertisement against wearing fur that was published in several leading magazines. "Killing an animal to make a coat is a sin," Doris said at the time. "At one time, before I became aware of the situation, I did buy fur coats. Today, when I look at them hanging in the closet, I could cry."

Years later she said, "It just breaks my heart that these films (most notably *That Touch of Mink*) are playing and I want everybody to know that I do not wear furs. I won't even sell them. I won't auction them. I won't do anything with them. They're in a big storage chest and that's where they're going to stay because I'm so against that."

Doris Day has been criticized for paying so much attention to animals when there are other charities concerning humans and the environment. Doris sees no difference. "A lot of people resent it when you work for animals, but I don't separate cruelty to animals from cruelty to people at all," she said. "I think we really have to study animals as they are—and then learn from them. That's why they are here. I'm *convinced* that's why they are here.... And I see in them the most loyalty, the most love, the most joy, the most purity, the most everything."

Doris took a leave of absence from Actors and Others for Animals when her mother became ill. After Alma Kappelhoff's death, Doris and then-husband Barry Comden established the non-profit Doris Day Pet Foundation in 1978. Starting on a small scale consisting of Doris, Comden and a group of volunteers, the foundation operated a small kennel in the San Fernando Valley to care for abandoned animals available for adoption. Doris and Comden contributed $100,000 to the operation.

Eventually, the foundation provided spaying and neutering, found homes for thousands of unwanted animals, gave medical attention to animals whose families could not afford it, and provided advice and counseling. The foundation's efforts were limited primarily to Southern California and Carmel. By mid–1982, the foundation had answered more than 12,500 telephone inquiries about pets needing assistance.

The pet foundation closed in 1996. The Doris Day Animal Foundation was established in 1998 to include services for areas outside of Southern California. The organization rents space in a kennel and if a homeless dog is found, it is put there and kept until a home is found. They never put a dog down unless it is very ill. The foundation also raises money to pay for food, medical care, vaccinations and other services for people who could not otherwise afford to keep their pets.

One of the Animal Foundation's main events is the annual Spay Day USA, held in February. Spay Day USA was created as a national effort to bring public awareness to the procedure and to complete the task of spaying and neutering cats and dogs. Pet overpopulation is a main concern of the organization, and Spay Day USA helps eliminate the growing problem. Between ten and twelve million dogs and cats are put to death each year because no one wants them. "That's almost a quarter of all the pets in the country," Doris pointed out. "It's a national shame. But we're doing something about it." Not only does the Foundation help prevent overpopulation, but saves millions of dollars in taxpayer money from housing and killing the animals.

"We should not breed," Doris stated, "except for pedigrees, and that should be very, very carefully done."

In 2002 alone, the organization spayed or neutered more than 200,000 cats and dogs, thus preventing millions of births and probable suffering and death. In just six years, one female dog and her offspring can produce 67,000 animals. In the case of cats, one female and her offspring are capable of producing 420,000 cats in just seven years.

Animal abuse awareness is another program of the Doris Day Animal Foundation. *The Violence Connection* assists people to help abused and neglected animals through the judicial system and informs people how animal abusers acquire their victims—in many instances, through newspapers ads in which people wish to give their unwanted pets to good homes. The organization advises against using such a tactic unless the owner is absolutely sure the new owner is capable of caring for the pet. The Foundation also made public a group of individuals, known as "bunchers," who seek out free pets only to eventually sell the animals to medical researchers for experimentation.

An additional item to which the Foundation brings attention is "The Vicious Circle," which explains the connection between violence toward animals and violence towards people. It explores the cases of children who had a history of animal abuse in their childhood, and who eventually turned their abuse toward humans.

In 1987, Doris formed the Doris Day Animal League headquartered in Washington D.C. The primary concern of the organization is lobbying for animal protection rights. It has grown to include over 280,000 members and supporters in the United States. The league is a non-profit organization and its main source of revenue is contributions.

Since its conception, the Doris Day Animal League's influence has been felt all over the United States, from small towns to Congress. It has grown to become one of the largest animal rights groups in the United States. The league encourages the public to write members of Congress to voice their opinions on the rights of animals. The organization has a web site (www.ddal.org) which details current legislation being targeted, and the status of legislation on both state and national levels.

For example, Minnesota has the lowest penalty in the country for cruelty to animals, with even the most violent abused deemed as a misdemeanor. The league urged residents to support Senator Don Betzold, who suggested the penalties for the severest crimes be raised to a felony level.

Publicity shot, 1989 (from the collection of Matt Tunia).

The league also lobbies for laws against using animals for unnecessary testing of household products and cosmetics and has managed to replace outdated and inhumane animal testing with safer and more effective alternatives. As a result, public awareness of animal testing has grown, which in turn creates more public protests and boycotting of animal-tested products. The league is now pushing for more legislation to prevent cruelty to animals in circuses and factory farms and on public land.

Both the Doris Day Animal League and the Doris Day Animal Foundation are extremely vocal organizations. Both post graphic stories of the horrific treatment of animals on the Internet. One topic on the subject of greyhound racing tells how prime greyhounds are bred. Often, the runts of the litter—each numbering up to eight puppies—are destroyed within three weeks of birth if they show little promise of being a champion runner. The survivors are sold and begin training for the racetrack. Those who fail to show signs of being turned into a racing dog are also destroyed. At around one year of age, the trained greyhounds are taken to the racetrack to begin their careers. Unfortunately, only one out of eight dogs lives to four years of age. In several instances, dogs are often buried in mass graves near the racetracks. In fact, the remains of 143 dogs were discovered in an Arizona lemon grove.

Of the retired dogs who are not put to death, several are subjected to a worse fate. Former racing dogs have been sold to the U.S. Army laboratory at the Presidio where they were used for "long term survival projects," including bone replacement experiments. In another instance, more than 80 retired dogs were used at the University of Arizona for reproductive, orthopedic, anesthetic and cardiopulmonary experiments.

Through the efforts of the Doris Day Animal League and other organizations and individuals, all but 16 states have banned greyhound racing.

The Doris Day Animal League also supported a lawsuit against the U.S. Air Force in the transfer of chimpanzees to the Coulston Foundation, an animal research facility. The 111 chimps given to Coulston are the survivors and descendants of the group of chimps used in America's space program in the 1960s before the historic flights of John Glenn and Alan Shepard. Although the Air Force considered retiring the unneeded chimps to a sanctuary, only 30 of them were sent into a comfortable retirement. In addition, Coulston has been investigated three times in the past several years for violating the Animal Welfare Act. All three investigations concerned the negligent deaths of chimps.

Not surprisingly, Doris Day is very political. At times she spends part of each evening listening to talk radio, and often writes letters to politicians. Many of them are requests urging them to help put a stop to testing products on animals. Her outspoken views have caused some to ask, "How could Doris Day say those things!?" One reason is the public's misconception of Doris Day the entertainer and Doris Day the person. While the former provided the public with decades of entertainment, the latter has resulted in the public's disbelief and at times, shock, over her beliefs—at times highly controversial.

Doris believes product experimentation should be performed on convicted killers instead of animals. "Why not?" she asked. "They owe society something. Don't stand aghast at that. They're sitting there having three meals a day and we're paying for it. What the hell are they going to do for society to pay us back?

"I think they'd want to do it," she later said, "to give back to society what they have taken from it. I should think it would make them feel better. I would volunteer if I'd done something so horrendous like those people on death row. Anyway, it's stupid to test on animals. They're not like us."

Of course, such stands have provoked controversy and individuals attempting to discredit Doris for being too supportive of animal rights. One rumor claimed that Doris catered to her animals as if they were human, feeding her pets on tables with gingham cloths. In truth she uses short step stools; as for the cloths, she had several mismatched placemats she had no use for, so she simply put them under the animal's feeding bowls to prevent spillage on the floors.

Doris Day is easily one of the twentieth century's most popular and versatile entertainers, with five decades of performing: dancing on a local level in her early years to big bands, music tours, radio shows, films, recordings and television. Her imprint on Hollywood is enshrined at Grauman's Chinese Theater where she set her signature, hand and footprints in 1961, and on the Hollywood Walk of Fame where she has been awarded different times for her work in films and music.

The only major award she has received for her body of work was in 1989. Doris made a rare appearance in Los Angeles at the Hollywood Foreign Press Association's Golden Globe Awards to receive the Cecil B. DeMille Award for lifetime achievement. She looked dazzling, relaxed, healthy and happy, perhaps more so because at the same event, Terry, was nominated as a co-writer for Best Song with "Kokomo" from the movie *Cocktail*.

When fellow Carmel resident Clint Eastwood presented the award to Doris, he stumbled over his words, and said he regretted not having had the chance to work with her. Doris received a standing ovation which lasted for over one minute (including a couple catcall whistles) as she kissed Eastwood. The orchestra played "Whatever Will Be, Will Be" as she stood looking around at the crowd, catching sight of a few people she knew personally, and simply glowed.

"I don't know what to say, I really don't," Doris began her speech. "I'm a wreck. You do this all time and I don't do it any more. I live in the country, and I've got to come to town more often." (*sustained applause*)

"I look around and I can't believe all this talent. I'm in awe, I really am, and for me to be standing up here with this award, I don't understand it. But I love it, and I am very grateful. And it's so wonderful seeing all of you again. I've been away much too long.

"This business has been such a great joy in my life. I've loved every minute of it. And there's so many people I'd love to thank: all the fabulous leading men I've worked with…. I've worked with the cream of the crop. And I'd love to work with you by the way," she said to a grinning Eastwood, at which time she tilted her head and rolled her eyes as the audience laughed and applauded.

"It's been a wonderful life and I'm not finished yet. I think the best is yet to come, I really do, and I'd like to do some more."

But the lure of offers and money have not been enough for her to return to performing. Countless times she has been asked to perform, including headlining in Las Vegas for top dollar, but she refused. She also turned down $1 million to appear in one diet food commercial. The company who made the offer agreed to film on location in Carmel, and promised that it would be no more than four hours work. Doris refused on the basis of integrity. "I've never had a weight problem and I don't use the product," she reasoned. "It wouldn't be honest." Les Brown asked Doris in 1985 to consider singing with his band again by holding a concert to raise money for her pet foundation. Doris said she'd think about it, but it never came to fruition.

After she sang harmony on "These Days" on Terry's self-titled 1974 album, was in top form in her 1975 television special, and recorded several cuts for *Doris Day's Best Friends*, Terry tried to convince Doris to record a new album. But she declined, not wishing to return to the studio as she suffers from an allergic reaction to the pine and oak trees surrounding her Carmel home. The result is a slightly husky quality according to writer Joseph F. Laredo, who believes Doris' vocal quality is completely intact. While researching in the mid–1990s for the Bear Family CD box sets of Doris' music career, Laredo heard Doris sing parts of her songs to refresh her memory. But Doris the perfectionist will not record again unless she can sing the way she wants to sing.

Instead of returning to the recording studio, Doris asked Terry what happened to the tapes she made for an album in 1968 after her Columbia contract expired. This was the first Terry had heard of the recordings. After an intense search, the missing tapes were found in storage.

Terry learned how Capitol Records improved the quality of Nat King Cole's recordings, so he had the master tapes transferred to a digital computer format, enhancing and upgrading the tapes. This resulted in *The Love Album*, released in 1993 as the first "new" Doris Day album in over 25 years.

Unlike a majority of her fellow actors and singers, who cling to the spotlight long after their time has passed, no Norma Desmond is she. Doris walked away when she felt it was time and entered a new life of her own making.

"Maybe without performing there isn't much of a life for them," Doris offered. "If they can't do that any more, life becomes dull. Well, my life is anything but dull. I'm so busy, they'd never believe everything I do.... To do a film just to be working, I don't need that."

For an entertainer who has not made a movie more than 35 years, has not recorded music for specific release in as many years, and has not appeared in a television series in 20 years, Doris Day remains popular. Her popularity continues to grow each year through the sales of videocassettes and DVDs of her film and reissues of her music on compact disc. "Her music catalogue each year seems to sell a multiple of two or three times what it did the previous year," says Terry, who primarily oversees his mother's business dealings when not working on his own projects. "I think she's very surprised—almost amazed—that there would be a continuing interest, with absolutely no encouragement on her part. I think she gets about as much mail today as she got did in 1960." Although Doris receives over 1,000 letters a week, she does make an attempt to answer her fan mail.

When Doris was invited to appear at a UCLA Film and TV Archives series in Los Angeles honoring her career, she did not reply to the invitation. Columnist Army Archerd telephoned Doris and asked her why she did not go or at least respond. Doris replied she knew nothing about the fete and sighed that the letter is "probably on my table with a stack of Christmas cards I'm still going through."

Although the requests to appear at industry fetes and personal letters from fans is overwhelming at times, Doris takes the time to visit whenever a fan happens to see her.

For some odd reason, the print media cannot accept how she could simply choose to lead a somewhat ordinary life after the glamour of Hollywood. Every so often, tabloid newspapers run stories on how Doris is a recluse, living in the past, and other untruths.

Perhaps the most damaging was a story printed in a July 23, 1991, edition of *The Globe* which claimed Doris looked like a bag lady, rummaged through garbage cans for food for her animals, and did not recognize her own voice when "Whatever Will Be, Will Be" was played in her presence. Doris retaliated by filing a $25 million lawsuit.

"People need to know that tabloids like *The Globe* are really cheating and deceiving the public," Doris said in a statement. "Many people, unfortunately, believe the lies these people print." The suit was withdrawn after *The Globe* agreed to run a public apology for the article. The apology was also printed in several newspapers around the world.

Perhaps in an effort to counteract the perception she was reclusive, Doris appeared in a couple of documentaries and interview shows in the 1990s that were recorded in Carmel. In them, she openly discussed her life and her career, and looked healthy and content.

Not that she doesn't value her privacy. When a 2000 census taker arrived at her gate and pushed the intercom button, Doris answered over the intercom, refusing to take part. When the person informed her it was the law, Doris replied, "I will not answer any questions." Doris participated in the census by telephone.

Today Doris Day is not locked up in her house, but loves to shop and entertain friends, both old and new. She watches television and listens to the radio, stays informed on both local and international activities, continues her work with her animal foundations, and is content with the life she now leads. Although she experienced back trouble in 2003 that required treatment, now in her ninth decade, Doris continues to remain active.

"My mother is somewhat unpredictable, totally spontaneous. She has an ability to actually enjoy herself with whatever she's doing," Terry Melcher summarized. "She never did develop an addiction to the spotlight. And one day she walked away and never looked back.

"She lives a very peaceful existence."

Day at the Movies

I think Doris Day is the most underrated, under appreciated actress to ever come out of Hollywood. —Molly Haskell

OVERVIEW

DORIS DAY HAD ONE of the most successful—and diverse—Hollywood acting careers. From lighthearted musicals and sophisticated comedies to a handful of dramatic roles, and a couple Westerns as well, Day succeeded in several film genres.

Day's film career can be arguably split into three periods: 1948 through 1954 (the Warner Bros. years); 1955 through 1962 (the diverse years); and 1963 through 1968 (the light comedy years).

The Warner Bros. years consisted mainly of musicals, with the exception of a couple dramatic roles including *Young Man with a Horn* and *Storm Warning*. The years 1955 through 1962 showcased Day's wide acting range, from dramas including *Julie* and the biography *Love Me or Leave Me*, to the suspense films *Midnight Lace* and Alfred Hitchcock's *The Man Who Knew Too Much*. This era also showed Day as a gifted comedienne with *Pillow Talk*, *Please Don't Eat the Daises*, *Lover Come Back* and *That Touch of Mink*. She also returned to her musical film roots twice more at this time: in the minor hit *The Pajama Game* and also in *Jumbo* which, despite positive reviews and a score by Rodgers and Hart, proved an inexplicable box office flop. The post–1962 era consisted entirely of comedies with hits like *The Thrill of It All* and *The Glass Bottom Boat* through critical and financial misses including *Caprice* and *The Ballad of Josie*.

73

Her acting ability and talent grew, from her debut in *Romance on the High Seas* in 1948 through her swan song *With Six You Get Eggroll* 20 years later; from overflowing enthusiasm in her musicals, to surprising resonance in atypical dramas, to subtle reformation of role interpretations in comedies. Although the viewer knew it was Doris Day on the screen, to her credit, Day skillfully did not act as herself in films, unlike several actors who tend to play themselves in a role rather than becoming and acting the role. Day's roles and films may have had similarities at times, but to the discerning eye, her portrayals differed.

Day realized this. "Unless you're a character actor, you're always playing your-self," she said. "It can't be any other way. Maybe a lot of actors would argue the point with me. But almost every motion picture star has his own personality com-ing through the character he plays. Brando plays many different roles but it's always Brando and a strong Brando. That's what people latch onto.

"Before I came to Hollywood I was a fan of Gary Cooper, Spencer Tracy, Jimmy Stewart, Ginger Rogers and Jean Arthur, because I knew what to expect them to do, and wanted them to do it. And that's what makes movie stars.

"I learn my lines and know my character and the rest is me. The inner per-son is manifest on the screen. And I think that's the way it is with all actors. But it's especially true of stars. Essentially they are themselves. Audiences expect them to be and are disappointed if they are not."

In the Warner Bros. years, critics labeled Doris Day "the girl next door" primarily because a majority of the Warner films had Day cast in such roles. While most were musicals, Day was pleased to move on to other genres after leaving Warner Bros. Musicals were "hard work," she recalled, especially perfecting the choreography which took much time to accomplish. Unlike today's musicals where a dance scene is severely edited into segments of a few seconds and pieced together to the beat of a song (pos-sibly because the actors cannot either dance or simultaneously execute routines with other performers), most of Day's choreography segments were presented with a small number of cuts in the finished film, as was the norm of that era.

During "the diverse years," that "girl next door" label disappeared because her acting style changed with each movie genre in which she appeared. From dramas to comedies, there was an effortlessness believability that emerged on-screen with each role. However, during the "light comedy" era, a handful of critics labeled her the "perennial virgin" because a few of her more successful films had centered around sexual innuendoes until the sexual act (off-screen of course) was performed with the blessing of matrimony. In fact, Oscar Levant, who co-starred in *Romance on the High Seas*, later joked that he "knew Doris Day before she was a virgin." Levant was not making fun of the woman inasmuch as he was the system that labeled her as such.

While Day largely ignored the "perennial virgin" tag, it had become some-thing of an international joke, though few took it seriously. Day simply brushed it off and said she could care less what people think about her. Day noted that she had played a wife and a mother in several films when many other actresses refused to play such roles, and specifically pointed out that Cary Grant never played a (biological) father in his films. When asked in the 1980s about the label, Day blamed the studios. "[It was] something to talk about, and it gives it a label. And that's what they like," she said, referring to publicity. "And they hope the audiences will go for it. I think it's rather silly."

In fact, a breakdown of her films show that in 19 of them, Day's characters were single, never-been-married women. In most, her character had a boyfriend, some of whom she married shortly before the end. Fourteen of these were made before 1954 when strict codes on film morals were enforced, whether it was a Doris Day film, an Elizabeth Taylor film or a Lassie film.

Of her post–1954 films where she played a non-married woman, in each of them Day's character plans to have sex with her leading man before matrimony. In most of them (*Pillow Talk, Lover Come Back*) she discovers the man is a scoundrel and dumps him before the act takes place. But what is overlooked is the fact that her character was going to bed the man but changed her mind after learning she had been lied to, save for her final film *With Six You Get Eggroll* when it was implied her character slept with the leading male before they married. In fact, in *Pillow Talk*, her character remarked she has been with a lot of men, but Rex/Rock Hudson is the jackpot. Only one film—*That Touch of Mink*—truly deals with the virginity issue, in which the character is protecting her honor. The others concentrate on the woman protecting her space and her integrity.

"[Doris Day] played a working girl when there were no working girl in movies," remarked Molly Haskell, who was among the first critics to credit Day for promoting the independent working woman striving for success without the aid of a man.

"When I remember her roles … it is as one of the few movie heroines who had to *work* for a living," noted Haskell. "Grace Kelly and Audrey Hepburn, bless their chic souls, floated through life. Voluptuous Ava Gardner ran barefoot and bohemian through exotic places. Marilyn Monroe was the sexual totem for the various fetishes of fifties America. Kim Novak, Debbie Reynolds and Shirley MacLaine, who, like Day, were not goddesses and hence had to exert themselves, still sought a man to lean on. One never felt in them the driving, single-minded ambition one felt in Day…."

It is, arguably, that quality women viewers found in Day that they admired. Men felt she represented what they wanted in a woman—pretty, smart, optimistic, friendly, driven, sexy—but not overtly so—and not seeking to emasculate. All of these qualities combined to make Doris Day one of the most popular performers of all time, and the most successful film actress of the twentieth century.

In regard to movies since leaving the big screen, Day prefers films of quality, no matter the genre. Her favorites, however, are mystery and action films. In 1975, Day was blunt about the subject: "I don't want to see junk. If I want realism, I'll become a social worker. But to come out thinking it's a shitty world …

it's like people who stop to look at an accident; they're not aware of what it does to them. I know what I want, and I know what I don't want. In this country you can do what you damn well please."

As for nudity in films she does not have a problem, but full frontal nudity oversteps the boundaries, and she personally would not have done nude scenes like so many other actresses if her career depended on it. "I have nothing against sex—I'm all for it," she remarked to Merv Griffin. "I don't want to be looking in a keyhole, and to me that's what it is, and it takes all the beauty out of it for me. I just don't want to go the theater and see it and watch people rising up on the bed and carrying on."

"She felt some sort of responsibility to people who had followed her work for years," Terry Melcher relayed, "to give them a portrayal of the type of person that's pretty much consistent with what they might expect. I think she really had a concept of what it meant to be Doris."

When asked how she'd like to be remembered in the annals of film history, Day replied: "So many people write to me and they say that when they're depressed or feeling really low, they'll go and see one of my films and they feel better. Now I don't know what that means except if what I do brings joy to the people, I would love that."

Interestingly, before the well-known Doris Day began her career in films, there was another actress by the same name who made a few movies in the 1930s and 1940s. The brunette appeared in *Thou Shalt Not Kill*, *Village Barn Dance* and *Saga of Death Valley* for Republic Pictures before fading into a private life and the arrival of the second Doris Day. This confusion leads some historians to erroneously list the initial Doris Day's films with the latter's work. Today, union rules prevent two entertainers with the same name to receive screen credit in films and television; an initial or middle name is added to distinguish between the two actors.

FILMOGRAPHY

Studio / Production Company (when applicable); Format / Running Time;
Month and Year of Release; Production Credits; Cast; Songs;
Story Plots; Film Reviews; Doris Day Reviews
*—denotes a song which features the vocals of Doris Day

Romance on the High Seas
Warner Bros. / Technicolor / 99 minutes / Released: July 1948

CREDITS:
Producer: Alex Gottlieb; *Director:* Michael Curtiz; *Screenplay:* Julius J. Epstein, Philip G. Epstein; *Additional Dialogue by* I.A.L. Diamond; *Photography:* Elwood

Bredell; *Art Direction:* Anton Grost; *Set Decoration:* Howard Winterbottom; *Costumes:* Milo Anderson; *Special Effects:* David Curtiz, Wilfred M. Cline, Robert Burks; *Musical Numbers:* Busby Berkeley; *Orchestrations:* Ray Heindorf; *Sound Recording:* Everett A. Brown, David Forrest; *Film Editing:* Rudi Fehr.

CAST:

Jack Carson (Peter Virgil); Janis Paige (Elvira Kent); Don DeFore (Michael Kent); Doris Day (Georgia Garrett); Oscar Levant (Oscar Ferrar); S.Z. Sakall (Uncle Laszlo); Fortunio Bonanova (Plinio); Eric Blore (Ship's Doctor); William Bakewell (Travel Agent); Franklin Pangborn (Hotel Clerk); Leslie Brooks (Miss Medwick); Johnny Berkes (Drunk); Kenneth Britton (Bartender); Frank Dae (Minister); John Holland (Best Man); Janet Warren (Organist); John Alvin (Travel Agent #2); Douglas Kennedy (Car Salesman); Mary Field (Maid); Tristram Coffin (Ship Headwaiter); Grady Sutton (Radio Operator); Barbara Bates (Stewardes); Sandra Gould (Telephone Operator) with Avon Long, Page Cavanaugh Trio, The Samba Kings, Sir Lancelot.

SONGS:

"I'm in Love"*; "It's Magic"*; "It's You Or No One"*; "Put 'Em in a Box, Tie It With a Ribbon (and Throw 'Em In the Deep Blue Sea)"*; "Run, Run, Run"; "The Tourist Trade"; "Two Lovers Met In the Night" by Sammy Cahn, Jule Styne.

PLOT:

Wealthy socialite Elvira Kent believes her husband, Michael, is having an affair. She tells Michael she plans to go on an ocean cruise to Rio, but she secretly plans to stay in New York to spy on him. Elvira hires nightclub singer Georgia Garrett to go in her place on the cruise, but Gloria must assume the Elvira Kent name and manners. Michael, meanwhile, becomes suspicious of Elvira going on the cruise without him. He hires private detective Peter Virgil to spy on Elvira during the trip. On the cruise, Peter mistakens Georgia for Elvira. Soon he falls in love with her, and when Georgia's friend Oscar Ferrar unexpectedly joins the cruise in pursuit of Georgia, Peter is torn between his loyalty to Michael and his jealousy of Oscar. When Georgia accepts a job singing in a new Rio nightclub, complications arise. The real Elvira Kent cannot sing a note. Soon, Elvira and Michael arrive separately to see what is happening. Elvira arrives on stage to sing, but introduces Georgia and allows her to sing instead. Peter realizes Georgia is not Elvira, and the Kents reunite with the understanding that each has remained faithful.

REVIEWS FOR *Romance on the High Seas*:

"...[a] musical that will give paying audiences more than their money's worth in laughs, tunes, romance and all-around good fun." —*Film Bulletin*

Ad, 1948.

"...a lush and exquisite Technicolor film—the first such ambitious presentation from Warners in several seasons."—*Hollywood Reporter*

"Sparkling dialogue, tuneful music, luxurious settings and an amusing story combine to make this film ideal light entertainment."—*Monthly Film Bulletin*

REVIEWS FOR DORIS DAY:

"Doris Day [is] a lass who is something to rave about.... Doris Day's singing is only one facet of a talent with genuine flair for acting."—*Hollywood Reporter*

"[Day] has much to learn about acting, but she has personality enough to take her time about it."—*New York Herald Tribune*

"...Doris Day, making her initial appearance in this musical, comedy, travelogue, song and dance production, and what you have is no less than devastating as a comedienne and singer ... she not only looks good in it but she is good."—*Film Daily*

My Dream Is Yours

Warner Bros. / Technicolor / 101 minutes / Released: April 1949

CREDITS:

Producer-Director: Michael Curtiz; *Screenplay:* Harry Kurnitz, Dane Lussier; *Adaptation:* Allen Rivkin, Laura Kerr; *Story:* Jerry Wald, Paul Moss; *Photography:* Ernest Haller, Wilfred M. Cline; *Art Direction:* Robert Haas; *Set Decoration:* Howard Winterbottom; *Costumes:* Milo Anderson; *Special Effects:* Edwin DuPar; *Musical Direction:* Ray Heindorf; *Musical Numbers Staging:* LeRoy Prinz; *Cartoon Sequence Director:* I. Freleng; *Sound Recording:* C.A. Riggs, David Forrest; *Film Editing:* Folmar Blangsted

CAST:

Jack Carson (Doug Blake); Doris Day (Martha Gibson); Lee Bowman (Gary Mitchell); Adolphe Menjou (Thomas Hutchins); Eve Arden (Vivian Martin); S.Z. Sakall (Felix Hofer); Selena Royle (Freda Hofer); Edgar Kennedy (Uncle Charlie); Sheldon Leonard (Grimes); Franklin Pangborn (Manager); John Berkes (Actor); Ada Leonard (Herself); Frankie Carle (Himself); Duncan Richardson (Freddie); Ross Wesson (Hilliard); Sandra Gould (Mildred); Iris Adrian (Peggy); Jan Kayne (Polly); Bob Carson (Jeff); Lennie Bremen (Louis); with Marion Martin, Chill Williams, Rudy Friml, James Flavin, Kenneth Britton, Frank Scannell, Art Gilmore.

SONGS:

"Love Finds A Way"; "My Dream Is Yours"*; "Someone Like You"*; "Tic, Tic, Tic"* by Ralph Freed, Harry Warren.

Jack Carson co-starred with Day in her first three films and dated her off-screen as well.

"Canadian Capers (Cuttin' Capers)"* by Guy Chandler, Bert White, Henry Cohen, Earle Burtnett.

"Freddie Get Ready"* (from "Hungarian Rhapsody II"); "I'll String Along With You" by Al Dubin, Harry Warren.

"Wicky, Wacky, Woo"*; "You Must Have Been a Beautiful Baby"*

PLOT:

When bobby-soxer idol Gary Mitchell quits his popular radio show, his agent, Doug Blake, hurries to find a replacement. Doug hears Martha Gibson singing over a selection-by-phone jukebox and takes her to audition for the show's sponsor, Felix Harper. Her style does not suit Harper, so she auditions for other shows, all to no avail. Martha meets Gary Mitchell and falls for him. Meanwhile, in an effort to cheer Martha, Doug brings her young son to live with her and his friend, Vivian Martin. Doug discovers Martha's singing strength lies in ballads. When Gary is fired after appearing drunk before a radio telecast, Martha is a hit as a last-minute replacement. As her star rises, Martha continues to carry a torch for Gary, who is practically unemployable. Doug sees Martha's love for Gary and, as a gesture to Martha, he decides to arrange a comeback for Gary. But at the return, Martha realizes not only Gary is a shallow, egotistical man but that she is in love with Doug.

REVIEWS FOR *My Dream Is Yours*:

"This is a reasonably entertaining variant of the tired, old backstage musical, due chiefly to Doris Day's fresh and appealing personality and Jack Carson's glib and amiable buffoonery."—*Film Bulletin*

"It's the old story of a newcomer trying to get a break—in this case, over the airwaves. But it's all dressed up with some sparkling tunes, sung by Doris, the lively vitriol of la Arden—plus the brash geniality of Jack Carson."—*Screen Stories*

"With a couple of bright new splashes here and there, a well-known rags to riches show business story serves again…. It is an entertainment of proven worth."—*Film Daily*

REVIEWS FOR DORIS DAY:

"…it is too much to expect [Day] to carry so many of the musical numbers, especially when they lack production values and consist essentially of solo singing spots. Naturally, the girl gives everything she has—which is plenty…."—*Hollywood Reporter*

"Unquestionably, Miss Day has what is called 'talent' in Los Angeles."—*New York Herald Tribune*

"Miss Day … turns in another exuberant performance that will win the favor of audiences; she is becoming a marquee asset."—*Film Bulletin*

It's a Great Feeling

Warner Bros. / Technicolor / 85 minutes / Released: August 1949

CREDITS:

Producer: Alex Gottlieb; *Director:* David Butler; *Screenplay:* Jack Rose, Mel Shavelson; *Story:* I.A.L. Diamond; *Photography:* Wilfred M. Cline; *Art Direction:*

Stanley Fleischer; *Set Decorator:* Lyle B. Reifsnider; *Costumes:* Milo Anderson; *Musical Director:* Ray Heindorf; *Orchestrations:* Sidney Cutner, Leo Shuken; *Choreography:* LeRoy Prinz; *Sound Recording:* Dolph Thomas, David Forrest; *Film Editing:* Irene Morra; *Makeup:* Perc Westmore.

CAST:

Dennis Morgan (Himself); Doris Day (Judy Adams); Jack Carson (Himself); Bill Goodwin (Arthur Trent); Irving Bacon (Information Clerk); Claire Carleton (Grace); Harlan Warde (Publicity Man); Jacqueline DeWitt (Secretary); Wilfred Lucas (Mr. Adams); Pat Flaherty (Gate Guard); Wendy Lee (Manicurist); Lois Austin (Saleslady); Tom Dugan (Man in the Bar); James Holden (Soda Jerk); Sandra Gould (Train Passenger); Errol Flynn (Jeffrey Bushdinkle); with Carol Brewster, Sue Casey, Nita Talbot, Joan Vohs, Eve Whitney; and appearing as themselves: David Butler, Michael Curtiz, Gary Cooper, Joan Crawford, Sydney Greenstreet, Danny Kaye, Patricia Neal, Eleanor Parker, Ronald Reagan, Edward G. Robinson, King Vidor, Raoul Walsh and Jane Wyman.

SONGS:

"At the Café Rendezvous"*; "Blame My Absent-Minded Heart"*; "Fiddle Dee Dee"; "Give Me a Song with a Beautiful Melody"; "It's a Great Feeling"*; "That Was a Big Fat Lie"*; "There's Nothing Rougher Than Love"* by Jule Styne, Sammy Cahn.

PLOT:

Actor-turned-director Jack Carson coerces Dennis Morgan and promising actress–studio commissary worker Judy Adams into appearing in his film *Mademoiselle Fifi*. When Judy realizes Jack was joking about the part, she announces she's returning home to Gurkeys Corners, Wisconsin. Both men feel awful, and offer Judy the lead in the film—but only after every major actress at Warners has refused it. Dennis, Jack and Judy resort to many ways for producer Arthur Trent to "discover" her, but Arthur thinks he's having problems when he sees a pert blonde everywhere. Jack and Dennis decide to sell Judy as a famous French actress who has arrived to Hollywood. The studio welcomes her at a party, but the plan falls through and Judy is exposed as an impostor. She decides to return home to marry her fiancé. Arthur Trent, on the same train taking Judy back, hears her sing a ballad and offers her a contract. Judy angrily refuses. Dennis and Jack rush to Wisconsin to convince her, but are too late. She has just been married to Jeffrey Bushdinkle, the boy next door who looks a lot like Errol Flynn.

REVIEWS FOR *It's a Great Feeling*:

"The feeling may not be great precisely, but it is pleasant."—*The New York Times*

"Since practically every actor and director on the Warner Bros. lot has a brief appearance in this movie, it is one of the biggest all-star productions yet.... [The film] is well-paced and amusingly staged, with bright costumes and many pleasant tunes."—*Movie Star Parade*

"[A] broad takeoff on Hollywood and picture-making. It has a gay, light air, color and a lineup of surprise guests that greatly enhance word-of-mouth values. Dialog has punch and it all plays well. [P]roduction is expertly set up to show off the comedy and the players."—*Variety*

REVIEWS FOR DORIS DAY:

"The addition of Doris Day is another attribute ... and in this film she proves she is a good comedienne, as well as a good singer."—*Showmen's Trade Review*

"Doris Day made this reviewer uncomfortable by insisting that she couldn't act throughout the proceedings. This sort of confession is too close to the truth for comfort."—*New York Herald Tribune*

Young Man with a Horn
Warner Bros. / Black and White / 112 minutes / Released: March 1950

CREDITS:

Producer: Jerry Wald; *Director:* Michael Curtiz; *Screenplay:* Carl Foreman, Edmund H. North; *Based on a novel by* Dorothy Baker; *Photography:* Ted McCord; *Art Direction:* Edward Carrere; *Set Decorator:* William Wallace; *Costumes:* Milo Anderson; *Musical Direction:* Ray Heindorf; *Musical Advisor:* Harry James (also Douglas' trumpet playing); *Sound Recording:* Everett A. Brown; *Film Editing:* Alan Crosland, Jr.; *Makeup:* Perc Westmore.

CAST:

Kirk Douglas (Rick Martin); Lauren Bacall (Amy North); Doris Day (Jo Jordan); Hoagy Carmichael (Smoke Willoughby); Juano Hernandez (Art Hazzard); Jerome Cowan (Phil Morrison); Mary Beth Hughes (Margo Martin); Nestor Paiva (Galba); Orley Lindgren (Rick as a Child); Walter Reed (Jack Chandler); Alex Gerry (Dr. Weaver); Jack Kruschen (Cab Driver); Jack Shea (Nurse); Dean Reisner (Joe); James Griffith (Walt); Everett Glass (Song Leader); Paul E. Burns (Pawnbroker); Julius Wechter (Boy Drummer); Ivor James (Boy Banjo Player); Dan Seymour (Mike); Paul Dubov (Maxie); Frank Cady (Hotel Clerk); Keye Luke (Ramundo); Paul Brinegar (Stage Manager); Bill Walker (Minister); Helene Heigh (Woman); Matharine Kurasch (Miss Carson).

SONGS:

"Get Happy" by Harold Arlen, Ted Koehler.
"I May Be Wrong"* by Henry Sullivan, Harry Ruskin.

"I Only Have Eyes For You"; "Lullaby of Broadway" by Harry Warren, Al Dubin.

"Limehouse Blues" by Philip Brahm, Douglas Furber.

"The Man I Love" by George & Ira Gershwin.

"Melancholy Rhapsody" by Sammy Chan, Ray Heindorf.

"Pretty Baby" by Egbert Van Alstyne, Tony Jackson.

"Too Marvelous for Words"* by Johnny Mercer, Richard Whiting.

"The Very Thought of You"* by Ray Noble.

"With a Song In My Heart"* by Richard Rodgers, Lorenz Hart.

PLOT:

A young boy, Rick Martin, listens to the music played in local bars and decides he wants to play the trumpet. Legendary jazzman Art Hazzard sees the potential in Rick and teaches him. Rick rises in the jazz world and finds love in singer Jo Jordan. He leaves Jo and friend Smoke when the sexy Amy North arrives on the scene, and with her he quits his friends and plays with a dance band. But beyond any human being, Rick's true love is music. After the death of Art, Rick comes to realize what is important. He leaves Amy, but with insecurities he loses his ability to play the trumpet and falls into the depths of alcoholism. He is rehabilitated and reunites with Jo and Smoke to begin a comeback.

REVIEWS FOR *Young Man with a Horn*:

"[T]here is considerable good entertainment in *Young Man with a Horn* despite the production's lack of balance."—*The New York Times*

"…a B-movie with pretentions."—*The New Republic*

"For the jazz devotee, it is nearly two hours of top trumpet notes. For the regular filmgoer, it is a good drama…."—*Variety*

REVIEWS FOR DORIS DAY:

"Songbird Doris Day turns in a topnotch performance."—*Film Bulletin*

"Doris Day is delightful as the girl singer and enacts her role with warmth and charm. She is a lovely gal, and her appeal is well-nigh irresistible."—*Showmen's Trade Review*

"Ex–dance band singer Doris Day is realistic and appealing as the torch-carrying friend."—*Look*

Tea for Two

Warner Bros. / Technicolor / 98 minutes / Released: September 1950

CREDITS:

Producer: William Jacobs; *Director:* David Butler; *Screenplay:* Harry Clork; *Based on the musical* No, No Nanette *by* Frank Mandel, Otto Harback, Vincent

With Gordon MacRae and S.Z. Sakall in *Tea for Two* **(Jerry Ohlinger's Movie Material Store, Inc.).**

Youmans, Emil Nyitray; *Photography:* Wilfred M. Cline; *Art Direction:* Douglas Bacon; *Set Decorator:* Lyle B. Reifsnider; *Costumes:* Leah Rhodes; *Musical Director:* Ray Heindorf; *Sound Recording:* Dolph Thomas, David Forrest; *Film Editing:* Irene Morra.

CAST:

    Doris Day (Nanette Carter); Gordon MacRae (Jimmy Smith); Gene Nelson (Tommy Trainor); Patrice Wymore (Beatrice Darcy); Eve Arden (Pauline Hastings); Billy DeWolfe (Larry Blair); S.Z. Sakall (J. Maxell Bloomhaus); Bill Goodwin (William Early); Virginia Gibson (Mabel Wiley); Craufurd Kent (Stevens); Mary Eleanor Donahue (Lynne); Johnny McGovern (Richard); Herschel Daugherty (Theater Manager); Abe Dinovitch (Taxi Driver); Elizabeth Flournoy (Secretary); with John Hedloe, Harry Harvey, George Baxter, Buddy Shaw, Art Gilmore, Jack Daley.

SONGS:

    "Charleston" by Cecil Mack, Jimmy Johnson.
    "Crazy Rhythm" by Irving Caeser, Roger Wolfe Kahn, Harry Warren.

Day co-starred with singer-actor Gordon MacRae in five films (Jerry Ohlinger's Movie Material Store, Inc.).

"Do Do Do"* by George & Ira Gershwin.
"Here in My Arms" by Richard Rodgers, Lorenz Hart.
"I Know That You Know"* by Anne Caldwell, Vincent Youmans.
"I Only Have Eyes for You" by Al Dubin, Harry Warren.
"No No Nanette"* by Otto Harback, Vincent Youmans.
"Oh Me, Oh My" by Arthur Francis, Vincent Youmans.
"I Want To Be Happy"*; "Tea For Two"* by Irving Caesar, Vincent Youmans.

PLOT:

In 1929, wealthy Nanette Carter decides to invest $25,000 in a Broadway musical in which she will star. But Wall Street crashes, along with her fortune. Her uncle and financial advisor, J. Maxwell Bloomhaus, does not have the heart to tell her the money is gone. When she asks for the money for the show, J. Maxwell devises a bet that she must not say the word "yes" for the next 24 hours. Despite several complications, Nanette succeeds, only to have her lawyer inform her that there is no money. However, the lawyer is wealthy. Friend Pauline Hastings schemes to win the lawyer's love and persuades him to back the show. The curtain finally rises on the successful musical *No, No Nanette*.

REVIEWS FOR *Tea for Two*:

"*Tea for Two* actually [is] filled with tuneful and popular melodies, plenty of laughs and ingratiating dances."—*Independent Film Journal*

"Good music and snappy comedy—dialogue variety—combine to make *Tea for Two* a pleasant entertainment in Technicolor."—*The New York Times*

"*Tea for Two* is in the bag. There is no reason why it should not be. The ace Technicolor production is generously endowed with all the ingredients that any musical intended for popular consumption is to possess—pace, catchy tunes, humor unconfined, perky dance numbers, color, femmes easy to behold and story pattern cut to the requirements of this type of film."—*Film Daily*

"A pleasant, entertaining musical with an amusing script, expertly presented dance scenes, and song of the 'Twenties sung by Doris Day and Gordon Mac-Rae."—*Monthly Film Bulletin*

REVIEWS FOR DORIS DAY:

"[Day and MacRae] complement each other like peanut butter and jelly. Their duet of the title song is just wonderful and the same goes for the other tunes they do singly and in tandem."—*The New York Times*

"...Doris Day dances for the first time on the screen and shows even greater potentialities as one of the top film entertainers."—*Independent Film Journal*

The West Point Story

Warner Bros. / Black and White / 107 minutes / Released: November 1950

CREDITS:

Producer: Louis F. Edelman; *Director:* Roy Del Ruth; *Screenplay:* John Monks, Jr., Charles Hoffman, Irving Wallace; *Based on a story by* Irving Wallace; *Photography:* Sid Hickox; *Art Direction:* Charles H. Clarke; *Set Decoration:* Armor E. Marlowe; *Costumes:* Milo Anderson, Marjorie Best; *Special Effects:* Edwin DuPar; *Musical Direction:* Ray Heindorf; *Dance Direction:* LeRoy Prinz; *Orchestrations:* Frank Perkins; *Sound Recording:* Francis J. Scheid; *Film Editing:* Owen Marks; *Makeup:* Otis Malcolm; *Hairstyles:* Gertrude Wheeler.

CAST:

James Cagney (Elwin Bixby); Virginia Mayo (Eve Dillon); Doris Day (Jan Wilson); Gordon MacRae (Tom Fletcher); Gene Nelson (Hal Courtland); Alan Hale, Jr. (Bull Gilbert); Roland Winters (Harry Eberhart); Raymond Roe (Bixby's "Wife"); Wilton Graff (Lt. Col. Martin); Jerome Cowan (Jocelyn); Frank Fergu-

The West Point Story: from left, Gene Nelson, Virginia Mayo, James Cagney, Day and Gordon MacRae (Jerry Ohlinger's Movie Material Store, Inc.).

son (Commandant); Russ Saunders (Acrobat); Jack Kelly (Officer-in-Charge); Glen Turnbull (Hoofer); Walter Ruick (Piano Player); Lute Crockett (Senator); with James Dobson, Bob Hayden, DeWitt Bishop, Joel Marston.

SONGS:

"Brooklyn"; "By the Kissing Rock"*; "It Could Only Happen in Brooklyn"; "Long Before I Knew You"; "Military Polka"*; "Ten Thousand Four Hundred Thirty Two Sheep"*; "You Love Me"* by Jule Styne, Sammy Cahn.

PLOT:

Performer Elwin Bixby accepts an offer to stage a show at West Point with his girlfriend Eve Dillon. Elwin is forced to enlist in the academy as a plebe after striking a cadet. Cadet Tom Fletcher has written the show, and through an agreement with Tom's uncle, producer Harry Eberhart, Elwin tries to convince Tom to take the show to Broadway. He is unsuccessful until he brings actress Jan Wilson to West Point, and she and Tom soon fall in love. When Jan is called back to her movie studio, Tom follows her, going AWOL from the Academy. Elwin brings Tom back to West Point, but the cadet is placed under arrest and the show is canceled. Elwin earned a French honor while he was a soldier, and remembers that a rule in which a visiting celebrity to the Academy can obtain amnesty for all punished cadets. He invites the French Premier to pay an official visit to West Point, and in turn the cadets are forgiven. The show is held, and Tom is reunited with Jan. In return, Tom presents Elwin with the stage rights to the show.

REVIEWS FOR *The West Point Story*:

"The net result is a great deal of fun, plenty of action and gusty, refreshing entertainment…. It rolls along pleasantly." — *Film Daily*

"The story is overlong and dated with corny situations that make the running time seem twice as long." — *Film Bulletin*

"…a little monster of a flag-waving, hip wagging musical." — *Time*

REVIEWS FOR DORIS DAY:

"For its best moment, *The West Point Story* depends on talented dancer Gene Nelson and the pleasant voices of Gordon MacRae and Doris Day…." — *Time*

"Miss Day is the femme lure for MacRae and this romantic lure clicks through their handling." — *Variety*

Storm Warning

Warner Bros. / Black and White / 92 minutes / Released: February 1951

CREDITS:

Producer: Jerry Wald; *Director:* Stuart Heisler; *Screenplay:* Daniel Fuchs, Richard Brooks; *Photography:* Carl Guthrie; *Art Direction:* Leo K. Kuter; *Set Decoration:* G.W. Berntsen; *Costumes:* Milo Anderson; *Music:* Daniele Amfitheatrof; *Sound Recording:* Leslie G. Hewitt; *Film Editing:* Clarence Kolster; *Makeup:* Perc Westmore; *Hairstyles:* Ray Forman.

CAST:

Ginger Rogers (Marsha Mitchell); Ronald Reagan (Burt Rainey); Doris Day (Lucy Rice); Steve Cochran (Hank Rice); Hugh Sanders (Charlie Burr); Lloyd Gough (Rummel); Raymond Greenleaf (Faulkner); Ned Glass (George Athens); Paul E. Burns (Houser); Walter Baldwin (Bledsoe); Lynn Whitney (Cora Athens); Stuart Randall (Walters); Sean McClory (Shore); Dave McMahon (Hollis); Robert Williams (Jaeger); Charles Watts (Wally); Dale Van Sickel (Walter Adams); Leo Cleary (Barnet); Alex Gerry (Basset); Charles Conrad (Jordan); Grandon Rhodes (Pike); Dabbs Greer (Attendant); with Paul Brinegar, Anthony Warde, King Donovan, Gene Evans, Dewey Robinson.

PLOT:

On a trip to visit her younger, married sister Lucy, New York model Marsha Mitchell arrives in a small Southern town to find it dark and unfriendly. Marsha then witnesses a brutal murder by a group of Ku Klux Klansmen. She discovers Lucy's husband, Hank, is one of the murderers, but keeps it to herself. When Marsha is interrogated by Burt Rainey, a lawyer who had grown up in the community, she tells him the group wore sheets. Burt files suit against the Ku Klux Klan, but when Marsha appears on the stand during the court proceedings, she denies knowing anything and all are cleared. An arrogant Hank brags about the Klan's win, and returns home drunk. Marsha belittles him and says she plans to tell the truth. Hank strikes and attempts to rape her. Lucy walks in and tries to calm him, but he also strikes her. Soon after, Klan members arrive at Hank's house, and they take Marsha to a secret meeting where she is whipped. Burt, Lucy and the police arrive, but a confrontation occurs with Hank accidentally shooting Lucy, and Hank being shot dead.

REVIEWS FOR *Storm Warning*:

"*Storm Warning* is a rip-roaring, spine-tingling film fare that keeps the customers on edge.... Wald ... artfully combines preachment and galloping entertainment."—*Variety*

"Played with dead seriousness all the way, *Storm Warning* permits a fine selection of players to demonstrate their talents with excellent results.... [The film] is potent, alert and stirring fare."—*Film Daily*

"A somber but stirring and thought-provoking story...."—*Hollywood Reporter*

REVIEWS FOR DORIS DAY:

"Surprise for the occasion is the successful casting of the singer Doris Day in a straight role that calls for considerable dramatic assurance."—*Variety*

"Songster Doris Day ... has her first crack at dramatic acting in this violent melodrama and comes off remarkably well."—*Photoplay*

"*We* were the first to hail Doris Day as a scintillating new discovery ... was the experiment to put her in *Storm Warning* really necessary?"—*Picturegoer* (UK)

Lullaby of Broadway

Warner Bros. / Technicolor / 92 minutes / Released: March 1951

CREDITS:

Producer: William Jacobs; *Director:* David Butler; *Screenplay:* Earl Baldwin; *Photography:* Wilfred M. Cline; *Art Direction:* Douglas Bacon; *Set Decoration:* Lyle

Opposite page: *Lullaby of Broadway* earned Day *Photoplay* magazine's Best Actress of 1951 (Jerry Ohlinger's Movie Material Store, Inc.).

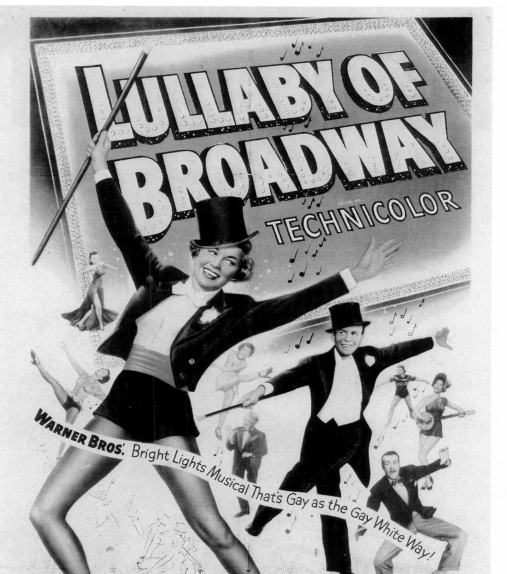

B. Reifsnider; *Costumes:* Milo Anderson; *Musical Director:* Ray Heindorf; *Musical Numbers:* Al White, Eddie Prinz; *Orchestrations:* Frank Perkins, Howard Jackson; *Sound Recording:* Stanley Jones; *Film Editing:* Irene Morra.

CAST:

Doris Day (Melinda Howard); Gene Nelson (Tom Farnham); S.Z. Sakall (Adolph Hubbell); Billy DeWolfe ("Lefty" Mack); Gladys George (Jessica Howard); Florence Bates (Mrs. Hubbell); Anne Triola (Gloria Davis); Hanley Stafford (George Ferndel); Sheldon Jett (Gus); Murray Alper (Joe); Edith Leslie (Nurse); Hans Herbert (Head Waiter); Herschel Daugherty (Sidney); Elizabeth Flournoy (Secretary); Jimmy Aubrey (Stewart); with Bess Flowers, Donald Kerr, Philo McCullough, Arlyn Roberts, Page Cavanaugh Trio, The DeMattiazzis.

SONGS:

"Fine and Dandy" by Paul James, Kay Swift.
"I Love the Way You Say Goodnight"* by Eddie Pola, George Wyle.
"In a Shanty in Old Shanty Town" by Little Jack Little, John Siras, Joe Young.
"Just One of Those Things"* by Cole Porter.
"Lullaby of Broadway"*; "You're Getting to Be a Habit with Me"* by Harry Warren, Al Dubin.
"Please Don't Talk About Me When I'm Gone" by Sam H. Slept, Sidney Clare.
"Somebody Loves Me"* by George Gershwin, B.G. DeSylva, Ballard Mac-Donald.
"We'd Like to Go on a Trip"; "You're Dependable" by Sy Miller, Jerry Seelen.
"Zing! Went the Strings of My Heart" by James F. Hanley.

PLOT:

Up-and-coming stage actress Melinda Howard arrives from London to visit her mother, Jessica, in New York. Melinda has no idea her mother has a drinking problem and is no longer a big Broadway star, but is singing in a small, dingy nightclub. When Melinda arrives "home," she lives in the basement, having been told the house is being rented by wealthy Adolph Hubbell and his wife. An attempt to clear the situation fails when, at a party hosted by the Hubbells, Jessica fails to appear. Despite not seeing her mother at the occasion, Melinda falls in love with dancing star Tom Farnham. Mrs. Hubbell, however, becomes jealous after seeing Melinda dancing and talking with her husband. A producer sees Melinda's talent for dancing and singing, and she is co-starred with Tom in a musical. But after her involvement with Mr. Hubbell, whispers of the Hubbells divorcing, a quarrel with Tom, and learning the truth about her mother, Melinda decides to return to England. Jessica comes forward and confronts her daughter, leading to reconciliation and understanding among all. Melinda appears with Tom in her first Broadway hit, *Lullaby of Broadway*.

REVIEWS FOR *Lullaby of Broadway*:

"Excellent musical. ... [The film] has been colorfully and lavishly produced, with quite a number of nostalgic songs featured throughout."—*Hollywood Reporter*

"A mildly diverting musical, stronger in the song-and-dance department than most of this type, but well in the rut insofar as story is concerned."—*Film Bulletin*

"This is a highly competent production from the same Warner team responsible for *Tea for Two*. Ideas and story are far from original, but the direction is polished and the musical numbers are excellently put across."—*Monthly Film Bulletin*

REVIEWS FOR DORIS DAY:

"Miss Day, it might be added, is a pert performer who, at this point, does not have to prove her right to sing a song. Though she is no Eleanor Powell, Miss Day ... has learned to dance effectively, too."—*The New York Times*

"Miss Day again demonstrates her musical comedy abilities for hefty reaction."—*Variety*

"Doris Day, pretty and irrepressible, sails through [her] songs ... with the grace and style of a big league performer. She's simply swell."—*Hollywood Reporter*

On Moonlight Bay

Warner Bros. / Technicolor / 95 minutes / Released: July 1951

CREDITS:

Producer: William Jacobs; *Director:* Roy Del Ruth; *Screenplay:* Jack Rose, Melville Shavelson; *Based on the* Penrod *Stories by* Booth Tarkington; *Photography:* Ernest Haller; *Art Direction:* Douglas Bacon; *Set Decoration:* William Wallace; *Costumes:* Milo Anderson, Marjorie Best; *Musical Director:* Ray Heindorf; *Musical Numbers:* LeRoy Prinz; *Sound Recording:* Francis J. Scheid, David Forrest; *Film Editing:* Thomas Reilly; *Makeup:* Gordon Bau.

CAST:

Doris Day (Marjorie Winfield); Gordon MacRae (Bill Sherman); Jack Smith (Hubert Wakley); Leon Ames (George Winfield); Rosemary DeCamp (Mrs. Winfield); Mary Wickes (Stella); Ellen Corby (Miss Stevens); Billy Gray (Wesley Winfield); Jeffrey Stevens (Jim Sherman); Esther Dale (Aunt Martha); Suzanne Whitney (Cora); Eddie Marr (Barker); Sig Arno (Dancing Instructor); Jimmy Dobson (Soldier); Rolland Morris (Soldier #2); Ray Spiker (Bartender); Creighton Hale (Silent Film Father); Lois Austin (Silent Film Mother); Ann Kimball (Silent Film Daughter); with Hank Mann, Ralph Montgomery, Jack Mower.

SONGS:

"Christmas Story"* by Pauline Walsh.

"Cuddle Up a Little Closer"; "Every Little Movement Has a Meaning All Its Own" by Otto Harback, Earl Hochna.

"I'm Forever Blowing Bubbles" by Jean Kenbrovin, John W. Kellette.

"Love Ya"* by Charles Tobias, Peter DeRose.

"(On) Moonlight Bay"* by Percy Wenrich, Edward Madden.

"Pack Up Your Troubles in Your Old Kit Bag" by Felix Powell, George Asaf.

"Tell Me (Why Nights Are Lonely)"* by Max Kortlander, W.J. Callahan.

"Till We Meet Again"* by Ray Egan, Richard Whiting.

PLOT:

In 1917, the Winfield family moves into a larger house closer to the bank where George Winfield works. George hopes that the move will help his tomboy daughter, Marjorie, meet a nice, acceptable young man to marry. Marjorie meets neighbor college boy Bill Sherman. While and the pair begin dating, George does not feel Bill is good enough for his daughter. When George's son Wesley misbehaves in school, he tells his teacher that his father drinks and beats Marjorie. Soon, the news spreads to Bill at college, who returns home to confront George and is promptly thrown out of the house. All is forgiven when it is revealed that Wesley was behind the story. At Bill's commencement exercises, the entire graduating class announce they have enlisted in the Army. Now engaged, Bill and Marjorie decide to wait to get married until Bill returns from the war.

REVIEWS FOR *On Moonlight Bay*:

"The stars are top-notch, the songs nostalgic and the production thoughtfully mounted but for all that, it just can't seem to get up the go and git. ... [T]he material handed the popular stars in this one has cooked too long in Hollywood's oven to be successfully camouflaged under Technicolor gravy."—*Photoplay*

"*Moonlight Bay* makes no pretense at being anything other than good, soundly-valued entertainment with popular appeal."—*Variety*

"...this production by William Jacobs is one easy-going entertainment sure to receive a good response from most any audience."—*Film Daily*

REVIEWS FOR DORIS DAY:

"Casting is nigh perfect. Miss Day and Mr. MacRae blend well in the romantic leads, both performance and song-wise."—*Variety*

"Doris Day is energetic and agreeable, although not quite of the period." —*Monthly Film Bulletin*

Starlift

Warner Bros. / Black and White / 103 minutes / Released: December 1951

CREDITS:

Producer: Robert Arthur; *Director:* Roy Del Ruth; *Screenplay:* John Klorer, Karl Kamb; *Photography:* Ted McCord; *Art Direction:* Charles H. Clarke; *Set Decoration:* G.W. Berntsen; *Costumes:* Leah Rhodes; *Musical Director:* Ray Heindorf; *Choreography:* LeRoy Prinz; *Sound Recording:* Francis J. Scheid, David Forrest; *Film Editing:* William Ziegler; *Makeup:* Gordon Bau; *Hairstyles:* Gertrude Wheeler.

CAST:

Janice Rule (Nell Wayne); Dick Wesson (Sgt. Mike Nolan); Ron Hagerthy (Cpl. Rick Williams); Richard Webb (Col. Callan); Hayden Rorke (Chaplain); Howard St. John (Steve Rogers); Ann Doran (Mrs. Callan); Tommy Farrell (Turner); John Maxwell (George Norris); Don Beddoe (Bob Wayne); Mary Adams (Sue Wayne); Bigelow Sayre (Dr. Williams); Eleanor Audley (Mrs. Williams); Pat Henry (Theater Manager); Ray Montgomery (Capt. Nelson); Bill Neff (Co-Pilot); Jill Richards (Nurse); Rush Williams (Virginia Boy); Doris Day, Gordon MacRae, Virginia Mayo, Gene Nelson, Ruth Roman, James Cagney, Gary Cooper, Virginia Gibson, Phil Harris, Frank Lovejoy, Lucille Norman, Louella Parsons, Randolph Scott, Jane Wyman and Patrice Wymore (as themselves).

SONGS:

"Good Green Acres of Home" by Irving Kahal, Sammy Fain.

"I May Be Wrong (But I Think You're Wonderful)" by Harry Ruskin, Henry Sullivan.

"Liza" by Gus Kahn, George & Ira Gershwin.

"'S Wonderful"* by George & Ira Gershwin.

"Look Out Stranger, I'm a Texas Ranger" by Ruby Ralesin, Phil Harris.

"Lullaby of Broadway"* by Harry Warren, Al Dubin.

"Noche Carib" by Percy Faith.

"What Is This Thing Called Love"; "You Do Something to Me"* by Cole Porter.

"You Ought to Be in Pictures"* by Edward Heyman, Dana Suesse.

"You're Gonna Lose Your Gal"* by Joe Young, Jimmy Monaco.

PLOT:

Lonely soldier Rick Williams discovers his former school friend Nell Wayne, now a movie star, is making a personal appearance visit in San Francisco. With the help of Mike Nolan, he devises a plan to meet her. Mike and Rick pass themselves off as soldiers who are about to leave for the Korean front, when in actuality they work the air route between Honolulu and the mainland United States. Gossip columnist Louella Parsons reports of Rick and Nell's romance, but then Nell discovers Rick is not a war hero. She wants nothing to do with him, but decides to publicly continue their "romance" to pacify the public and the press. A variety show with several film stars takes place at Travis Air Base to entertain the troops before they leave for Korea. On their return, however, Rick does get assigned to overseas duty, and he is reconciled with Nell.

REVIEWS FOR *Starlift*:

"As all-star pictures go, *Starlift* ranks among the better exhibits, although it suffers from the usual faults of such extravaganzas—an excuse for a plot on which to hang disjointed comedy and musical numbers...."—*Film Bulletin*

"All things considered, *Starlift* is suitably glittering."—*Screen Stories*

"When *Starlift* exploits a wardful of wounded veterans to raise a lump in the throat, it raises only a gorge."—*Time*

REVIEWS FOR DORIS DAY:

"Among the acts, Doris Day's several warblings of old songs are the easiest to take, while a hula dance by Virginia Mayo reaches the other extreme."—*The New York Times*

"Doris Day and Gordon MacRae, singly and as a vocal duo, perform yeoman work, while Gene Nelson's dancing is another highlight."—*Film Bulletin*

"As stars playing themselves, Doris Day and Gordon MacRae wind up and deliver strongly...."—*Variety*

I'll See You in My Dreams

Warner Bros. / Black and White / 110 minutes / Released: January 1952

CREDITS:

Producer: Louis F. Edelman; *Director:* Michael Curtiz; *Screenplay:* Melville Shavelson, Jack Rose; *Story:* Grace Kahn, Louis F. Edelman; *Photography:* Ted McCord; *Art Direction:* Douglas Bacon; *Set Decoration:* George James Hopkins; *Costumes:* Leah Rhodes; *Musical Director:* Ray Heindorf; *Musical Numbers*: LeRoy Prinz; *Sound Recording:* Oliver S. Garretson, David Forrest; *Film Editing:* Owen Marks.

CAST:

Doris Day (Grace LeBoy Kahn); Danny Thomas (Gus Kahn); Frank Lovejoy (Walter Donaldson); Patrice Wymore (Gloria Knight); James Gleason (Fred Thompson); Mary Wickes (Anna); Julie Oshins (Johnny Martin); Jim Backus (Sam Harris); Minna Gombell (Mrs. LeBoy); Harry Antrim (Mr. LeBoy); William

Forrest (Florenz Ziegfeld); Bunny Lewbel (Irene); Mimi Gibson (Young Irene); Robert Lyden (Donald); Christy Olsen (Young Donald); Else Neft (Mrs. Kahn); Ray Kellogg (John McCormack); George Neise (Isham Jones); with Vince Barnett, Don Barton, Clarence Landry, Jack Williams.

SONGS:

"Ain't We Got Fun," "Ukulele Lady" by Gus Kahn, Richard Whiting; "Carioca" by Gus Kahn, Edward Eliscu, Vincent Youman; "Carolina In the Morning"; "Love Me or Leave Me"; "Makin' Whoopee!"*; "My Buddy"*; "Yes Sir, That's My Baby"* by Gus Kahn, Walter Donaldson; "I Never Knew" by Gus Kahn, Ted Fiorito; "I Wish I Had a Girl"* by Gus Kahn, Grace LeBoy Kahn; "I'll See You in My Dreams"*; "It Had to Be You"; "The One I Love Belongs to Somebody Else"*; "Swingin' Down the Lane"* by Gus Kahn, Isham Jones; "I'm Through with Love" by Gus Kahn, Matt Melneck, Fud Livingston; "Liza" by Gus Kahn, George & Ira Gershwin; "Memories" by Gus Kahn, Egbert Van Alstyne; "My Island of Golden Dreams," "Your Eyes Have Told Me So" by Gus Kahn, Walter Blaufuss; "No No Nora"* by Gus Kahn, Ted Fiorito, Ernie Erdman; "Nobody's Sweetheart"* by Gus Kahn, Billy Meyers, Elmer Schoebel, Ernie Erdman; "Pretty Baby" by Gus Kahn, Egbert Van Alstyne, Tony Jackson; "San Francisco" by Gus Kahn, Bronislaw Kaper, Walter Jurmann; "Shine on Harvest Moon" by Nora Beyes, Jack Norworth; "Toot Toot Tootsie Goodbye"* by Gus Kahn, Ernie Erdman.

PLOT:

Aspiring songwriter Gus Kahn offers his patriotic songs to a Chicago music publishing firm. Assistant Grace Leboy reads his music, but tells him he should write simpler songs. After reading the works of Browning, Gus writes the lyrics "I Wish I Had a Girl," which Grace writes the music for and gets published. The two spend several years writing together, and later marry. The inspiration of Grace and his family life results in Gus composing "Pretty Baby," and during the birth of a child, "It Had to Be You." Gus is offered a contract with Florenz Ziegfeld in New York while Grace and the children remain in Chicago. He composes "Love Me or Leave Me" for the star of the Ziegfeld show, which causes insecurity in Grace. She travels to New York to find her marriage still intact. After the 1929 stock market crash, the demand for published music diminishes, bringing financial hardships to the Kahns. After an unsuccessful tenure in Hollywood, Gus suffers a mental breakdown. With the help of collaborator Walter Donaldson, Gus returns to success, and to the spotlight when a tribute is held in his honor.

REVIEWS FOR *I'll See You in My Dreams*:

"A dream of a movie, warm and tender. A movie that gives abundantly of song and happiness of simple pleasure and abiding love...."—*Photoplay*

"[The film] has a warmth that few musicals possess, and this is the quality

Michael Curtiz stresses in his direction. The pathos is nicely balanced by humor and the dialogue is sprightly and gay...."—*Film Bulletin*

"Well produced, excellently directed and acted by the principals, it will amuse and hold the interest of music lovers...."—*Showmen's Trade Review*

REVIEWS FOR DORIS DAY:

"Miss Day sells the Kahn tunes given her with a wallop and lends likable competence to the portrayal of Grace LeBoy Kahn."—*Variety*

"Doris Day does a good, solid job, contributing most of the sweetness with which she sings some songs."—*The New York Times*

"Doris Day again proves herself an able actress as well as an excellent singer."
—*Showmen's Trade Review*

The Winning Team
Warner Bros. / Black and White / 98 minutes / Released: June 1952

CREDITS:

Producer: Bryan Foy; *Director:* Lewis Seiler; *Screenplay:* Ted Sherdeman, Seelag Lester, Merwin Gerard; *Photography:* Sid Hickox; *Art Direction:* Douglas Bacon; *Set Decoration:* William Kuehl; *Special Effects:* H.F. Koenekamp; *Costumes:* Leah Rhodes; *Makeup:* Gordon Bau; *Music:* David Buttolph; *Orchestrations:* Maurice de Packh; *Sound Recording:* Stanley Jones; *Film Editing:* Alan Crosland, Jr.

CAST:

Doris Day (Aimee); Ronald Reagan (Grover Cleveland Alexander); Frank Lovejoy (Hornsby); Eve Miller (Margaret); James Millican (Bill Killefer); Rusty [Russ] Tamblun (Willie Alexander); Gordon Jones (Glasheen); Hugh Sanders (McCarthy); Frank Ferguson (Sam Arrants); Walter Baldwin (Pa Alexander); Dorothy Adams (Ma Alexander); Bonnie Kay Eddie (Sister); James Dodd (Fred); Fred Millican (Catcher); Pat Flaherty (Bill Klem); Tom Greenway (Foreman); Frank MacFarland (Johnson); Arthur Page (Preacher); Tom Browne Henry (Lecturer); Larry Blake (Detective); Frank Marlowe (Taxi Driver); Kenneth Patterson (Dr. Conant); with Bob Lemon, Peanuts Lowrey, Gene Mauch, George Metkovich, Irving Noren, Jerry Priddy, Hank Sauer, Al Zarilla.

SONGS:

"Ain't We Got Fun" by Gus Kahn, Richard Whiting.
"I'll String Along with You" by Al Dubin, Harry Warren.
"Lucky Day" by B.G. De Sylva, Lew Brown, Ray Henderson.
"Take Me Out to the Ball Game"* by Albert von Tilzer, Jack Norworth.
"Ol' St. Nicholas" (traditional)*.

With Ronald Reagan in *The Winning Team*, **1952 (Jerry Ohlinger's Movie Material Store, Inc.).**

PLOT:

Telephone lineman Grover Cleveland Alexander rises to become a leading baseball pitcher and player. An accident while playing baseball in his youth has caused him to suffer from double vision, and the results of the injury rise unexpectedly. After serving in World War I and at the peak of his baseball career, blackouts occur, and a doctor suggests he quit baseball and live a quiet life. But Grover ignores the advice and refuses to tell anyone that anything is wrong. Soon, his playing is affected and there are rumors surfacing that Grover has a drinking problem. His career slides and his wife, Aimee, leaves him. Grover resorts to drinking and, appearing with a circus sideshow, tells of his past triumphs. Aimee learns her husband has epilepsy and seeks him out. She convinces him to get help and, with her by his side, he rises not only back to the top of the sport, but wins the World Series.

REVIEWS FOR *The Winning Team*:

"Foy handles the story with discrimination, covering the epilepsy angle ... with excellent taste."—*Hollywood Reporter*

"As baseball pictures go, *The Winning Team* is not a home run, nor even a triple. We would say it's a fairly well hit two bagger...." — *Film Bulletin*

"Although the facts may not be quite up to par, you'll find *The Winning Team* exciting film fare...." — *Screen Stories*

REVIEWS FOR DORIS DAY:

"Miss Day gives her finest dramatic performance to date, playing Aimee with sensitiveness and understanding." — *Hollywood Reporter*

"Miss Day is a straight and narrow version of a fretful but loving wife." — *New York Herald Tribune*

"Doris Day brings warmth to her portrayal of Alex's loyal and loving wife...." — *Screen Stories*

April in Paris

Warner Bros. / Technicolor / 101 minutes / Released: January 1953

CREDITS:

Producer: William Jacobs; *Director:* David Butler; *Screenplay:* Jack Rose, Melville Shavelson; *Photography:* Wilfred M. Cline; *Art Direction:* Leo K. Kuter; *Set Decoration:* Lyle B. Reifsnider; *Costumes:* Leah Rhodes; *Music Director:* Ray Heindorf; *Musical Numbers:* LeRoy Prinz; *Orchestrations:* Frank Comstock; *Sound Recording:* C.A. Riggs, David Forrest; *Film Editing:* Irene Morra; *Makeup:* Gordon Bau.

CAST:

Doris Day (Ethel "Dynamite" Jackson); Ray Bolger (S. Winthrop Putnam); Claude Dauphin (Philippe Forquet); Eve Miller (Marcia); George Givot (Francois); Paul Harvey (Secretary Sherman); Herbert Farjeon (Joshua Stevens); Wilson Millar (Sinclair Wilson); Raymond Largay (Joseph Weimar); John Alvin (Tracey); Jack Lomas (Taxi Driver); Mimi Fouquet (Veronica Pataky); Donald Kerr (Usher); Harry Tyler

Dancing in fine form with 1953's *April in Paris*.

(Doorman); Maurice Marsac (Representative); Eugene Borden (Master Chef); Nestor Paiva (Ship's Captain); Andrew Berner (Jacques); Robert Scott Campbell (Charles); Pat Mitchell (Marie); Patsy Weil (Jeanne); Delfina Salazar (Yvonne); with Don Brodie, Dee Carroll, Jill Richards.

SONGS:

"April in Paris"* by E.Y. Harburg, Vernon Duke.

"Give Me Your Lips"; "I Know a Place"*; "I'm Gonna Ring the Bell Tonight"*; "Isn't Love Wonderful?"*; "That's What Makes Paris Paree"*; "It Must Be Good"*; "The Place You Hold in My Heart"* by Sammy Cahn, Vernon Duke.

PLOT:

Chorus girl Ethel "Dynamite" Jackson is accidentally chosen to represent the American Theater at the International Festival of Arts in Paris. S. Winthrop Putnam of the Department of State travels to New York to tell her he made a mistake, and that the letter she received was supposed to go to Ethel Barrymore. Word leaks out about the unknown Ethel Jackson representing the United States, and Ethel sets sail for Paris.

On the ship, Ethel is befriended by Philippe, a Frenchman returning to his homeland. Winthrop and the delegation, however, believe she should follow their lead and do as they say. But the fun-loving Ethel refuses. Although Winthrop is engaged to Marcia, the daughter of his boss, he becomes involved with Ethel, and the two are married on board. Philippe halts the honeymoon when he discovers the newlyweds were not married by the captain, but by a ship worker.

When they arrive in Paris, Marcia meets them, having flown into the city. Winthrop decides not to tell either woman about the circumstances; however, each becomes jealous of the other, and a catfight ensues between the two at the opening day of the festival. Ethel is told to return to the U.S. Before leaving, Ethel learns from Philippe that she was never married. She stays in Paris and finds work on the Paris stage with Philippe. After Winthrop and Marcia sees her on stage, he tells Marcia he loves Ethel. But when Winthrop tells her, she insinuates that Philippe is her lover. Winthrop discovers the truth that Philippe is married with children, and he and Ethel finally divulge to each other they are in love with each other.

REVIEWS FOR *April in Paris*:

"An average musical sparked by Doris Day and Ray Bolger ... David Butler's direction makes the most of the material in the screen story [by] cloaking the sagging spots when the plot becomes too thin and pointing up a number of very amusing sequences." — *Variety*

"[The film] is ably equipped to exert appeal to those customers for whom mirth-and-melody offerings are prime draws. Under David Butler's expert direction, the feature unfolds as bright and breezy fare." — *Boxoffice*

"...if [the plot] sound artless to you, we're afraid that you'll not be too happy with the knock-about humors of this film."—*New York Times*

REVIEWS FOR DORIS DAY:

"Miss Day's winning personality and pipes aid her character, and Bolger is okay...."—*Variety*

"Miss Day spends much time sniping at [Bolger] ... Miss Day puts her skill at rhythm singing to frequent and favorable use."—*New York Times*

"The warm presence and the musical gifts of Doris Day and Ray Bolger breathe life into a flimsy farce plot, and it's done so spontaneously that even the waits between numbers are easy to take."—*Photoplay*

By the Light of the Silvery Moon
Warner Bros. / Technicolor / 102 minutes / Released: May 1953

CREDITS:

Producer: William Jacobs; *Director:* David Butler; *Screenplay:* Robert O'Brien, Irving Elinson; *Based on the* Penrod *stories by:* Booth Tarkington; *Photography:* Wilfred M. Cline; *Art Direction:* John Beckman; *Set Decoration:* William K. Kuehl; *Costumes:* Leah Rhodes; *Music Adaptation:* Max Steiner; *Musical Numbers:* Donald Saddler; *Vocal Arrangements:* Norman Luboff; *Sound Recording:* Stanley Jones, David Forrest; *Film Editing:* Irene Morra; *Makeup:* Gordon Bau.

CAST:

Doris Day (Marjorie Winfield); Gordon MacRae (Bill Sherman); Leon Ames (George Winfield); Rosemary DeCamp (Mrs. Winfield); Mary Wickes (Stella); Billy Gray (Wesley Winfield); Russell Arms (Chester Finley); Maria Palmer (Miss LaRue); Howard Wendell (Mr. Harris); Walter Flannery (Pee Wee); Geraldine Wall (Mrs. Harris); John Maxwell (Ike Hickey); Carol Forman (Dangerous Dora); Minerva Urecal (Mrs. Simmons); Harry Tyler (Mr. Simmons); Gayle Kellogg (Doughboy); with Lucille Curtis, Merv Griffin, Florence Ravenal.

SONGS:

"Ain't We Got Fun"* by Gus Kahn, Richard A. Whiting.

"Be My Little Baby Bumble Bee"* by Stanley Murphy, Henry I. Marshall.

"By the Light of the Silvery Moon"* by Gus Edwards, Edward Madden.

"I'll Forget You"* by Ernest R. Ball, Annelu Burns.

"If You Were the Only Girl in the World"* by Clifford Grey, Nat D. Ayer.

"Just One Girl" by Lyn Udall, Karl Kennett.

"King Chanticleer"* by A. Seymour Brown, Nat D. Ayer.

Billy Gray played Day's younger brother in the period musicals *On Moonlight Bay* and its sequel, *By the Light of the Silvery Moon* (Jerry Ohlinger's Movie Material Store, Inc.).

"My Home Town Is a One-Horse Town" by Alex Gruber, Abner Silver.
"Your Eyes Have Told Me So"* by Gus Kahn, Egbert Van Alstyne.

PLOT:

Bill Sherman returns from World War I to his fiancée, Marjorie Winfield, and announces that he wishes to postpone the wedding until he has earned some money. When Bill later changes his mind, it is Marjorie who wants to postpone the nuptials. Although she feels she cannot explain to Bill her reasons for the change, it is to protect her father.

George Winfield is on the board of trustees of the local theater group. When a glamorous actress wishes to present a play in the town, George reads the script and makes some alterations, rewriting parts that he feels may offend the audience. George's son, Wesley, read the note, shows it to Marjorie, and the pair believe their father is having an affair. Bill also sees the note and believes Marjorie is romantically involved with Wesley's music teacher, Chester Finlay. Bill breaks off the engagement, but he is later told that the note was written by George Winfield.

While celebrating the Winfields' twentieth anniversary, the truth is revealed and the family and relationships are restored.

REVIEWS FOR *By the Light of the Silvery Moon*:

"The movie is a spun-sugar musical, prettily pink to go with the season of bunnies, lilacs and new bonnets, generous-looking in Technicolor but mostly air and melting at the slightest touch...."—*New York Herald Tribune*

"[The film] is a warm, good-natured comedy of nostalgia that pleasantly combines charm, music and humor to an entertaining degree...." *Hollywood Reporter*

"Lots of fun, with a spoof and a song evident in David Butler's directing." —*Screenland*

REVIEWS FOR DORIS DAY:

"Doris Day gives her typical bright and refreshing performance, and as always her vocals are mighty pleasing to the ear."—*Film Bulletin*

"Miss Day is thoroughly charming in the feminine lead and seems to sing better than ever, which is saying a lot for the always good singing star."—*Hollywood Reporter*

"Miss Day and MacRae make a strong pairing to put over the romantic, comedic and musical moments of the film."—*Variety*

Calamity Jane
Warner Bros. / Technicolor / 101 minutes / Released: November 1953

CREDITS:

Producer: William Jacobs; *Director:* David Butler; *Screenplay:* James O'Hanlon; *Photography:* Wilfred M. Cline; *Art Direction:* John Beckman; *Set Decoration:* G.W. Berntsen; *Costumes:* Howard Shoup; *Musical Direction and Numbers:* Jack Donohue; *Sound Recording:* Stanley Jones, David Forrest; *Film Editing:* Irene Morra.

CAST:

Doris Day (Calamity Jane); Howard Keel (Wild Bill Hickok); Allyn McLerie (Katie Brown); Philip Carey (Lt. Gilmartin); Dick Wesson (Francis Fryer); Paul Harvey (Henry Miller); Chubby Johnson (Rattlesnake); Gale Robbins (Adelaide Adams); Lee Shumway (Bartender); Rex Lease (Buck); Francis McDonald (Hank); Monte Montague (Pete); Emmett Lynn (Artist); Forrest Taylor (MacPherson); with Billy Bletcher, Stanley Blystone, Budd Buster, Lane Chandler, Kenne Duncan, Terry Frost, Bill Hale, Reed Howes, Tom London, Tom Monroe, Lee Morgan, Zon Murray, Buddy Roosevelt, Glenn Strange.

Howard Keel and Day in *Calamity Jane* (Jerry Ohlinger's Movie Material Store, Inc.).

SONGS:

"The Black Hills of Dakota" *; "The Deadwood Stage" *; "Higher Than a Hawk"; "I Can Do Without You" *; "I've Got a Hive Full of Honey"; "Just Blew in from the Windy City" *; "Keep It Under Your Hat"; "Secret Love"*; "'Tis Harry I'm Plannin' to Marry"; "A Woman's Touch"* by Sammy Fain, Paul Webster.

PLOT:

When dance hall owner Henry Miller hires a man to sing in his business instead of a woman, tomboy Calamity Jane travels to Chicago to bring the famous Adeline Adams back to Deadwood. Unknowingly, Calamity instead offers the job to Katie Brown, Adams' maid.

In Deadwood, Katie falters and reveals what she has done, but after the crowd gives her a chance, she succeeds. Both Wild Bill Hickok (who is Calamity's friend) and Lt. Gilmartin (who Calamity loves) fall for Katie. Calamity believes the town is not safe for Katie, so she moves her into her cabin. Katie in turn decides to help her friend become more feminine. Together the pair makes their home livable, and Katie shows Calamity how to dress properly.

At a dance, Calamity sees Katie and Gilmartin embrace. Her jealousy causes her to tell Katie to get out of town. Wild Bill tells Calamity she's been a fool. During their talk, the pair realize they love each other. When Calamity goes to town to tell Katie the news, she finds she has already left. Calamity races and stops the stagecoach tells Katie of the engagement. A double wedding follows.

REVIEWS FOR *Calamity Jane*:

"A rollicking musical filled with humor, vitality and sure-fire song hits, *Calamity Jane* stands out as one Warner's brightest filmusicals to explode on the screen."—*Hollywood Reporter*

"Doris Day has given Warners one of its best—if not the best—musicals in years."—*Film Bulletin*

"The story is shamelessly reminiscent of *Annie Get Your Gun*, but the picture is lighter and fresher than *Annie*, though the score—ballads and novelty numbers—don't measure up."—*Photoplay*

REVIEWS FOR DORIS DAY:

"In this musical, it is the performance of Miss Day which keys the production. She cavorts through each scene, giving the action all that she has, imparting sensational verve to the songs and stepping adroitly through her dance routines."—*Independent Film Journal*

"As for Miss Day's performance, it is tempestuous to the point of becoming just a bit frightening—a bit terrifying—at times…. David Butler, who directed, has wound her up tight and let her go. She does everything but hit the ceiling in lashing all over the screen."—*The New York Times*

"Rowdy, bouncy, rough and punching across tunes like a Marciano left, the Day gal converts an ordinary story into topflight entertainment."—*Film Bulletin*

Lucky Me

Warner Bros. / Technicolor-CinemaScope / 100 minutes / Released: April 1954

CREDITS:

Producer: Henry Blanke; *Director:* Jack Donohue; *Screenplay:* James O'Hanlon, Robert O'Brien, Irving Elinson; *Story:* James O'Hanlon; *Photography:* Wilfred M. Cline; *Art Direction:* John Beckman; *Set Decoration:* William Wallace; *Musical Direction:* Ray Heindorf; *Orchestrations:* Frank Comstock; *Sound Recording:* Oliver Garretson; *Film Editing:* Owen Marks.

CAST:

Doris Day (Candy); Robert Cummings (Dick); Phil Silvers (Hap); Eddie Foy, Jr. (Duke); Nancy Walker (Flo); Martha Hyer (Lorraine); Bill Goodwin (Thayer); Marcel Dalio (Anton); Hayden Rorke (Tommy Arthur); James Burke (Mahoney); Herb Vigran (Theater Manager); George Sherwood (Smith); Percy Helton (Brown); James Hayward (Jones); Jack Shea (Officer Elmer); William Bakewell (Motorist); Cliff Ferre (Orchestra Leader); Charles Cane (Sergeant); Jean DeBriac (Captain); Ann Tyrrell (Fortune Teller); Gladys Hurlbut (Dowager); Jac George (Waiter Captain); with Angie Dickinson, Dolores Dorn, Emmaline Henry, Lucy Marlow, Tom Powers, Ray Teal.

SONGS:

"Bluebells of Broadway"*; "High Hopes"*; "I Speak to the Stars"*; "Love You Dearly"*; "Lucky Me"; "Men"*; "Parisian Pretties"*; "Superstition Song"*; "Take a Memo to the Moon"; "Wanna Sing Like an Angel"* by Sammy Fain, Paul Francis Webster.

PLOT:

Traveling troupe Hap, Flo, Duke and the superstitious Candy find themselves running out of luck. With little money, they dine at an expensive Miami hotel restaurant and are forced to pay for it by working in the kitchen.

Registered in the same hotel is successful songwriter Dick, who is working on a production he hopes will be financed by wealthy oilman Thayer. Dick begins paying attention to Thayer's daughter Lorraine, hoping to influence Thayer. When Candy meets Dick, she thinks he works in an auto garage. He continues the facade until Hap reveals the truth. Dick suggests to Candy that she could play a leading role in his production. When Lorraine discovers this, she threatens to tell her father not to invest in Dick's show.

A birthday party for Thayer provides an outlet for the show's songs to be heard. Lorraine attempts to sabotage the performance, but doesn't recognize the foursome as they enter the party in disguise. Candy taunts Lorraine throughout the house and outside to the swimming pool, where Lorraine is pushed in. With

Lorraine unable to stop the group, the songs are presented to Thayer. He agrees to invest in the show, with Candy ignoring her superstitions as she and Dick move to Broadway.

REVIEWS FOR *Lucky Me*:

"Lightweight musical romance. Is tuneful, ingratiating. Has its moments, frequently...."—*Film Daily*

"Except for occasional sparks flying from Miss Day and Mr. Cummings, *Lucky Me* is one of those factory-made shows produced when the machine isn't quite running right."—*New York Herald Tribune*

"No fresh angles have been added to a familiar musical comedy plot about a burlesque troupe stranded in Miami Beach; nothing, that is, except CinemaScope, which is an asset."—*Film Bulletin*

REVIEWS FOR DORIS DAY:

"It's up to Day to carry this musical to success, and she responds nobly...."
—*Photoplay*

"Doris Day is in fine voice and she applies herself to the action of the comedy-romance in a manner calculated to render complete satisfaction."—*Film Daily*

"Doris Day handles tunes and performance in usual vivacious manner that will score with her fans."—*Film Bulletin*

Young at Heart

Warner Bros. / An Arwin Production / WarnerColor-Technicolor /
117 minutes / Released: January 1955

CREDITS:

Producer: Henry Blanke; *Director:* Gordon Douglas; *Screenplay:* Liam O'Brien; *Adapted from the screenplay by:* Julius J. Epstein, Lenore Coffee; *based on the story* Sister Act *by* Fanny Hurst; *Photography:* Ted McCord; *Art Direction:* John Beckman; *Set Decoration:* William Wallace; *Costumes:* Howard Shoup; *Musical Direction, Arrangements and Conducted by:* Ray Heindorf; *Piano Solos:* André Previn; *Sound Recording:* Leslie G. Hewitt, Charles David Forrest; *Film Editing:* William Ziegler; *Makeup:* Gorden Bau.

CAST:

Doris Day (Laurie Tuttle); Frank Sinatra (Barney Sloan); Gig Young (Alex Burke); Ethel Barrymore (Aunt Jessie); Dorothy Malone (Fran Tuttle); Robert Keith (Gregory Tuttle); Elizabeth Fraser (Amy Tuttle); Alan Hale, Jr. (Robert Neary); Lonny Chapman (Ernest Nichols); Frank Ferguson (Bartell); Marjorie Bennett (Mrs. Ridgefield); John Maxwell (Doctor); William McLean (Husband);

From left: Ethel Barrymore, Robert Keith, Dorothy Malone, Alan Hale, Jr., Elizabeth Fraser, Lonny Chapman, Day and Frank Sinatra in *Young at Heart* (Jerry Ohlinger's Movie Material Store, Inc.).

Barbara Pepper (Wife); Robin Raymond (Girl); Tito Vuolo (Man); Grazia Narciso (Man's Wife); Ivan Browning (Porter); Joe Forte (Minister); Cliff Ferre (Bartender); Harte Wayne (Conductor); Celeste Bryant (Young Girl).

SONGS:
"Hold Me in Your Arms"* by Ray Heindorf, Charles Henderson, Don Pippin.

"Just One of Those Things" by Cole Porter.

"One for My Baby" by Harold Arlen, Johnny Mercer.

"Ready, Willing and Able"* by Floyd Huddleston, Al Rinker.

"Someone to Watch Over Me" by George & Ira Gershwin.

"There's a Rising Moon for Every Falling Star"* by Paul Francis Webster, Sammy Fain.

"Till My Love Comes Back to Me"* by Paul Francis Webster (from Mendelssohn's "On Wings of Song").

"You, My Love"* by Mack Gordon, James Van Heusen.

"Young at Heart" Johnny Richards, Carolyn Leigh.

PLOT:

In a small Connecticut town lives the Tuttle family, Fran, Amy and Laurie, along with their music teacher father, Gregory, and Aunt Jessie. When Alex Burke arrives in town, the girls are delighted to learn that he is a boarder in their home and working with their father.

Alex invites his self-pitying but talented friend Barney Sloan to orchestrate his music score. Although Alex and Laurie are engaged, Barney falls in love with her. On the wedding day, Laurie discovers Amy also loves Alex. Rather than hurt her sister, Laurie runs off with Barney and the two elope.

Amy forgets Alex and later marries happily. Even though they are far from the family, Barney feels Laurie is still in love with Alex. After a suicide attempt, Barney fully accepts his wife's devotion, and the couple has a baby.

REVIEWS FOR *Young at Heart*:

"*Young at Heart* proves that Hollywood has not lost its knack for making indifferent new pictures out of good old pictures."—*The Saturday Review*

"It's always disheartening to see a film end poorly after a good beginning." —*New York Post*

"Musically entertaining…. Falters in heart, pathos and gentle humor that graced [the] original. Major drawback is rambling script, synthetic motivation in romantic complications of [the] screenplay."—*Film Bulletin*

REVIEWS FOR DORIS DAY:

"Miss Day delivers a fresh-faced and warmhearted performance."—*The Saturday Review*

"For both Miss Day and Sinatra, *Young at Heart* is a topflight credit. They give the songs the vocal touch that makes them solid listening, and score just as strongly on the dramatics…."—*Variety*

Love Me or Leave Me

MGM / Eastmancolor-CinemaScope / 122 minutes / Released: June 1955

CREDITS:

Producer: Joe Pasternak; *Director:* Charles Vidor; *Screenplay:* Daniel Fuchs, Isobel Lennart; *Story:* Daniel Fuchs; *Photography:* Arthur E. Arling; *Art Direction:* Cedric Gibson; *Set Decoration:* Edwin B. Willis; *Costumes:* Helen Rose; *Musical Direction:* George Stoll; *Miss Day's Music:* Percy Faith; *Choreography:* Alex Romero; *Sound Recording:* Wesley C. Miller; *Film Editing:* Ralph E. Winters.

CAST:

Doris Day (Ruth Etting); James Cagney (Marty "The Gimp" Snyder); Cameron Mitchell (Johnny Alderman); Robert Keith (Bernard V. Loomis); Tom Tully (Frobisher); Harry Bellaver (Georgie); Richard Gaines (Paul Hunter); Peter Leeds (Fred Taylor); Claude Stroud (Eddie Fulton); Audrey Young (Song Girl); John Harding (Greg Trent); Dorothy Abbott (Dancer); Phil Schumacher (Bouncer #1); Otto Reichow (Bouncer #2); Henry Kulky (Bouncer #3); Jay Adler (Orry); Mauritz Hugo (Customer); Veda Ann Borg (Hostess); Claire Carleton (Claire); Benny Burt (Stage Manager); Robert B. Carson (Mr. Brelston); James Drury (Assistant Director); Richard Simmons (Choreographer); Roy Engel (Reporter #1); John Damler (Reporter #2).

Love Me or Leave Me with James Cagney proved Day as a dramatic actress.

SONGS:

"At Sundown"*; "Sam, the Old Accordion Man"* by Walter Donaldson.
"Everybody Loves My Baby"* by Jack Palmer, Spencer Williams.
"I Cried for You"* by Arthur Freed, Gus Arnheim, Abe Lyman.
"I'll Never Stop Loving You"* by Nicholas Brodzky, Sammy Cahn.
"It All Depends on You"* by B.G. DeSylva, Lew Brown, Ray Henderson.
"Love Me or Leave Me"* by Gus Kahn, Walter Donaldson.
"Mean to Me"* by Roy Turk, Fred Ahlert.
"My Blue Heaven"* by Walter Donaldson, Richard Whiting.
"Never Look Back"* by Chilton Price.
"Shaking the Blues Away"* by Irving Berlin.
"Stay on the Right Side, Sister"* by Joe McCarthy, James Monaco.
"Ten Cents a Dance"* by Richard Rodgers, Lorenz Hart.
"What Can I Say (After I Say I'm Sorry)"* by Walter Donaldson, Abe Lyman.

PLOT:

Marty Snyder, a limping gangster covering as a laundryman, meets ten-cents-a-dance woman Ruth Etting in a small Chicago club. Marty offers her a job in a floor show. But Ruth wants to sing, so Marty persuades Johnny Alderman to teach her.

Ruth's singing career climbs from nightclubs to radio, but Johnny tells her that Marty is not a manager and just wants to use her. Johnny quits and Ruth ignores his warning as she receives a contract and continued success with the Ziegfeld Follies. Marty finds himself being needed less and less, and in a confrontation, he rapes Ruth. Although she does not love him, Ruth marries Marty.

Ruth's career continues after she leaves the Follies, with recording and a tour, and eventually a Hollywood film contract. In California she is pleased to learn Johnny is signed as the musical director for her first film. When Marty and Ruth break up, he has his right hand man, Georgie, spy on his wife. Georgie tells Marty that Ruth and Johnny are serious, and one evening Marty shoots Johnny. The event does not change Ruth and Johnny's relationship, but she feels compelled to help Marty realize that their marriage is over. When Marty is released from jail, Ruth appears at the opening of his nightclub to thank him for his help with her career.

REVIEWS FOR *Love Me or Leave Me*:

"The story is the solidest, strongest, most credible film biography yet. What makes this all the more surprising is the fact that *Love Me or Leave Me* is essentially a song-and-dance picture...."—*The New York Times*

"It is a musical that combines all the producer's ability to make sure-fire box-office with a story so true to human characterization, so powerful in its emotional conflict and so honest in its inquiry into the harsh as well as the exalting side of love that it qualifies, in every way, as a work of art."—*Hollywood Reporter*

"...the film had plenty for the box office. In all situations. [It] is unique and sufficiently offbeat to enjoy a distinction all its own ... it's a rich canvas of the Roaring 20s with gutsy and excellent performances...."—*Variety*

REVIEWS FOR DORIS DAY:

"Doris Day graduates out of her world of peppy collegiate revels with this picture, and the change is all to the good. She gives a mature performance...."
—*New York Herald Tribune*

"Miss Day comes through as a subtle and sure emotional actress ... she makes every sullen glance, every cautious smile and every murmured commonplace phrase speak volumes. A great popular star has become a great actress."—*Hollywood Reporter*

"Under the direction of Charles Vidor, Doris Day and James Cagney give dazzling performances as the mismatched pair."—*Look*

Alfred Hitchcock's
The Man Who Knew Too Much
Paramount / A Filwite Production / Technicolor-VistaVision /
120 minutes / Released: June 1956

CREDITS:

Producer-Director: Alfred Hitchcock; *Screenplay:* John Michael Hayes, Angus MacPhail; *Story:* Charles Bennett, D.B. Wyndham-Lewis; *Photography:* Robert Burks; *Art Direction:* Hal Pereira, Henry Bumstead; *Set Decoration:* Sam Comer, Arthur Krams; *Costumes:* Edith Head; *Sound Recording:* Paul Franz, Gene Garvin; *Film Editing:* George Tomasini.

CAST:

James Stewart (Ben McKenna); Doris Day (Jo Conway-McKenna); Brenda de Banzie (Mrs. Drayton); Bernard Miles (Mr. Drayton); Christopher Olsen (Hank McKenna); Ralph Truman (Buchanan); Daniel Gelin (Louis Bernard); Magens Wieth (Ambassador); Alan Mowbray (Val Parnell); Hillary Brooke (Jan Peterson); Reggie Nalder (Rien); Richard Wattis (Assistant Manager); Noel Willman (Woburn); Alix Talton (Helen Parnell); Yves Brainville (Police Inspector); Carolyn Jones (Cindy Fontaine); Alexi Bobrinskoy (Foreign Prime Minister); Abdelhaq Chraibi (Arab); Betty Baskcomb (Edna); Leo Gordon (Chauffeur); Patrick Aherne (English Handyman); Louis Mercier (French Policeman #1); Anthony Warde (French Policeman #2); Lewis Martin (Detective); Gladys Holland (Bernard's Girlfriend); with Peter Camlin, Ralph Neff, Eric Snowden.

SONGS:

"Storm Cloud Cantata" by Arthur Benjamin.
"We'll Love Again"*; "Whatever Will Be, Will Be (Qué Será, Será)"* by Jay Livingston, Ray Evans.

PLOT:

American Dr. Ben McKenna, his wife Jo and their son Hank vacation to French Morocco where they become acquainted with Frenchman Louis Bernard. While at dinner, the pair are befriended by an English couple, the Draytons, who recognized Jo, a famous, but now-retired singer.

While in the market, Bernard, who is an intelligence spy, is stabbed. He finds Ben and, before he dies, tells Ben that a statesman is to be assassinated in London. The Draytons kidnap Hank before Ben can tell the police what he knows about the plot. Ben and Jo travel to London in search of their son, and discover the Draytons have him hidden away in Ambrose Chapel. The couple attends a service at the chapel and discover the Draytons there. While Jo leaves to inform

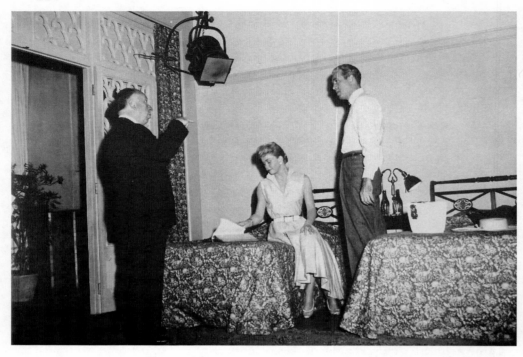

With director Alfred Hitchcock and co-star James Stewart, preparing to film the kidnapping confession in *The Man Who Knew Too Much*, **1956 (Jerry Ohlinger's Movie Material Store, Inc.).**

the police, Ben stays after Mr. Drayton dismisses the congregation. Ben is knocked unconscious and the Draytons flee with Hank to an embassy.

Jo meanwhile goes to the Royal Albert Hall, where the assassination is to occur. She sees the assassin and his target in the balcony, and at a crucial moment—the crash of the cymbals—during the concert, she screams, causing the assassin to not only miss his target, but fall to his death. Jo and Ben invite themselves to the embassy of the foreign Prime Minister, where Jo sings a couple of songs for the group. Hank hears his mother's voice and whistles to her from upstairs. Ben finds Hank and, after a struggle with Mr. Drayton, reunites with Jo.

REVIEWS FOR *The Man Who Knew Too Much*:

"Even in mammoth VistaVision, the old Hitchcock thriller-stuff has punch ... a fast, lively, sharp, suspenseful show."—*The New York Times*

"With Alfred Hitchcock pulling the suspense strings, *The Man Who Knew Too Much* is a good thriller...."—*Variety*

"While the current product ... is unquestionably much bigger and shinier than the original, it doesn't move along with anything like the agility of its predecessor."—*New Yorker*

1984 THEATRICAL REISSUE REVIEWS:

"[The film originally was] invariably dismissed as a minor work in the master's canon, [it is] so much better than any new movie that one feels both elated and dismayed."—David Denby, *New York*

"...a thrilling piece of cinema for anyone who can appreciate the working out of formal problems as a means of stirring the murky depths of the unconscious.... If you come out of the movie relieved that Stewart and Day are back together and happy again ... then you have missed the whole point of Stewart's implacability and Day's delirium. This is no ordinary nuclear family."—Andrew Sarris, *Village Voice*

REVIEWS FOR DORIS DAY:

"Miss Day functions very nicely opposite [Stewart], proving she does not need a predominately singing role to click with an audience."—*Hollywood Reporter*

"Miss Day again proves that she is a better actress than her early musicals would have us believe, and she has some anguished moments before the family is reunited."—*New York Herald Tribune*

"Mrs. McKenna is remarkably well played by Doris Day, who, until she appeared in the role of Ruth Etting in *Love Me or Leave Me*, was considered just a pretty girl who had a way with a song. She is now rapidly developing into a fine actress."—*New York Daily News*

Julie

MGM / An Arwin Production / Black and White /
97 minutes / Released: November 1956

CREDITS:

Producer: Martin Melcher; *Director-Screenplay:* Andrew L. Stone; *Photography:* Fred Jackman, Jr.; *Music:* Leith Stevens; "Midnight on the Cliffs" *Composed and Performed by* Leonard Pennario; *Sound Recording:* Francis J. Scheid; *Film Editing:* Virginia Stone; *Makeup:* Armand Del Mar; *Hairstyles:* Marie Walter.

CAST:

Doris Day (Julie Benton); Louis Jourdan (Lyle Benton); Barry Sullivan (Cliff Henderson); Frank Lovejoy (Detective Capt. Pringle); John Gallaudet (Detective Cole); Harlan Warde (Detective Pope); Jack Kruschen (Detective Mace); Hank Patterson (Ellis); Alene Towne (Denise Martin); Ann Robinson (Valerie); Ed Hinton (Pilot); Jack Kelly (Co-Pilot); Barney Phillips (Doctor); Carleton Young (Field Man); Pamela Duncan (Peggy); Mae Marsh (Passenger); Edward Marsh (Airline Official).

SONGS:

"Julie"* by Leith Stevens, Tom Adair.

PLOT:

Julie Benton discovers that her second husband, concert pianist Lyle, murdered her first husband. When Julie tries to leave him, Lyle threatens her. After the police are unable to provide her with any protection, Julie resumes her old job as an airline stewardess through the help of Cliff Henderson. Lyle stalks Cliff, attempts to murder him, and discovers where Julie is hiding. After Julie has been called in at the last minute for a flight, Lyle follows her and boards the same airplane. When she learns he is aboard, Lyle enters the captain's cabin with a pistol. A struggle follows, with both Lyle and the pilot shot to death. Julie is left to land the plane herself with help from personnel in the control tower.

REVIEWS FOR *Julie*:

"The charm and appeal of Doris Day lifts this MGM suspense melodrama a bit above conventional standards. The action under Andrew L. Stone's direction moves at a good pace, but the plotting lacks plausibility."—*Film Bulletin*

"This film is not for sophisticates. It's strictly meller and well staged for excitement values, but still suggestive of *The Perils of Pauline*...."—*Variety*

"The picture maintains a tension from beginning to end that will keep fans riveted with attention ... even though the story here and there shows the mark of contrivance...."—*Film Daily*

REVIEWS FOR DORIS DAY:

"Actually, the story seems a waste of talent for Doris Day and it will not advance her career as a straight actress, although she lends the picture more believability than it merits."—*Hollywood Reporter*

"Performances are adequate all around, although Miss Day has a time of it trying to behave convincingly in landing that big airplane."—*Variety*

"[T]he whole thing is contrivance and the acting is in the same vein. Miss Day wrings her hands and looks frantic not so much because she feels it as because she gets her cues."—*The New York Times*

The Pajama Game

Warner Bros. / A George Abbott and Stanley Donen Production /
WarnerColor / 101 minutes / Released: August 1957

CREDITS:

Producers-Directors: George Abbott, Stanley Donen; *Screenplay:* George Abbott, Richard Bissell; *Based on their Musical Based on the Novel 7½ Cents by*

Richard Bissell; *Photography:* Harry Stradling; *Art Direction:* Malcolm Bert; *Set Decoration:* William Kuehl; *Costumes:* William and Jean Eckart; *Orchestrations:* Nelson Riddle, Buddy Bregman; *Vocal Arrangements:* Charles Henderson; *Choreography:* Bob Fosse; *Sound Recording:* M.A. Merrick, Dolph Thomas; *Film Editing:* William Ziegler.

CAST:

Doris Day (Katie "Babe" Williams); John Raitt (Sid Sorokin); Carol Haney (Gladys Hotchkiss); Eddie Foy, Jr. (Vernon Hines); Reta Shaw (Mabel); Barbara Nichols (Poopsie); Thelma Pelish (Mae); Jack Straw (Prez); Ralph Dunn (Hasler); Owen Martin (Max); Ralph Chambers (Charlie); Mary Stanton (Brenda); Jack Waldron (Salesman); Franklyn Fox (Pop Williams); William A. Forester (Joe); Elmore Henderson (Waiter); Fred Villani (Tony); Kathy Marlowe (Holly); Otis Griffith (Otis); with Peter Gennaro, Jackie Kelk, Kenneth LeRoy, Buzz Miller, Ralph Volkie.

SONGS:

"Hernando's Hideaway"; "Hey There"*; "I'll Never Be Jealous Again"; "I'm Not at All in Love"*; "Once-a-Year Day"*; "The Pajama Game"; "Racing with the Clock"*; "Seven-and-a-Half Cents"*; "Small Talk"*; "Steam Heat"; "There Once Was a Man"* by Richard Adler, Jerry Moss.

PLOT:

At the Sleeptite Pajama Factory, superintendent Sid Sorokin shoves a member of the factory's labor union. Babe Williams, head of the union's grievance committee, investigates the matter and decides that Sid was not at fault. At the annual picnic, Babe and Sid fall in love. The union wants a seven-and-a-half cent hourly raise, but factory manager Hasler refuses. The employees decide to work slower, and mess up the sizes in the orders so that Hasler will listen to their demands. When Babe makes her sewing machine short out, causing an electrical blowout in the factory, Sid fires her. Sid later discovers Hasler had allotted an increase for the workers but has been putting the money toward non-business ventures. To risk being exposed, Hasler agrees to the hourly raise, and Babe and Sid reunite.

REVIEWS FOR *The Pajama Game*:

"The whole thing is splendid, the color is gay and strong...."—*The New York Times*

"With zip and zest and a proper, precise knowledge of what a musical comedy is intended to be, George Abbott and Stanley Donen have staged the best one of the year for Warners ... a triumph in every department."—*Hollywood Reporter*

"[A] socko filmusical.... Having the advantage ... of longtime association with the original, the celluloid version is an extension and an enhancement of the original."—*Variety*

REVIEWS FOR DORIS DAY:

"...even Miss Day, the interloper, is right in the spirit of things. Her high point, we'd say is when she couple with Mr. Raitt in 'There Once Was A Man....'"—*The New York Times*

"Doris Day makes a very likable Babe."—*Monthly Film Bulletin*

"Miss Day, freckled, short blonde locks and all, is as pretty as a Fourth of July picnic and as spirited...."—*Hollywood Reporter*

Teacher's Pet

Paramount / A Perlberg-Seaton Production / Black and White-VistaVision /
120 minutes / Released: April 1958

CREDITS:

Producer: William Perlberg; *Director:* George Seaton; *Screenplay:* Fay & Michael Kanin; *Photography:* Haskell Boggs; *Art Direction:* Hal Pereira, Earl Hedrick; *Set Decoration:* Sam Comer, Robert Benton; *Costumes:* Edith Head; *Sound Recording:* Hugo Grenzbach, Winston Leverett; *Film Editing:* Alma Macrorie.

CAST:

Clark Gable (Jim Gannon); Doris Day (Prof. Erica Stone); Gig Young (Dr. Hugo Pine); Mamie Van Doren (Peggy DeFore); Nick Adams (Barney Kovac); Peter Baldwin (Harold Miller); Marion Ross (Katy Fuller); Charles Lane (Assistant); Jack Albertson (Guide); Florenz Ames (J.L. Ballentine); Harry Antrim (Lloyd Crowley); Vivian Nathan (Mrs. Kovac); Terry Becker (Mr. Appino); Elizabeth Harrower (Clara Dibney); Margaret Muse (Miss Gross); Merritt Smith (Mr. Cory); Steffi Sidney (Book Store Worker); Cyril Delevanti (Copy Man); Norton Mockridge (Harry); Sandra Gould (Tess); Frank Richards (Cab Driver); with (as themselves) Army Archerd, Joe Hyams, Erskine Johnson, Paine Knickerbocher, Frank P. Quinn, Vernon Scott, Sidney Skolsky.

SONGS:

"The Girl Who Invented Rock and Roll"*; "Teacher's Pet"* by Joe Lubin. (Doris Day sings an excerpt of "The Girl Who Invented Rock and Roll," which was sung in its entirety in the film by Mamie Van Doren.)

PLOT:

Tough city editor Jim Gannon is invited to lecture at Prof. Stone's journalism class. Although Jim had never taken a college course in his life and believes the best education is learning by experience, he reluctantly goes at the insistence of his boss. After seeing Prof. Stone is an attractive single woman, Jim decides to enroll as a student. His first writing assignment impresses Prof. Stone; while feeling he possesses talent, she encourages him to continue with his writing. Jim feels he is paving the way for a romance with Prof. Stone until he discovers she already has a man in her life, the intelligent author Dr. Hugo Pine. Jim tries to beat Hugo at several games, only to find Hugo excels in almost all—except drinking. After Hugo passes out, Jim moves in for Prof. Stone. When Prof. Stone visits his boss to solicit a job for her talented pupil, Jim is called in and the truth comes to light. The pair later understand each other's point of view, and Jim agrees to deliver a series of lectures for her classes.

REVIEWS FOR *Teacher's Pet*:

"*Teacher's Pet*, as one of its principals remarks, does not succeed entirely in 'wedding old pros to eggheads.' But all concerned have welded romance, ribbing and reality into a cheerful and charming entertainment."—*The New York Times*

"[The film] is a deliciously funny comedy, rib-tickling from start to finish." —*Film Daily*

"Humming with sex like (an open wire) to Reno and clicking off laughs like a telegrapher's key on the third day of a Shriner's convention, *Teacher's Pet* is a hit newspaper comedy...."—*Hollywood Reporter*

REVIEWS FOR DORIS DAY:

"Doris Day ... is developing into a capable comedienne and plays well with Gable. Men will enjoy watching her, and women can still enjoy watching Gable." —*Films in Review*

"Miss Day, who apparently can do almost any kind of a role, is as bright and fresh as a newly set stick of type."—*Variety*

"Perhaps Miss Day is a mite too exotic for the role of an instructor of journalism. But she does convey some of the dedication needed for teaching the finer aspects of the craft and she certainly has the equipment to turn the head of so tough a citizen as Mr. Gable."—*The New York Times*

The Tunnel of Love
MGM / Black and White–CinemaScope / 98 minutes / Released: November 1958

CREDITS:

Producers: Joseph Fields, Martin Melcher; *Director:* Gene Kelly; *Screenplay:* Joseph Fields; *Based on the Play by* Joseph Fields, Peter DeVries; *Based on the Novel by* Peter DeVries; *Photography:* Robert Bronner; *Art Direction:* William A. Horning, Randall Duell; *Set Decoration:* Henry Grace, Robert Priestley; *Costumes:* Helen Rose; *Sound Recording:* Wesley C. Miller; *Film Editing:* John McSweeney, Jr.

CAST:

Doris Day (Isolde Poole); Richard Widmark (Augie Poole); Gig Young (Dick Pepper); Elisabeth Fraser (Alice Pepper); Gia Scala (Estelle Novick); Elizabeth Wilson (Miss MacCracken); Vikki Dougan (Actress); Doodles Weaver (Escort); Charles Wagenheim (Hotel Man #1); Robert Williams (Hotel Man #2); with The Esquire Trio.

SONGS:

"Run Away, Skidaddle Skidoo"* by Ruth Roberts, Bill Katz.

"(Have Lips, Will Kiss in) The Tunnel of Love"* by Patty Fisher, Bob Roberts.

PLOT:

Happily married but childless, Augie and Isolde Poole want a baby and decide to adopt. When the adoption agency's Estelle Novick investigates the Pooles, she finds Augie unsuitable as he is drinking, is undressed, and claims to chase a mouse out of his house. Depressed by making the wrong impression, Augie takes Miss Novick out to dinner to convince her that he and Isolde would be good parents. But Augie drinks too much and finds himself the next morning in a motel, remembering nothing from the night before. Several months later, Miss Novick writes Augie to ask him for a loan as she is pregnant, while also hinting that she may be able to help with his application to the agency. A baby boy is sent to the Pooles, and Augie is convinced the child is his with Miss Novick. Just as Isolde begins to suspect the same, Miss Novick arrives to repay the loan and explains that she had a girl. Soon after, Isolde discovers she is pregnant.

REVIEWS FOR *The Tunnel of Love*:

"Wit, appeal and sophistication range all over the film version of the hit Broadway play *The Tunnel of Love*.... As a box office candidate [the film] belongs up there with the big ones."—*Film Daily*

"With such basically meager material, director Gene Kelly has done wonders. Every situation is carefully contrived, every laugh milked bone dry...."—*Photoplay*

"Kelly's expert direction has none of the artiness he sometimes has been accused of. ...Field's script adroitly cleans everything up so that the audience leaves the theater loving the characters."—*Hollywood Reporter*

REVIEWS FOR DORIS DAY:

"A lot of the picture's quality comes from Miss Day's clean playing of sexy situations. She's a wholesome as wheat germ, as bubbly as champagne."—*Hollywood Reporter*

"Doris Day, the epitome of the wholesome American girl, again displays a likable warmth."—*Film and Filming*

"Miss Day and Widmark make a fine comedy team, working as smoothly as if they had been trading gags for years."—*Variety*

It Happened to Jane

Columbia–An Arwin Production / Technicolor-CinemaScope / 98 minutes / Released: June 1959 / Re-released in 1960 under the title *Twinkle and Shine*

CREDITS:

Producer-Director: Richard Quine; *Screenplay:* Norman Katkor; *Story:* Max Wilk, Norman Katkor; *Photography:* Charles Lawton, Jr.; *Art Direction:* Cary Odell; *Set Decoration:* Louis Diage; *Music:* George Duning; *Orchestration:* Arthur Morton; *Sound Recording:* John Livadary, Harry Mills; *Film Editing:* Charles Nelson; *Makeup:* Clay Campbell; *Hairstyles:* Helen Hunt.

CAST:

Doris Day (Jane Osgood); Jack Lemmon (George Denham); Ernie Kovacs (Harry Foster Malone); Steve Forrest (Larry Hall); Teddy Rooney (Billy Osgood); Russ Brown (Uncle Otis); Walter Greaza (Crawford Sloan); Parker Fennelly (Homer Bean); Mary Wickes (Matilda Runyon); Philip Coolidge (Wilbur Peterson); Casey Adams (Selwyn Harris); John Cecil Holm (Aaron Caldwell); Gina Gillespie (Betty Osgood); Dick Crockett (Clarence Runyon); Napoleon Whiting (Porter); with Bill Cullen, Dave Garroway, Steve McCormick, Jayne Meadows, Terry Melcher, Garry Moore, Henry Morgan, Bob Paige, Betsy Palmer, Gene Rayburn, Bess Myerson.

SONGS:

"Be Prepared"* by Fred Karger, Richard Quine.
"It Happened to Jane"* by Joe Lubin, I.J. Roth.

PLOT:

Widow and lobster dealer Jane Osgood of Cape Ann becomes angry when her shipment of lobsters is ruined due to the inefficiency of the railroad company. She enlists the help of her friend and lawyer, George Denham, and becomes involved in a long battle with railroad head Harry Foster Malone. Jane wins for damages, and Harry appeals. When Jane legally seizes one of the company's trains, Harry retaliates by canceling all train stops at Cape Ann. Although she has received much publicity for her efforts, the townspeople blame Jane for Harry's actions. Eventually they bind together to help her. Jane and George, determined to deliver the lobsters via the train, discover Harry has given them a different and lengthy route around New England. Harry's lawyer persuades him to finally give in, and Jane rejects a wedding proposal from a New York reporter to marry George.

REVIEWS FOR *It Happened to Jane*:

"A bouncy, good-natured little comedy…. For one thing, it moves. Mr. Quine must have told his personable cast to get in there and run. The picture also provides one of the prettiest comedy backgrounds we've seen in a long time…."—*The New York Times*

"If Columbia's sales and advertising departments do what they should, [the film] could be the harbinger of a return to the Capra-like comedy-cum-Americana of the '30s. There hasn't been much of that in the last two decades—and it's about time…. In short, [the film is] *entertainment*, and the kind of entertainment people go out the theater feeling better for. The U.S. population needs *more* of it…."—*Films In Review*

REVIEWS FOR DORIS DAY:

"Miss Day, a beguiling figure of outraged womanhood, doesn't lose her essential femininity in the glory of the cause. She is pugnacious but perceptibly female."—*Variety*

"The breezy Miss Day, especially at the beginning, gallops away like Paul Revere's horse…."—*The New York Times*

Pillow Talk

Universal / An Arwin-Universal Production / Eastmancolor-CinemaScope / 110 minutes / Released: October 1959

CREDITS:

Producers: Ross Hunter, Martin Melcher; *Director:* Michael Gordon; *Screenplay:* Stanley Shapiro, Maurice Richlin; *Story:* Russell Rouse, Clarence Greene; *Photography:* Arthur E. Arling; *Art Direction:* Alexander Golitzen, Richard H. Riedel; *Set Decoration:* Russell A. Gausman, Ruby Levitt; *Costumes:* Bill Thomas; *Miss Day's Gown:* Jean Louis; *Music:* Frank DeVol; *Music Direction:* Joseph Gershenson; *Sound Recording:* Leslie I. Carey, Bob Pritchard; *Film Editing:* Milton Carruth; *Makeup:* Bud Westmore.

CAST:

Rock Hudson (Brad Allen); Doris Day (Jan Morrow); Tony Randall (Jonathon Forbes); Thelma Ritter (Alma); Nick Adams (Tony Walters); Julia Meade (Marie); Allen Jenkins (Harry); Marcel Dalio (Pierot); Lee Patrick (Mrs. Walters); Mary McCarty (Nurse Resnick); Alex Gerry (Dr. Maxwell); Hayden Rorke (Mr. Conrad); Valerie Allen (Eileen); Jacqueline Beer (Yvette); Arlen Stuart

Pillow Talk revealed a sexy, intelligent Day and a humorous Rock Hudson (Jerry Ohlinger's Movie Material Store, Inc.).

(Tilda); Perry Blackwell (Singer); Don Beddoe (Mr. Walters); Robert B. Williams (Mr. Graham); William Schallert (Hotel Clerk); Karen Norris (Miss Dickenson); Lois Rayman (Jonathon's Secretary); with Muriel Landers, Harry Tyler, Joe Mell, Boyd "Red" Morgan, Dorothy Abbott.

SONGS:
"I Need No Atmosphere"; "Inspiration"; "Possess Me"*; "You Lied" by Joe Lubin, I.J. Roth.
"Pillow Talk"* by Buddy Pepper, Inez James.
"Roly Poly"* by Elsa Doran, Sol Lake.

PLOT:
Unmarried interior designer Jan Morrow has a good life except that she shares a party telephone line with playboy Brad Allen, who is constantly talking on it with his conquests. Brad sees Jan at a nightclub and is attracted to his "other end of the party line." Because he knows she would never meet with him, Brad disguises himself as a wealthy Texan, Rex Stetson. The two begin dating and Jan

realizes she has fallen for him. Brad's friend and employer, Jonathon Forbes, also pursues Jan, but she has declined his offers. Jonathon discovers that Rex is really Brad, and tells him to get out of town and leave Jan alone. Brad leaves, but takes Jan with him on what will be a romantic weekend. However, Jan discovers the truth, and Jonathon arrives to take the broken-hearted Jan back to New York. In order to win her back, Brad hires Jan to redecorate his apartment. She designs it to resemble a bordello. When the enraged Brad sees her work, he goes to her place and carries her back to his. There he tells her that he loves her, and wants to marry her. Jan smiles and accepts.

REVIEWS FOR *Pillow Talk*:

"One of the most lively and up-to-date comedy-romances of the year...." —*The New York Times*

"...[the film] is a first class bit of fun ... slick, polished and admirably acted...."—*London Evening News*

"In a happy combining of talents, skills and showmanly appreciation of high-comedy values, producer Ross Hunter of U-I and Martin Melcher of Arwin Prods. have come up with a comedy to be laughed at—by the adults, the juniors, and the exhibitor on his way to the bank."—*Film Daily*

REVIEWS FOR DORIS DAY:

"Doris Day gives possibly her best comedy performance to date...."—*Monthly Film Bulletin*

"Miss Day has never looked more attractive or acted better."—*London Evening News*

"Miss Day discards her usual hairstyle, displays a brace of smart Jean Louis gowns, and delivers crisply."—*Variety*

Please Don't Eat the Daisies

MGM / A Euterpe Production / MetroColor/CinemaScope /
110 minutes / Released: April 1960

CREDITS:

Producer: Joe Pasternak; *Director:* Charles Walters; *Screenplay:* Isobel Lennart; *Based on the book by* Jean Kerr; *Photography:* Robert Bronner; *Art Direction:* George W. Davis, Hans Peters; *Set Decoration:* Henry Grace, Jerry Wunderlich; *Costumes:* Morton Haack; *Music:* David Rose; *Sound Recording:* Franklin Milton; *Film Editing:* John McSweeney, Jr.; *Makeup:* William Tuttle; *Hairstyles:* Sydney Guilaroff.

CAST:

Doris Day (Kate MacKay); David Niven (Larry MacKay); Janis Paige (Deborah Vaughn); Spring Byington (Suzie Robinson); Richard Haydn (Alfred North);

Patsy Kelly (Maggie); Jack Weston (Joe Positano); John Harding (Rev. Dr. McQuarry); Margaret Lindsay (Mona James); Carmen Phillips (Mary Smith); Mary Patton (Mrs. Hunter); Charles Herbert (David MacKay); Stanley Livingston (Gabriel MacKay); Flip Mark (George MacKay); Baby Gellert (Adam MacKay); Marina Koshetz (Jane March); Geraldine Wall (Dr. Sprouk); Kathyrn Card (Miss Yule); Donald Foster (Justin Winters); Irene Tedrow (Mrs. Greenfield); Anatole Winogradoff (Paul Foster); Benny Rubin (Pete); Madge Blake (Mrs. Kilkinny); Peter Leeds (Larry's Secretary); Leo Cronin (Pianist); Hobo (Hobo the dog).

SONGS:
    "Anyway the Wind Blows"* by Marilyn & Joe Hooven, By Dunham.
    "Please Don't Eat the Daisies"* by Jay Lubin.
    "Whatever Will Be, Will Be (Qué Será, Será)"* by Jay Livingston, Ray Evans.

PLOT:
    A former professor of drama, Larry MacKay launches his new career as a New York drama critic by reviewing his friend Alfred North's new play. Larry gives the production a bad notice, worded as kindly as possible. Alfred confronts Larry, as does the show's lead, Deborah Vaughn, who slaps him in public. The feud is widely publicized, and Larry's wife Kate worries that his success as a critic has affected his judgment. When the lease on their apartment expires, Kate finds an abandoned house for them and their four sons in Hooten, 70 miles from New York City. She renovates the house and becomes involved in local activities, including a drama group. To meet a book publishing deadline, Larry decides to stay in the city, where he is pursued by the now-friendly Deborah. Larry returns to Hooten and discovers that the drama group plans to produce a play that he wrote years ago which had been given to the group by Alfred. Angered, Larry leaves for the city where he reviews the play before it is presented, and admits his own mortality as a critic. As he prepares to return to Hooten, he meets Kate and the two reconcile.

REVIEWS FOR *Please Don't Eat the Daisies*:
    "*Please Don't Eat the Daisies* is a light and frothy comedy, and boffo family fare...."—*Variety*
    "Most of this is merely foolish, but some of it is also amiable, and the two principals bring off an occasional funny bit of business. Summing up: Oopsy-Daisy."—*Newsweek*
    "Charles Walters had directed his two stars, Doris Day and David Niven, to full advantage, theirs and the audience's.... Pasternak, Walters and Miss Lennart have collaborated to create a bright, clean film, sparkling with all the attributes of comedy."—*Hollywood Reporter*

Ad, 1960.

REVIEWS FOR DORIS DAY:

"Doris Day charms continually as the harried but madly coping mother."
—*Monthly Film Bulletin*

"Miss Day is both kookie and human, totally believable as the mother of four small (but ruthless) boys, and also as the wife Niven keeps coming home to despite professional competition."—*Hollywood Reporter*

"Doris Day is almost always pleasant to watch, even in such uneven material as [this film]. Much of the vitality she possessed in her early days as a song-belter is still with her, and as she has aged her acting range has widened."—*Films in Review*

Midnight Lace

Universal / A Hunter-Arwin Production / Eastmancolor /
108 minutes / Released: November 1960

CREDITS:

Producers: Ross Hunter, Martin Melcher; *Director:* David Miller; *Screenplay:* Ivan Goff, Ben Roberts; *Based on the Play* Matilda Shouted Fire *by* Janet Green; *Photography:* Russell Metty; *Art Direction:* Alexander Golitzen, Robert Clatworthy; *Set Decoration:* Oliver Emert; *Costumes:* Irene; *Music:* Frank Skinner; *Music Direction:* Joseph Gershenson; *Sound Recording:* Waldon O. Watson, Joe Lapis; *Film Editing:* Russell F. Schoengarth, Leon Barsha; *Makeup:* Bud Westmore; *Hairstyles:* Larry Germain.

CAST:

Doris Day (Kit Preston); Rex Harrison (Tony Preston); John Gavin (Brian Younger); Myrna Loy (Aunt Bea); Roddy McDowall (Malcolm); Herbert Marshall (Charles Manning); Natasha Perry (Peggy Thompson); John Williams (Inspector Byrnes); Hermione Baddeley (Dora Hammer); Richard Ney (Daniel Graham); Rhys Williams (Victor Elliot); Anthony Dawson (Ash); Richard Lupino (Simon Foster); Doris Lloyd (Nora); Hayden Rorke (Dr. Garver); Rex Evans (Basil Stafford); Keith McConnell (Police Officer); Terence DeMarney (Tim); Jimmy Fairfax (Bus Driver); Anthony Eustrel (Salesman); Jack Livesey (MP); Roy Dean (Harry); Paul Collins (Kevin); Richard Peel (Tommy); with Gage Clarke, Pamela Light, Elspeth March, Joan Staley.

SONGS:

"Midnight Lace" by Joe Lubin, Jerome Howard.
"What Does a Woman Do?" by Allie Wrubel, Maxwell Anderson.

Ad, 1960.

PLOT:

Wealthy American Kit Preston lives in London with her new husband, Tony. One evening she hears a mysterious voice threaten her life as she walks through the London fog. Tony convinces her that someone was pulling a prank, but later the same voice threatens her on the telephone, and at one point she is pushed in front of an oncoming bus. The police are skeptical of the threats, and eventually Tony and Kit's Aunt Bea believe that Kit is either delusional or lying for attention. When the time arrives, it is revealed that Tony and his mistress, Kit's friend Peggy, have been behind the scheme in order for Kit to die, which then could have been ruled a suicide. Kit rushes out onto the scaffolding to flee Tony. Scotland Yard, who have been keeping the Preston residence under surveillance, arrive in time to save her.

REVIEWS FOR *Midnight Lace*:

"In the uncrowded field of mystery melodrama, Alfred Hitchcock continues to reign supreme, but his position is currently being challenged by David Miller and his tense new shocker, *Midnight Lace*."—*Saturday Review*

"Doris Day is off and running again in *Midnight Lace*, a contrived and not very mysterious mystery melodrama that most audiences will love."—*Variety*

REVIEWS FOR DORIS DAY:

"Doris Day, let us be early to confess it, gives one of her best performances, ranging from her usual well-dressed charm into phases of hysteria which she has never before achieved."—*New York Post*

"Doris Day switches from sunny charm to stark terror with virtuoso skill."—*Saturday Review*

"Doris Day in *Midnight Lace* gives the kind of performance that Oscars are made of."—columnist Earl Wilson

Lover Come Back

Universal / A 7 Pictures–Arwin–Nob Hill Production /
Eastmancolor / 107 minutes / Released: March 1962

CREDITS:

Producers: Stanley Shapiro, Martin Melcher; *Director:* Delbert Mann; *Screenplay:* Stanley Shapiro, Paul Henning; *Photography:* Arthur E. Arling; *Art Direction:* Alexander Golitzen, Robert Clatworthy; *Set Decoration:* Oliver Emert; *Costumes:* Irene; *Music:* Frank DeVol; *Music Direction:* Joseph Gershenson; *Sound Recording:* Waldon O. Watson, Joe Lapis; *Film Editing:* Marjorie Fowler; *Makeup:* Bud Westmore; *Hairstyles:* Larry Germain.

CAST:

Rock Hudson (Jerry Webster); Doris Day (Carol Templeton); Tony Randall (Peter Ramsey); Edie Adams (Rebel Davis); Jack Oakie (J. Paxton Miller); Jack Kruschen (Dr. Linus Tyler); Ann B. Davis (Millie); Joe Flynn (Hadley); Karen Norris (Kelly); Howard St. John (Brackett); Jack Albertson (Fred); Charles Watts (Charlie); Donna Douglas (Deborah); Ward Ramsey (Hodges); John Leitel (Board Member).

SONGS:

"Lover Come Back"* by Alan Spilton, Frank DeVol.
"Should I Surrender?"* by Adam Ross, William Landan.

PLOT:

New York advertising executive Jerry Webster snares the big account of J. Paxton Miller through the help of alcohol and girls. Carol Templeton, an executive from a rival agency, reports Jerry's misconduct to the Advertising Council. When Jerry learns of this, he convinces one of the girls, Rebel Davis, to speak in his favor. In return, Jerry tells Rebel she will be the new VIP girl, and films television commercials of her promoting this fictitious product. However, the neurotic Peter Ramsey, head of the advertising company, puts Jerry's ads on television. Jerry and Peter engage the services of inventor Linus Tyler to produce VIP. Carol discovers what Jerry is doing and pays Linus a visit, only to mistake Jerry for the inventor. Jerry plays along, and almost manages to sleep with Carol. But when she discovers the truth and rushes to the Ad Council, Jerry emerges with a box of VIP candy wafers full of alcohol. All become intoxicated after eating the wafers, and Carol and Jerry wake up together in a motel room the next morning. Although they had married in their drunken state, Carol has the marriage annulled. However, she is pregnant. As Carol is being wheeled into the delivery room, she and Jerry reconcile and are remarried.

REVIEWS FOR *Lover Come Back*:

"In *Lover Come Back* we are graced with the sauciest, brightest, most blithe of sophisticated romantic comedies to show up in a long, long time."—*New York Herald Tribune*

"The funniest picture of the year.... If you thought *Pillow Talk* was a 'sleeper' when it popped up in 1959 as a comedy hit uniting Rock Hudson and Doris Day, wait until you see their latest."—*The New York Times*

"The comedy is breezily paced, full of zest and bounce, and designed for mass appeal. Just about everyone should like it...."—*Film Daily*

REVIEWS FOR DORIS DAY:

"Mr. Hudson and Miss Day are delicious ... she in her wide-eyed, pert, pugnacious and eventually melting vein...."—*The New York Times*

"Miss Day is strictly pinup material, and she can pout with the best of them."
—*Variety*

That Touch of Mink

Universal / A Granley–Arwin–Nob Hill Production /
Eastmancolor-Panavision / 99 minutes / Released: July 1962

CREDITS:

Producers: Stanley Shapiro, Martin Melcher; *Director:* Delbert Mann; *Screenplay:* Stanley Shapiro, Nate Monaster; *Photography:* Russell Metty; *Art Direction:* Alexander Golitzen, Robert Clatworthy; *Set Decoration:* George Milo; *Music:* George Duning; *Costumes:* Norman Norell; *Furs:* Leo Ritter; *Mr. Grant's Suits:* Cardinal; *Sound Recording:* Waldon O. Watson, Corson Jowett; *Film Editing:* Ted Kent; *Makeup:* Bud Westmore; *Hairstyles:* Larry Germain.

CAST:

Cary Grant (Philip Shayne); Doris Day (Cathy Timberlake); Gig Young (Roger); Audrey Meadows (Connie); Alan Hewitt (Dr. Gruber); John Astin (Beasley); John Fiedler (Mr. Smith); Willard Sage (Hodges); Jack Livesey (Dr. Richardson); John McKee (Collins); June Ericson (Millie); Laiola Wendroff (Mrs. Golden); Art Passarella (Empire); Dorothy Abbott (Stewardess); Ralph Manza (Taxi Driver); William Lanteau (Leonard); Kathryn Givney (Mrs. Haskell); Alice Backes (Miriam); Richard Deacon (Mr. Miller); Fred Essler (Mr. Golden); Helen Brown (Mrs. Farnum); Yogi Berra, Mickey Mantle, Roger Maris (As Themselves); with Joey Faye, Laurie Mitchell, Richard Sargent.

PLOT:

When wealthy businessman Philip Shayne's limousine splashes water on unemployed Cathy Timberlake, he sends his assistant Roger to apologize. Roger finds Cathy and convinces her to demand an apology from Philip in person. When she sees him, Cathy is attracted to Philip. He invites her on a one-day business trip around the East Coast, and discovers he is interested in her. Philip invites Cathy on a trip to Bermuda, but she understands his intentions and declines the offer. She later changes her mind, but when it comes time to go to bed, she develops a rash. A doctor tells her she should rest, and thus the affair cannot take place. On a second visit, Cathy becomes intoxicated and falls off the balcony, also preventing a romance. Back in New York, Cathy plots to arouse Philip's jealousy by announcing she is going to elope with another man, Beasley. Although Philip has no idea that Cathy has no intention of marrying Beasley, he sets off to convince her to marry him instead. He arrives in time and the couple marry, only to find the bridegroom has developed spots on their honeymoon.

On the set of *That Touch of Mink* with Cary Grant (left), 1962 (Jerry Ohlinger's Movie Material Store, Inc.).

REVIEWS FOR *That Touch of Mink*:

"Gay, sprightly romantic comedy. Top marquee names. Sophisticated dialogue. Outstanding entertainment ... [the film] breezes merrily along its gilt way, turning up delightful situations and gales of laughter...."—*Film Daily*

"Shapiro has a lively facility with verbal wit, and the film has a thousand gags, but they are practically all literary, very little comedy being strictly cinematic except for Miss Day's occasional amusing grimaces...."—*New York Herald Tribune*

"The adroit Stanley Shapiro has written a lively, lilting script that has as much glittering verbal wit as [his] *Pillow Talk* and *Lover Come Back*...."—*The New York Times*

REVIEWS FOR DORIS DAY:

"Miss Day ... certifies herself an adept farceur with this outing."—*Variety*

"Mr. Grant and Miss Day fit snugly into their roles."—*Film Daily*

Billy Rose's Jumbo

MGM / An MGM–Euterpe–Arwin Production / MetroColor-Panavision /
125 minutes / Released: December 1962

CREDITS:

Producers: Joe Pasternak, Martin Melcher; *Director:* Charles Walters; *Second Unit Director:* Busby Berkeley; *Screenplay:* Sidney Sheldon; *Based on the Musical Play and Book by* Ben Hecht, Charles MacArthur; *Photography:* William H. Daniels; *Art Direction:* George W. Davis, Preston Ames; *Set Decoration:* Henry Grace, Hugh Hunt; *Costumes:* Morton Haack; *Musical Direction:* George Stoll; *Orchestrations:* Conrad Salinger, Leo Arnaud, Robert Van Eps; *Vocal Arrangements:* Bobby Tucker; *Sound Recording:* Franklin Milton; *Film Editing:* Richard W. Farrell; *Makeup:* William Tuttle; *Hairstyles:* Sydney Guilaroff.

CAST:

Doris Day (Kitty Wonder); Stephen Boyd (Sam Rawlins); Jimmy Durante (Pop Wonder); Martha Raye (Lulu); Dean Jagger (John Noble); Charles Watts (Ellis); James Chandler (Parsons); Robert Burton (Madison); Wilson Wood (Hank); Norman Leavitt (Eddie); Pat Anthony, The Barbettes, Billy Barton, Richard Berg, The Carlisles, Corky Cristiani, Adolph Dubsky, The Hannefords, Ron Henon, Victor Julian, Miss Lani, Joe Monahan, The Pedrolas, Janos Prohaska, The Wazzans (Circus Performers); with Grady Sutton, Charles Waring, Lynn Wood.

SONGS:

"The Circus Is on Parade"*; "Little Girl Blue"*; "The Most Beautiful Girl in the World"; "My Romance"*; "Over and Over Again"*; "Sawdust, Spangles and Dreams"*; "This Can't Be Love"*; "Why Can't I?"* by Richard Rodgers, Lorenz Hart.

PLOT:

Co-owner of the Wonder Circus, Kitty Wonder spends much of her time managing and performing, and keeping Pop from gambling away the income. When Sam Rawlins arrives for a job, Kitty eventually offers one to him when he doubles as a high-wire artist. Unbeknownst to Kitty, Sam was sent by his father, circus owner John Noble, to help acquire the Wonder Circus. Kitty and Sam fall in love, and he tries to convince his father to change his mind. But it is too late, and the Noble Circus acquires the Wonder Circus and its assets including Jumbo the elephant. Heartbroken Kitty, Pop and Pop's fiancée Lulu begin doing one-night stands on their own. Sam reappears, having broken with his father, and helps the trio start a new circus with Jumbo. Kitty forgives Sam and the pair reconcile as the new circus group begins to rebuild.

REVIEWS FOR *Jumbo*:

"A great entertainment film...."—*Variety*

"A great big blubbery amiable polka-dotted elephant of a show, just the ticket for a holiday hoot with the wife and the kiddies."—*New York Herald Tribune*

"To reproduce any kind of stage presentation on celluloid is purely journeyman's work, a matter of picking the pieces and pasting them together. True adaptation, on the other hand, calls for imagination, finesse, and creativity. Perhaps that is why it is so rare. It is, therefore, a special pleasure to be able to report that *Billy Rose's Jumbo* fully meets the above specifications."—*Saturday Review*

REVIEWS FOR DORIS DAY:

"Doris Day may never have sung better than she does in *Jumbo*. While the story is no challenge to her thespic talents, her return to the thing she does so well could (and should) persuade her to make more musicals...."—*Variety*

"Day as usual is blindingly sunny, but in a circus the glare seems suitable."—*Time*

The Thrill of It All

Universal / A Hunter-Arwin Production / Eastmancolor-Technicolor /
108 minutes / Released: August 1963

CREDITS:

Producers: Ross Hunter, Martin Melcher; *Director:* Norman Jewison; *Screenplay:* Carl Reiner; *Story:* Carl Reiner, Larry Gelbart; *Photography:* Russell Metty; *Art Direction:* Alexander Golitzen, Robert Boyle; *Set Decoration:* Howard Bristol; *Costumes:* Jean Louis; *Music:* DeVol; Music *Direction:* Joseph Gershenson; *Sound Recording:* Waldon O. Watson, William G. Russell; *Film Editing:* Milton Carruth.

CAST:

Doris Day (Beverly Boyer); James Garner (Dr. Gerald Boyer); Arlene Francis (Mrs. Fraleigh); Edward Andrews (Mr. Fraleigh); Reginald Owen (Tom Fraleigh); Zasu Pitts (Olivia); Elliott Reid (Mike Palmer); Alice Pearce (Woman); Kym Karath (Maggie Boyer); Brian Nash (Andy Boyer); Lucy Landau (Mrs. Goethe); Paul Hartman (Dr. Taylor); Hayden Rorke (Billings); Alex Gerry (Stokely); Robert Gallagher (Van Camp); Anne Newman (Miss Thompson); Burt Mustin (Butler); Hedley Mattingly (Chauffeur); Bernie Kopell (stage director); cameo by Carl Reiner; with William Bramley, Pamela Curran, Maurice Gosfield, Robert Strauss

SONGS:

"The Thrill of It All" by Arnold Schwarzwald, Frederick Herbert.

PLOT:

When wealthy Happy soap executive Mr. Fraleigh and his wife discover they are going to have a baby, they invite Mrs. Fraleigh's obstetrician Dr. Gerald Boyer and his wife Beverly to dinner. After Beverly tells of an incident with her daughter and how she liked Happy soap, she is hired to tell the story in a television commercial. Beverly's naturalness leads to a contract as the Happy soap girl, much to the chagrin of Gerald, who does not like his wife being a celebrity who earns $80,000 a year. This leads to an argument between the couple over whose money belongs to who.

At a party to celebrate Beverly's success, Mrs. Fraleigh goes into labor. She, Mr. Fraleigh, Beverly and

Preparing for the homemade ketchup scene in 1963's *The Thrill of It All* (Jerry Ohlinger's Movie Material Store, Inc.).

the chauffeur race to the hospital, but are caught in two traffic jams. Gerald arrives with the help of a policeman and a horse, and a lane is cleared for the limousine. When they arrive to the hospital, Mrs. Fraleigh has already given birth to a girl. Gerald and Beverly embrace and reconcile.

REVIEWS FOR *The Thrill of It All*:

"Like most Ross Hunter productions, *The Thrill of It All* is lavishly mounted and technically glossy. It also has an excellent script and director, Norman Jewison, who can calculate exactly how far to develop a gag...."—*Monthly Film Bulletin*

"[The film] is different from the other Doris Day–Ross Hunter concoctions that have preceded it and it's easy to figure out wherein and why. It's funny, thanks to a Carl Reiner screenplay that lets Miss Day forget about preserving her virginity and concentrate on the comedy at hand."—*New York Herald Tribune*

"*The Thrill of It All*, the kind of vague, all-purpose title they used to put on Esther Williams' water-logged spectaculars, [is] one of the few comedies to have come out of Hollywood in some time, which also happens to be funny." — *Show*

REVIEWS FOR DORIS DAY:

"[Day] is also now an expert at the throwaway line and throwaway glance. She is one of the screen's best comediennes and she has plenty of good material to work with in Reiner's bright script and Jewison's inventive direction." — *Hollywood Reporter*

"Miss Day is remarkably uncoy in her devotion to farce rather than cuteness and an eyeful in all the lavish dressing-up the role calls for...." — *New York Herald Tribune*

"[Director Jewison's] particularly triumph is in having wrung most of the cuteness out of snub-nosed Doris Day. In doing it, he has given her what always lacked in her long series of nice-virgin comedies: a dry farce style." — *Show*

Move Over, Darling

Twentieth Century-Fox / An Arcola-Arwin Production /
DeLuxe Color–CinemaScope / 103 minutes / Released: December 1963

CREDITS:

Producers: Aaron Rosenberg, Martin Melcher; *Director:* Michael Gordon; *Screenplay:* Hal Kanter, Jack Sher; *Story:* Bella & Samuel Spewack, Leo McCarey; *Photography:* Daniel L. Fapp; *Art Direction:* Jack Martin Smith, Hilyard Brown; *Set Decoration:* Walter M. Scott, Paul S. Fox; *Costumes:* Moss Mabry; *Music:* Lionel Newman; *Orchestrations:* Arthur Morton, Warren Baker; *Sound Recording:* Alfred Bruzlin, Elmer Raguse; *Film Editing:* Robert Simpson.

CAST:

Doris Day (Ellen Wagstaff Arden); James Garner (Nick Arden); Polly Bergen (Bianca Steele Arden); Chuck Connors (Stephen Burkett); Thelma Ritter (Grace Arden); Fred Clark (Mr. Codd); Don Knotts (Shoe Salesman); Elliott Reid (Dr. Herman Schlick); Edgar Buchanan (Judge Bryson); John Astin (Clyde Prokey); Pat Harrington, Jr. (District Attorney); Eddie Quillan (Bellboy); Max Showalter (Desk Clerk); Alvy Moore (Waiter); Pami Lee (Jenny Arden); Leslie Farrell (Didi Arden); Rosa Turich (Maria); Harold Goodwin (Bailiff); Alan Sues (Court Clerk); Pat Moran (Drunk); Bess Flowers (Woman); Rachel Roman (Injured Man's Wife); Jack Orrison (Bartender); Ed McNally (Commander); James Patridge (Skipper); Christopher Connelly (Executive Seaman); Michael Romanoff (Floorwalker).

Ad, 1963.

SONGS:

"Move Over, Darling"* by Joe Lubin, Hal Kanter, Terry Melcher.
"Twinkle Lullaby"* by Joe Lubin.

PLOT:

Ellen Arden disappeared after a plane crash; five years later, when she is finally rescued, she finds that her two daughters no longer recognize her. Ellen also learns she had been legally declared dead and that her husband, Nick, remarried the same day. She rushes to the newlyweds before the marriage can be consummated, but after seeing Nick having trouble telling his neurotic and frustrated bride Bianca the truth, Ellen storms off alone. At home, Ellen and her mother-in-law Grace devise a plan to disguise Ellen as a Swedish nurse to care for Nick, who has faked a fall and is returning with Bianca. Meanwhile, Nick discovers that Ellen had spent the past years with the athletic Stephen Burkett. Ellen denies that anything happened between them, but Nick suspects there had to have been a romance interlude. Witnessing the problems in the household, Grace informs the authorities that her son is a bigamist. All converge into a courtroom where the mess is sorted out, including the annulment of Nick's second marriage. Bianca leaves with her psychiatrist and the Ardens return home to their children, who also learn the truth of their mother.

REVIEWS FOR *Move Over Darling*:

"Something old, something new, something borrowed, something blue is the nature of *Move Over, Darling*...."—*Variety*

"*Move Over, Darling* appears to be straining and shouting for effects that should be natural and uncontrived."—*The New York Times*

REVIEWS FOR DORIS DAY:

"Ellen is a good role for Doris Day. It gives her chances to run the gamut of funny faces, to be deeply hurt, to get raving and fighting mad, to sing a couple of songs. And as no Doris Day movie would be complete without the star's tears, it gives her a chance to cry over the two little daughters who don't recognize the strange lady as their mommy."—*New York Daily News*

"Miss Day and James Garner play it to the hilt, comically, dramatically and last, but not least (particularly in the case of the former), athletically."—*Variety*

Send Me No Flowers

Universal / A Martin Melcher Production / Technicolor /
100 minutes / Released: November 1964

CREDITS:

Producer: Harry Keller; *Director:* Norman Jewison; *Screenplay:* Julius Epstein; *Based on a Play by* Norman Barasch, Carroll Moore; *Photography:* Daniel Fapp;

Art Direction: Alexander Golitzen, Robert Clatworthy; *Set Decoration:* John McCarthy, Oliver Emert, John Austin; *Costumes:* Jean Louis; *Music:* DeVol; *Choreography:* David Winters; *Sound Recording:* Waldon O. Watson; *Film Editing:* J. Terry Williams; *Makeup:* Bud Westmore; *Hairstyles:* Larry Germain.

CAST:

Rock Hudson (George); Doris Day (Judy); Tony Randall (Arnold); Clint Walker (Bert); Paul Lynde (Mr. Akins); Hal March (Winston Burr); Edward Andrews (Dr. Morrissey); Patricia Barry (Linda); Clive Clerk (Vito); Dave Willock (Milkman); Alene Towne (Cora); Helene Winston (Commuter); Christine Nelson (Nurse).

SONGS:

"Send Me No Flowers"* by Burt Bacharach, Hal David.

PLOT:

Hypochondriac George Kimball overhears his doctor discuss a patient's case and impending death. George erroneously believes that *he* is the one who is dying, and confides in his friend and neighbor Arnold, who in turn finds solace in alcohol. George sets out to find his wife Judy a suitable husband after he is gone. He decides an old college friend of Judy's, the wealthy Bert. Judy, however, suspects that George is having an affair. Her suspicions are confirmed when she sees George in the arms of a recently separated neighbor. George then tells Judy that he is dying. She decides to take him to the Mayo Clinic for tests, but after George's doctor tells her George is healthy, Judy suspects her husband is indeed having an affair. Before leaving for a quick divorce, Judy learns that George truly believed he was dying because he had purchased burial plots for them and possibly a second husband. The couple reconcile.

REVIEWS FOR *Send Me No Flowers*:

"It is a beautiful farce [and] stays within the bounds of good taste, is never cruel or insensitive, and makes something good of every gag."—*The New York Times*

"*Send Me No Flowers* doesn't carry the same voltage, either in laughs or originality, as Doris Day and Rock Hudson's two previous entries, *Pillow Talk* or *Lover Come Back*. Film is amusing, however...."—*Variety*

REVIEWS FOR DORIS DAY:

"Miss Day looks like a tow-headed little Pekinese when she yips in anger or cuddles in devotion and when she goes in for really high comedy she looks like Carol Burnett doing an imitation of Shirley Temple."—*New York Herald Tribune*

"Miss Day is full of puffs and sputters, initially at her husband's mystery and then, when she learns what is cooking, at his misplaced chivalry...."—*The New York Times*

"[A]ctress Day, who at 40 should maybe stop trying to play Goldilocks, comes off as a cheerful, energetic and wildly over decorated Mama Bear."—*Time*

Do Not Disturb

Twentieth Century-Fox / An Arcola-Melcher Production /
DeLuxe Color–CinemaScope / 102 minutes / Released: December 1965

CREDITS:

Producers: Aaron Rosenberg, Martin Melcher; *Director:* Ralph Levy; *Screenplay:* Milt Rosen, Richard Breen; *Based on a Play by* William Fairchild; *Photography:* Leon Shamroy; *Art Direction:* Jack Martin Smith, Robert Boyle; *Set Decoration:* Walter M. Scott, Jerry Wunderlich; *Costumes:* Ray Aghayan; *Music:* Lionel Newman; *Orchestrations:* Mort Garson, Alexander Courage, Warren Baker; *Sound Recording:* Alfred Bruzlin, Elmer Raguse; *Film Editing:* Robert Simpson.

CAST:

Doris Day (Janet Harper); Rod Taylor (Mike Harper); Hermione Baddeley (Vanessa Courtwright); Sergio Fantoni (Paul Bellasi); Reginald Gardiner (Simmons); Maura McGiveney (Claire Hackett); Aram Katcher (Culkos); Leon Askin (Langsdorf); Lisa Pera (Alicia); Albert Carrier (Reynard); Barbara Morrison (Mrs. Ordley); Dick Winslow (One-Man Band); Michael Romanoff (Man).

Do Not Disturb promotional still 1965. The film was not a hit (Jerry Ohlinger's Movie Material Store, Inc.).

SONGS:
"Au Revoir"* by Bob Hilliard, Mort Garson.
"Do Not Disturb"* by Ben Raleigh, Mark Barkan.

PLOT:
Wool fashion manufacturer Mike Harper and his wife Janet move to England, where Janet finds a place in the country for them to live. Mike spends most of his time at the office, so to make him jealous, Janet flirts with Paul Bellari, a Continental antique dealer. Paul tells Janet he has a special dining room table in Paris, so the pair fly there. After getting drunk and finding that a fog has postponed all flights back to England, Janet and Paul stay overnight in his shop. Mike believes the two were intimate. Janet learns that Mike will be attending a convention party, and arrives there to explain that nothing happened between her and Paul. To gain admittance to the party, Janet pretends she is Mike's secretary Claire, of whom she's suspected Mike of having an affair with. She learns, however, that this is not true, and while trying to surprise Mike, she enters the wrong hotel bedroom. After discovering she is in bed with Willie Langsford, a wool buyer whom Mike is trying to charm, Janet leaves, only to be chased by Willie. She eventually finds Mike and the pair reconcile.

REVIEWS FOR *Do Not Disturb*:
"*Do Not Disturb* is a light, entertaining comedy, set in England but filmed in Hollywood...."—*Variety*

"Doris Day has saved worse productions than this, however, and she desperately tries to keep the whole thing going.... Yet the material defeats everyone in the end...."—*Monthly Film Bulletin*

"*Do Not Disturb* is the most foolish piece of comic trivia [Day has] been caught in since her pre–Rock Hudson days. It is without wit, in script and direction...."—*The New York Times*

REVIEWS FOR DORIS DAY:
"Miss Day's followers—and they are legion, judging from box-office figures—will probably get a bang out of their Doris as she works hard at being a typical housewife in a London suburb."—*New York Herald Tribune*

"Doris Day approaches her career as Hollywood's No. 1 lady money-maker with a sense of responsibility toward what amounts to a public trust. When people go to a Doris Day movie, they apparently want to see an ordinary, awshucksy sort of girl with a sunny disposition and a $100,000 wardrobe, who sooner or later wakes up somewhere and mutters something like: 'Paul, what happened last night?' Doris never disappoints."—*Time*

"It will surprise no one at all that *Do Not Disturb* ... is a typical Day product.... There's no question that forever-freckled Doris is a pro, when it comes to her specialty—the coy little comedy."—*New York Daily News*

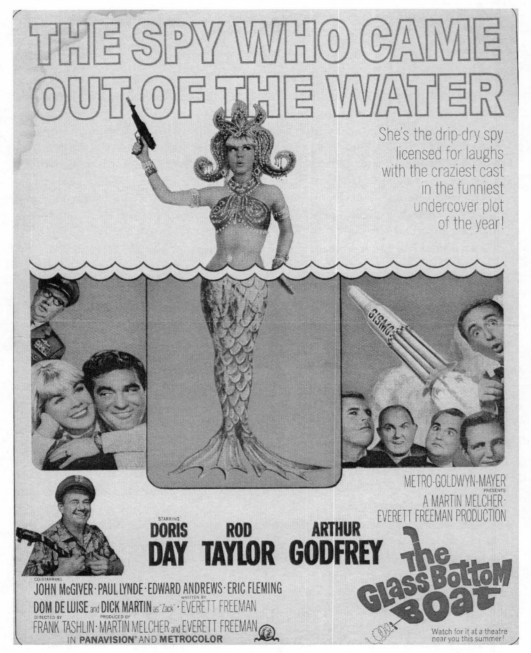

Ad, 1966.

The Glass Bottom Boat

MGM / An Arwin-Reame Production / MetroColor-Panavision /
110 minutes / Released: July 1966

CREDITS:

Producers: Martin Melcher, Everett Freeman; *Director:* Frank Tashlin; *Screenplay:* Everett Freeman; *Photography:* Leon Shamroy; *Art Direction*: George W. Davis, Edward Carfagno; *Set Decoration:* Henry Grace, Hugh Hunt; *Costumes:* Ray Aghayan; *Music:* DeVol; *Sound Recording:* Franklin Milton; *Film Editing:* John McSweeney; *Makeup:* William Tuttle; *Hairstyles:* Barbara Lampson.

CAST:

Doris Day (Jennifer Nelson); Rod Taylor (Bruce Templeton); Arthur Godfrey (Axel Nordstrom); John McGiver (Ralph Goodwin); Paul Lynde (Homer Cripps); Edward Andrews (Gen. Wallace Bleeker); Eric Fleming (Edgar Hill); Dom DeLuise (Julius Pritter); Dick Martin (Zach Malloy); Elisabeth Fraser (Nina); George Tobias (Mr. Fenimore); Alice Pearce (Mrs. Fenimore); Ellen Corby (Bruce's Housekeeper); Dee J. Thompson (Donna); Robert Vaughn (Party Guest Mirage).

SONGS:

"The Glass Bottom Boat"* by Joe Lubin.
"Soft As a Starlight"* by Joe Lubin, Jerome Howard.
"Whatever Will Be, Will Be (Qué Será, Será)"* by Jay Livingston, Ray Evans.

PLOT:

While swimming in a mermaid outfit for her father's glass bottom boat tours, widow Jennifer Nelson gets caught in the fishline of Bruce Templeton, an inventor at a space laboratory where she works. When Bruce learns that Jennifer works in public relations at the laboratory, he decides to spend time with her. He contrives to have her help him write his autobiography. While at work, Jennifer telephones her dog Vladimer several times a day. She does this so that he will get some exercise, because when the dog hears the phones ring, he runs around the house. Jennifer's actions arouses the suspicions of the security and intelligence men at the space laboratory. Soon they are convinced she is a spy, as do her nosy neighbors. At a party, Jennifer learns of the accusation, so she pretends to *be* a spy. The secret formula for the new discovery GIZMO is planted on her by double agent Edgar Hill. When Edgar goes to Jennifer's house to retrieve the formula, a chase ensues, but Jennifer is saved and later marries Bruce.

REVIEWS FOR *The Glass Bottom Boat*:

"Old numbers with puddling in the kitchen and legs stuck in wastepaper baskets, as well as a new routine with a radio-controlled rogue motor-boat, come up fresh as a daisy in Doris Day's cool fingers...."—*The London Observer*

"Strong points of the picture are its highly polished production, its easy performances, and the science-fiction complexity of the slapstick at one time and the reduction to basic procedure with pie-in-the-face...."—*New York Post*

"[W]hile this movie is as glossy and improbable as all the rest [of Day's films], it is easily the funniest. It was undoubtedly made so by that expert at farce, Frank Tashlin, who has taken a not entirely brilliant screenplay by Everett Freeman and generously larded it with slapstick."—*The Saturday Review*

REVIEWS FOR DORIS DAY:

"The script is unoriginal, and Mata Hari acts are not for Doris Day. She is, however, consistently delightful and well-dressed...."—*Monthly Film Bulletin*

"Worshipers, millions and millions, of the most popular actress in the nation will get their money's worth in laughs."—*New York Daily News*

"Miss Day delivers one of her customary wide-eyed romantic portrayals as she's caught in a web of circumstances in which she's suspected of being a Russian spy."—*Variety*

Caprice
Twentieth Century-Fox / A Rosenberg-Melcher Production /
Deluxe Color–CinemaScope / 98 minutes / Released: June 1967

CREDITS:

Producers: Aaron Rosenberg, Martin Melcher; *Director:* Frank Tashlin; *Screenplay:* Jay Johnson, Frank Tashlin; *Story:* Martin Hale, Jay Jayson; *Photography:* Leon Shamroy; *Aerial Photography:* Nelson Tyler; *Art Direction:* Jack Martin Smith, Walter Creber; *Set Decoration:* Walter M. Scott, Jerry Wunderlich; *Costumes:* Ray Aghayan; *Music:* DeVol; *Sound Recording:* Harry M. Lindgren, David Dockendorf; *Film Editing:* Robert Simpson; *Makeup:* Ben Nye, Harry Maret; *Hairstyles:* Margaret Donovan.

CAST:

Doris Day (Patricia Foster); Richard Harris (Christopher White); Ray Walston (Stuart Clancy); Jack Kruschen (Matthew Cutter); Edward Mulhare (Sir Jason Fox); Lilia Skala (Mme. Piasco); Irene Tsu (Su Ling); Larry D. Mann (Inspector Kapinsky); Maurice Marsac (Auber); Michael Romanoff (Butler); Lisa Seagram (Mandy); Michael J. Pollard (Barney); Fritz Field (Swiss Innkeeper); Cherie Foster (Usherette); Romo Vincent (Man); Penny Antine (Waitress); Roxanne Sprio (Teenage Girl); John Woodjack (Boy); John Bleifer (Doctor); Wayne Lundy (Swiss Officer); Madge Cleveland (Woman in Bra); Murial Landers (Nude

Woman); Consuela Neal (Secretary); Bob Gunner (Farley); Kirk Crivello (Ski Guest).

SONGS:
   "Caprice"* by Larry Marks.

PLOT:
   Undercover agent Patricia Foster is arrested while attempting to sell a stolen secret formula for a new cosmetic to her employer's rival. Patricia questions the intentions of Christopher White, whom she learns is also a double agent. She becomes a pawn in a battle between two cosmetic companies, both interested in the inventions of scientist Stuart Clancey. Patricia discovers Stuart's inventions are really his mother-in-law's findings, and have been available for sale in a remote European village. Patricia's motive for acting as a double agent: She wishes to avenge the death of her father, an Interpol agent who was murdered on the Swiss Alps by a narcotics ring. After being saved by Christopher from a similar fate, Patricia reveals that the cosmetic concern is merely a cover for distributing narcotics. She exposes Stuart Clancey as the villain and he then kidnaps her. Patricia is caught in a helicopter but manages to land it on top of the Eiffel Tower. Patricia and Christopher are reunited for an evening of romance.

REVIEWS FOR *Caprice*:
   "*Caprice* receives better direction from Frank Tashlin than it deserves. Even the subject—cosmetic espionage—conspires to remind us that we have been on a long Day's journey into night."—*Village Voice*
   "A spy thriller, *Caprice* is a slick, handsome production for 20th Century-Fox presenting our heroine as her worshipers love her: looking as young as springtime, done up in conservative mods ... pulling off comedy scenes with a straight face, making fools of men [trying] to make a fool of her...."—*New York Daily News*
   "[If] you've seen all those other Doris Day movies, *Caprice* adds very little new to the conversation that you haven't already heard before.... Oh well, to paraphrase the old saying, another Day, another Doris. Only trouble is, it's the same Day and the same Doris."—*New York Morning Telegram*

REVIEWS FOR DORIS DAY:
   "Miss Day? Well, let's just of her that she appears to have reached that stage where massive wigs and nutty clothes and acrobatics cannot conceal the fact that she is no longer a boy."—*The New York Times*
   "Miss Day of course has been many things; this time, thanks to a variety of wigs, soft lenses and mod costumes, she looks like an aging transvestite.... Miss Day is not as young as she used to be for this sort of caper but she does have the energy, and I guess energy is about the one distinction of *Caprice*."—Judith Crist, *Today*

Caprice was another spy spoof, but the film failed both critically and commercially (the Movie Market).

The Ballad of Josie

Universal / Technicolor-TechniScope / 103 minutes / Released: November 1967

CREDITS:

Producer: Norman Macdonnell; *Director:* Andrew V. McLaglen; *Screenplay:* Harold Swanton; *Photography:* Milton Krasner; *Art Direction:* Alexander Golitzen, Addison Hehr; *Set Decoration:* John McCarthy, James Redd; *Costumes:* Jean Louis; *Music:* DeVol; *Music Direction:* Joseph Gershenson; *Sound Recording:* Waldon O. Watson; *Film Editing:* Otho S. Lovering, Fred A. Chulak; *Makeup:* Bud Westmore; *Hairstyles:* Larry Germain.

CAST:

Doris Day (Josie Minick); Peter Graves (Jason Meredith); George Kennedy (Arch Ogden); Andy Devine (Judge Tatum); William Talman (Charlie Lord); David Hartman (Fonse Pruitt); Guy Raymond (Doc); Audrey Christie (Annabelle

Pettijohn); Karen Jensen (Deborah Wilkes); Elisabeth Fraser (Widow Renfrew); Linda Meiklejohn (Jenny); Shirley O'Hara (Elizabeth); Timothy Scott (Klugg); Don Stroud (Bratsch); Paul Fix (Alpheus Minick); Harry Carey (Mooney); John Fiedler (Simpson); Robert Lowery (Whit Minick); Teddy Quinn (Luther Minick).

SONGS:
"The Ballad of Josie" by Don Costa, Floyd Huddleston.
"Wait Till Tomorrow" by Gene DuPaul, Jack Lloyd.

PLOT:
After her drunken, abusive husband accidentally falls down the stairs and dies during an argument, Josie Minick is brought to trial for murdering him with a billiard cue. She is acquitted, but her father-in-law, Alpheus Minick, convinces her that he should take her son Luther until she finds a way to support him. Josie decides to renovate her ranch at Willow Creek to raise sheep, much to the chagrin of the men and the support of the women in the community. She and her hired hands bring the sheep through town en route to her ranch. A group of ranchers, led by Arch Ogden, plot to slaughter Josie's herd, but they are stopped by a rival group headed by Jason Meredith. Meanwhile, the impending range war, coupled with the women's rights support of Josie, appears to affect Wyoming's chances of statehood. The dispute is settled when attorney Charlie Lord persuades Ogden to stock Josie's ranch with cattle. Josie and Luther are reunited, while Josie and Jason plan to marry.

REVIEWS FOR *The Ballad of Josie*:
"*The Ballad of Josie* is a pleasant, innocuous Doris Day oater comedy about sheep-cattle range wars, and women's rights, in pre–1890, pre-statehood Wyoming."—*Variety*

"[T]he boo-of-the-week. It isn't funny enough to be viable comedy, but it's certainly too funny in many other respects to be taken seriously."—*New York Post*

"If it weren't for the presence of Miss Day ... one might believe that the film had really been turned out for immediate television airing."—*The New York Times*

REVIEW FOR DORIS DAY:
"The hot-headed, stubborn, gun-toting, riot-rousing female of this Western is no fittin' role for the actress who has successfully alternated between smart career girl and typical housewife of suburbia."—*The New York Daily News*

Where Were You When the Lights Went Out?

MGM / An Everett Freeman Production / MetroColor-Panavision /
95 minutes / Released: May 1968

CREDITS:

Producers: Everett Freeman, Martin Melcher; *Director:* Hy Averback; *Screenplay:* Everett Freeman, Karl Tunberg; *Based on the Play* Monsieur Masure *by* Claude Magnier; *Photography:* Ellsworth Fredricks; *Art Direction:* George W. Davis, Urie McCleary; *Set Decoration:* George W. Davis, Dick Pefferle; *Costumes:* Glenn Connelly; *Music:* Dave Grusin; *Sound Recording:* Franklin Milton; *Film Editing:* Rita Roland; *Makeup:* Harry Maret; *Hairstyles:* Sydney Guilaroff.

CAST:

Doris Day (Margaret Garrison); Robert Morse (Waldo Zane); Terry-Thomas (Ladislau Walichek); Patrick O'Neal (Peter Garrison); Lola Albright (Roberta Lane); Steve Allen (Radio Announcer); Jim Backus (Car Salesman); Ben Blue (Shaving Man); Pat Paulsen (Train Conductor); Robert Emhardt (Otis J. Hendershot, Sr.); Dale Malone (Otis J. Hendershot, Jr.); Harry Hickox (Detective Capt. Watson); Parley Baer (Dr. Dudley Caldwell); Randy Whipple (Marvin Reinholtz); Earl Wilson (as himself).

SONGS:

"Where Were You When the Lights Went Out?" by Dave Grusin, Kelly Gordon.

PLOT:

Broadway star Maggie Garrison finds herself too busy to have a baby with her architect husband Peter. But on November 9, 1965, a blackout occurs in New York and the show is canceled, so Maggie returns to her home to find Peter with another woman. Maggie storms out and hitches rides to her Connecticut home. She makes herself comfortable by drinking part of a liquid sedative. Executive Waldo Zane, who has stolen millions of dollars from the corporation he works for, has run out of New York but his car breaks down outside of Maggie's house. He enters the house and drinks the remainder of Maggie's liquid sedative. Peter travels to Connecticut to get Maggie's forgiveness only to find her and Waldo sleeping on the same couch. Although nothing happened between Maggie and Waldo, Peter leaves but is arrested when the money that Waldo stole is discovered in his car. Peter is released when Waldo appears and explains he took the money as a security measure during the blackout. Waldo is made president of the corporation, though his contentment dims when the boss' son flees the country with the money. Peter is convinced of Maggie's fidelity and the pair reconciles. Nine months later, Maggie gives birth to their first child.

The 1968 *Where Were You When the Lights Went Out?* with Terry-Thomas (right) and a cameo by columnist Earl Wilson (the Movie Market).

REVIEWS FOR *Where Were You When the Lights Went Out?*:

"[It] rates on the high end of the Doris Day movie scale, due to the presence of such assured professionals as Robert Morse, Patrick O'Neal and Terry-Thomas.... [The film] is such an uneven movie that misses so many opportunities for real comedy, that its few funny jokes are to be appreciated."—*Newsday*

"This picture goes to show that black-out or no, an ordinary plot remains an ordinary movie. You probably saw much more interesting things yourself."—*New York Post*

"Averback's comedy direction lifts things out of a well-plowed rut, making for an amusing, while never hilarious, film."—*Variety*

REVIEWS FOR DORIS DAY:

"Miss Day ... emerges from this piece of self-parody as a likable and almost credible character."—*Monthly Film Bulletin*

"[A] good part of the movie permits Miss Day to play an actress something like herself, and this might be fresh and almost poignant. She is clearly an actress who needs to be let out, and yet she is doomed to exclaim some version of the 'Oh Peter, I'm tarnished' line she has in this one...."—*The New York Times*

With Six You Get Eggroll

Warner-Pathé / A National General Picture / A Cinema Center Film / An Arwin Production / Color by Deluxe-Panavision / 99 minutes / Released August 1968

CREDITS:

Producer: Martin Melcher; *Director:* Howard Morris; *Screenplay:* Gwen Bagni, Paul Dubov, Harvey Bullock, R.S. Allen; *Story:* Gwen Bagni, Paul Dubov; *Photography:* Ellsworth Fredricks, Harry Stradling, Jr.; *Art Direction:* Cary Odell; *Set Decoration:* James I. Berkey; *Costumes:* Glenn Connelly, Constance Edney, Ray Summers; *Music:* Robert Mersey; *Sound:* Philip Mitchell, Sr., Dean Spencer; *Film Editing:* Adrienne Fazan; *Makeup:* Harry Maret, Emile LaVigne; *Hairstyles:* Barbara Lampson.

CAST:

Doris Day (Abby McClure); Brian Keith (Jake Iverson); Pat Carroll (Maxine Scott); Barbara Hershey (Stacy Iverson); George Carlin (Herbie Flack); Alice Ghostley (Housekeeper); John Findlater (Flip McClure); Jimmy Bracken (Mitch McClure); Richard Steele (Jason McClure); Herbert Voland (Harry Scott); Elaine Devry (Cleo); Jackie Joseph (Georgia Watson); Allan Melvin (Desk Sergeant); Peter Leeds (Officer Joelson); Victor Tayback, Jr. (Chicken Truck Driver); Jamie Farr (JoJo); William Christopher (Zip); Pearl Shear (Woman); Mickey Deems (Sam Bates); Milton Frome (Bud Young); John Copage (Lumberyard Worker); Lord Nelson (Calico, the dog); with The Grass Roots.

SONGS:

"You Make Me Want You" by Robert Mersey, Robert Hilliard.

PLOT:

Widow Abby McClure runs a lumberyard, raises three boys and constantly deals with her sister Maxine's determination to find her a man. Maxine reacquaints Maggie with widower Jake Iverson, but their meeting at a dinner party fails to ignite a romance. The pair later meet once again, but Maggie believes Jake has another woman in his life. She learns the other woman is Jake's teenage daughter, Stacy, and Jake and Maggie find themselves in love. The two quietly elope, but when they return, they find that the children disapprove of the marriage. To make life fair for the children, the couple decide to spend equal time at each other's homes. When this doesn't work out, Jake purchases a trailer for Abby and himself to live in. Because of the children's unbending ways, the newlyweds quarrel,

The minor 1968 hit *With Six You Get Eggroll* with (left to right) Brian Keith, Day, John Findlater, Barbara Hershey, Richard Steele and Jimmy Bracken.

and Abby drives off with the trailer, leaving Jake stranded in his underwear. A series of chases ensues involving the police and a local group of hippies. At the police station, the children understand their selfish attitude, marking the beginning of a happy family.

REVIEWS FOR *With Six You Get Eggroll*:
"This family comedy is little more than a variation on *Yours, Mine and Ours*, but its saving grace is that it is much more incisively and inventively done."—*Monthly Film Bulletin*

"Miss Day's widow is a sophisticated lady, but never fear, no passionate bed scenes here. This Doris Day comedy is still family fare—and enjoyable."—*New York Daily News*

"A bright and inventive family comedy."—*Halliwell's Film Guide*

REVIEWS FOR DORIS DAY:
"There are ... hints of the very real comic talent that has, over the years, become hermetically sealed inside a lacquered personality, like a butterfly in a Mason jar."—*The New York Times*

"Miss Day's sunniness, her husky-voiced humor and her gaiety really deserve a fresher setting than this stale situation comedy."—*Christian Science Monitor*

"The point is, with deft support from Brian Keith and a wittily dialogued script from a quartet of writers, Miss Day has moved brightly and engagingly into the area of character comedy."—*The Saturday Review*

FILM AWARDS AND STATISTICS

THE QUIGLEY POLL:

The annual Quigley Poll is a survey of 18,000 film exhibitors and distributors to determine the top box office draws (i.e., those whose films brought in the largest audience). In 1949, Quigley named Day a "Star of Tomorrow," a title given to screen newcomers who showed the most promise.

Doris Day made the Quigley top ten list ten times in the 20 years from her film debut in 1948 through her last film in 1968. In seven of those years, Day was the top female draw, and 30 years after her last film, she continues to hold the record with the most years an actress was number one: 4.

QUIGLEY'S DORIS DAY TOP TEN BOX OFFICE RANKINGS:

The following is a listing of Day's box office status in the years she made the top ten. Also listed are the top actors and actresses and their rankings:

Year	Rank	Top Male & Female Stars/Rank
1951	9	John Wayne (1); Betty Grable (3)
1952	7	Martin & Lewis (1); Susan Hayward (9)
1959	4	Rock Hudson (1); Debbie Reynolds (5)
1960	1	Rock Hudson (2); Elizabeth Taylor (4)
1961	3	Elizabeth Taylor (1); Rock Hudson (2)
1962	1	Rock Hudson (2); Elizabeth Taylor (6)
1963	1	John Wayne (2); Elizabeth Taylor (6)
1964	1	Jack Lemmon (2); Shirley MacLaine (7)
1965	3	Sean Connery (1); Julie Andrews (4)
1966	8	Julie Andrews (1); Sean Connery (2)

THE QUIGLEY TOP BOX OFFICE DRAWS OF THE 1960S:

1. John Wayne
2. Doris Day
3. Cary Grant, Rock Hudson, Elizabeth Taylor (tied)
6. Jack Lemmon
7. Julie Andrews

8. Paul Newman
9. Sean Connery
10. Elvis Presley

THE LAUREL AWARD:

The Laurel Award (also known as the Golden Laurel) is voted on by theater owners. Categories include the most popular actors and actresses of the year, as well as the best comedy and dramatic performances. The results were published in *Motion Picture Exhibitor* magazine. Doris Day won several of these awards and, like with the Quigley Poll, remains the publication's Top Female Star more than 30 years after her last film appearance:

1950	Leading new personality in the motion picture industry
1958	Top Female Star (winner)
1959	Top Female Star (winner)
1960	Top Female Star (winner)
	Female Comedy Performance for *Pillow Talk* (winner)
1961	Top Female Star (winner)
1962	Top Female Star (winner)
	Female Comedy Performance for *Lover Come Back* (winner)
1963	Top Female Star (winner)
	Female Comedy Performance for *That Touch of Mink* (winner)
1964	Top Female Star (winner)
	Female Comedy Performance for *Send Me No Flowers* (winner)
1967	Female Comedy Performance for *The Glass Bottom Boat* (runner-up)

Photoplay's GOLD MEDAL AWARD:

1951	Best Actress for *Lullaby of Broadway*
1959	Most Popular Actress of the Year / Best Actress for *Pillow Talk*

The New York Times ANNUAL TEN BEST FILMS:

1958	*Teacher's Pet*
1959	*Pillow Talk*
1962	*Lover Come Back*

HOLLYWOOD WOMEN'S PRESS CLUB SOUR APPLE AWARD:

1953	Most uncooperative actress of the year
1964	Most uncooperative actress of the year

1975 *Family Weekly* MAGAZINE POLL—FAVORITE MOVIE ACTRESS:

#3 Doris Day

1987 *People* MAGAZINE POLL—GREATEST ACTRESS OF ALL TIME:
#11 Doris Day

THE COMEDY AWARDS:

1991   Lifetime Achievement (first one given)

1999 ARTS & ENTERTAINMENT TELEVISION POLL—
FAVORITE MOVIE STAR OF ALL TIME:
#10 Doris Day

     (The only other actress to make the A&E Top Ten was Audrey Hepburn at #9 with two percent more votes. Marilyn Monroe ranked #11 and Shirley Temple #13.)

GOLDEN GLOBE AWARDS AND NOMINATIONS
(HOLLYWOOD FOREIGN PRESS ASSOCIATION):

     The following is a list of Golden Globe awards and nominations that Doris Day's films received. Following each nomination is the film which received the award. Unfortunately, complete nomination listings for the years 1948 through 1955 do not exist. At the very least, both *Calamity Jane* and *Love Me or Leave Me* more than likely received several nominations including musical, actress and actor (if not Howard Keel for *Calamity Jane*, then James Cagney for *Love Me or Leave Me*).

1950   *Tea for Two*
             Most Promising Newcomer Gene Nelson (winner)

1952   *I'll See You In My Dreams*
             Best Picture Musical or Comedy (*With a Song In My Heart*)

1954   World Film Favorite—Female Doris Day (Audrey Hepburn)

1957   World Film Favorite—Female Doris Day (winner)

1958   *Tunnel of Love*
             Best Actress in a Musical or Comedy Doris Day (Rosalind Russell, *Auntie Mame*)

             Teacher's Pet
             Best Actor in a Musical or Comedy Clark Gable (Danny Kaye, *Me and the Colonel*)
             Best Supporting Actor Gig Young (Burl Ives, *The Big Country*)

1960   *Pillow Talk*
             Best Picture Comedy (*Some Like It Hot*)
             Best Actress in a Musical or Comedy Doris Day (Marilyn Monroe, *Some Like It Hot*)

Best Supporting Actor Tony Randall (Stephen Boyd, *Ben-Hur*)

World Film Favorite—Female Doris Day (winner)

1960   *Midnight Lace*
        Best Actress in a Drama Doris Day (Greer Garson, *Sunrise at Campobello*)

1961   *Lover Come Back*
        Best Supporting Actor Tony Randall (George Chakiris, *West Side Story*)

1962   *That Touch of Mink*
        Best Picture Comedy (winner)
        Best Actor in a Musical or Comedy Cary Grant (Marcello Mastroianni, *Divorce, Italian Style*)

        Billy Rose's Jumbo
        Best Picture Musical (*The Music Man*)

With the Cecil B. DeMille award for lifetime achievement at the 1989 Golden Globe Awards (from the collection of Matt Tunia).

        Best Actress in a Musical or Comedy Doris Day (Rosalind Russell, *Gypsy*)
        Best Actor Musical or Comedy Stephen Boyd (Marcello Mastroianni, *Divorce, Italian Style*)
        Best Actor Musical or Comedy Jimmy Durante (Marcello Mastroianni, *Divorce, Italian Style*)
        Best Supporting Actress Martha Raye (Angela Lansbury, *The Manchurian Candidate*)

        World Film Favorite—Female Doris Day (winner)

1963   *Move Over, Darling*
        Best Actress in a Comedy or Musical Doris Day (Shirley MacLaine, *Irma la Douce*)

1965   *Do Not Disturb*
        New Star of the Year—Female Maura McGiveney (Elizabeth Hartman, *A Patch of Blue*)

        World Film Favorite—Female Doris Day (Natalie Wood)

1989   Cecil B. DeMille Award (Lifetime Achievement)—winner

OSCARS/ACADEMY AWARDS AND NOMINATIONS:

The following is a list of Academy Awards and nominations that Doris Day's films received. Following each nomination is the film which received the Oscar. Interestingly, Day herself was nominated only once for her acting performances (1959's *Pillow Talk*).

1948   *Romance on the High Seas*
        Best Song "It's Magic" ("Buttons and Bows" *The Paleface*)
        Best Scoring of a Musical Picture (*Easter Parade*)

1949   *It's A Great Feeling*
        Best Song "It's A Great Feeling" ("Baby, It's Cold Outside" *Neptune's Daughter*)

1950   *The West Point Story*
        Best Scoring of a Musical Picture (*Annie Get Your Gun*)

1953   *Calamity Jane*
        Best Song "Secret Love" (winner)
        Best Scoring of a Musical Picture (*Call Me Madam*)
        Best Sound Recording (*From Here to Eternity*)

1955   *Love Me or Leave Me*
        Best Actor James Cagney (Ernest Borgnine, *Marty*)
        Best Writing Motion Picture Story (winner)
        Best Writing Screenplay (*Marty*)
        Best Sound Recording (*Oklahoma!*)
        Best Song "I'll Never Stop Loving You" ("Love Is a Many Splendored Thing" *Love Is a Many Splendored Thing*)
        Best Scoring of a Musical Picture (*Oklahoma!*)

1956   *The Man Who Knew Too Much*
        Best Song "Whatever Will Be, Will Be" (winner)

        Julie
        Best Song "Julie" ("Whatever Will Be, Will Be" *The Man Who Knew Too Much*)

1958   *Teacher's Pet*
        Best Supporting Actor Gig Young (Burl Ives, *The Big Country*)
        Best Writing Story and Screenplay Written Directly for the Screen (*The Defiant Ones*)

1959   *Pillow Talk*
        Best Actress Doris Day (Simone Signoret, *Room at the Top*)
        Best Supporting Actress Thelma Ritter (Shelley Winters, *The Diary of Anne Frank*)

Best Writing Story and Screenplay Written Directly for the Screen (winner)

Best Art Direction-Set Direction Color (*Ben-Hur*)

Best Scoring of a Dramatic or Comedy Picture (*Ben-Hur*)

1961   *Lover Come Back*

Best Writing Screenplay Written Directly for the Screen (*Splendor in the Grass*)

1962   *That Touch of Mink*

Best Writing Story and Screenplay Written Directly for the Screen (*Divorce, Italian Style*)

Best Art Direction—Set Direction Color (*Lawrence of Arabia*)

Best Sound (*Lawrence of Arabia*)

Billy Rose's Jumbo

Best Scoring of Music—Adaptation or Treatment (*The Music Man*)

THE TOP DORIS DAY FILMS

by rental fees*, first-time run, approximate in millions US $:

1. *Lover Come Back* $8.5
2. *That Touch of Mink* $8.5
3. *Pillow Talk* $7.7
4. *Please Don't Eat the Daisies* $5.31
5. *The Thrill of It All* $5.3
6. *The Man Who Knew Too Much* $5.1
7. *Move Over Darling* $5.1
8. *The Glass Bottom Boat* $4.6
9. *With Six You Get Eggroll* $4.5
10. *Love Me Or Leave Me* $4.2
11. *Send Me No Flowers* $4.1
12. *Midnight Lace* $3.5
13. *I'll See You In My Dreams* $2.9
14. *On Moonlight Bay* $2.5

ALSO KNOWN AS...

A handful of Doris Day's film titles were changed when distributed to countries outside of the United States. This was done to either shorten the film's title

---

The rental fee is the payment from theater owners to film distributors to show a film; these are not the box office gross, the actual money generated by moviegoers who paid to see a film in a theater to see the film (i.e., the money generated by the sales of tickets). Also, figures are for the US and Canada, and not worldwide. Figures do not include reissues, television and videocassette-DVD sales and rentals, and are not adjusted for inflation. It was noted in 1967, however, that Day's six Universal films (1959 to 1965) alone grossed $70 million worldwide, when the average ticket price in the U.S. was well under $1.

to make it more memorable or to provide a more provocative title. Among them include:

Romance on the High Seas [also known as]	*It's Magic*
It's a Great Feeling	*Mademoiselle FiFi*
Young Man With a Horn	*Young Man of Music*
Tea for Two	*No, No Nanette*
The West Point Story	*Fine and Dandy*
It Happened to Jane	*Twinkle and Shine*
Jumbo	*The Most Beautiful Girl in the World*
The Glass Bottom Boat	*The Spy in Lace Panties*
With Six You Get Eggroll	*A Man in Mommy's Bed*

In the case of *Young Man with a Horn*, the title was changed for the U.K. release because it was too provocative for British censors. "Horn" implied an erection.

FILMS THAT MIGHT HAVE BEEN

There have been dozens—if not numbering over 100—roles Doris Day was offered but declined to play for various reasons. Many of these were never realized as a finished film. Even today, the money and requests of movie producers is not enough to lure Doris back to the big screen "unless it's a script I'm dying to do," she said, "and I can be filmed in or near Carmel." Thus far, no script or offer has enticed her to return to the screen, on which she was last seen more than 30 years ago. Below are a few of the films that could have been Doris Day films but weren't:

The follow-up to *Romance on the High Seas* was to be *The '49ers* with Michael Curtiz directing. Instead she made *My Dream Is Yours*.

After the release of *My Dream Is Yours*, Warner Bros. announced *Broadway Revisited* in which Doris was to share top billing with Joan Crawford, Jack Carson, Virginia Mayo and Gordon MacRae. It was not made.

Miss America, with Virginia Mayo and set at the Miss America contest, was planned but ultimately not produced with Day. Nor was the musical comedy *Painting the Clouds with Sunshine*.

There were also rumors that Doris would star with Gordon MacRae in a musical version of *Brother Rat*. It appeared that the studio was rushing to pair the two together in a film. This was finally done in *Tea for Two*.

Warner Bros. planned to star Doris Day in *Sunny*, the musical by Jerome Kern and Otto Harbach. It had been filmed twice before with Marilyn Miller in the original and Anna Neagle in the 1941 version. The Day-*Sunny* project was shelved for unknown reasons.

It was announced that Doris was to play the lead role in *The Helen Morgan Story*. The movie was later made with Ann Blyth and Paul Newman.

After appearing with Danny Thomas in the hit *I'll See You in My Dreams*, Warners wanted Doris and Thomas to reteam in a remake of *The Jazz Singer*. But the studio decided that the part was not up to Doris's then-present standing as an attraction, and the role was played by Peggy Lee.

The first movie produced by Martin Melcher Productions was to be *Yankee Doodle Girl* in 1954. The story takes place around 1910 when two new stars were about to be added to the U.S. flag (New Mexico and Arizona). There were opponents as well as supporters of this measure in the treatment of the proposed film, but it was never made.

Doris had wanted to play the lead in MGM's *Annie Get Your Gun*, but as she was bound to her Warner Bros. contract, the studio refused to loan her out to make the film. "It's my nature to be a go-along kind, never complaining—no suspensions—never balking," Doris said in 1955 after she completed her contract with Warner Bros. "Except once, maybe, when I was dying to do *Annie Get Your Gun*." The role went to Betty Hutton.

Marty Melcher and Doris Day's Arwin Productions announced that Doris was earmarked to star in her company's film *Nothing But a Woman*, a musical–Western. The project did not go further than the planning stage. Nor did *Anniversary Waltz* with Gene Kelly, who was to star and direct. Kelly, however, later directed Doris in *Tunnel of Love*.

When MGM decided to remake its 1939 hit *The Women* as a musical with male roles added, Doris and Howard Keel were offered the two leading roles. Although Doris allegedly wanted to be in the film (retitled *The Opposite Sex*), she was committed to other projects and had to turn it down. MGM contract player June Allyson was given the part. (Keel also turned down the offer, and *The Opposite Sex* failed with the critics and audiences.)

Doris declined to appear in the remake of the Irene Dunne tearjerker *Love Affair*. Deborah Kerr and Cary Grant were cast in the retitled *An Affair To Remember*, which became a classic in its own right.

In 1958, a newspaper column stated Doris was to film *Roar Like a Dove* in England the following year.

Sol Siegel began negotiating with Doris and Marty Melcher in 1958 for her to play *The Life of Elsie Janis*, but no deal was reached.

She was seriously considered for the lead role of Nellie Forbush in *South Pacific*, and Doris desperately wanted to be in the film. But because her asking price was too high for the already costly production, the lesser-known Mitzi Gaynor was cast instead. The film became a hit, but critics have since noted that it is not the classic film it could—or should—have become.

A proposed remake of the Ginger Rogers–Katharine Hepburn film *Stage Door* was announced with Doris Day and Carol Channing, but the idea was shelved.

Although it received favorable critical reviews, Doris Day's MGM film *Jumbo* was a financial flop—her only complete financial "miss" in a seven-year period, from *Pillow Talk* through *The Glass Bottom Boat*. It was rumored that *Jumbo*'s failure cost Doris the lead in MGM's *The Unsinkable Mollie Brown*, which ultimately went to Debbie Reynolds.

Darryl Zanuck, head of Twentieth Century-Fox, wanted Doris Day to play Maria in *The Sound of Music*. Doris had recorded and released the title song in the early 1960s and was nominated for a Grammy, but the role went to newcomer Julie Andrews. It was rumored that the dismal flop of *Jumbo* had cost her the role. James Harbert, one of Doris' accompanists-arrangers, stated that Doris herself had turned down *The Sound of Music*. Doris, however, said she did not decline *The Sound of Music* or another plum musical, 1960's *Can-Can*. If those roles were indeed offered, Doris knew nothing about them. "It was probably Marty who turned them down," she says.

One role that Doris herself declined to play was Mrs. Robinson in 1967's *The Graduate*. Doris' reason for not taking the role: The nudity required by the role offended her sense of values. The role proved to be a career advancement move for Anne Bancroft, who earned an Academy Award nomination for it.

In 1983, Jimmy Hawkins, who had acted in "The Donna Reed Show," "The Ruggles" and "The Adventures of Ozzie and Harriet" among other projects, met with Rock Hudson to discuss a sequel to *Pillow Talk*. Hudson was very interested, as was Delbert Mann, the director of *Lover Come Back*. By the spring of 1984, Hudson was ready to commit to do the project, and Doris was contacted. She was interested and suggested a few changes and her own ideas. But the project was never made as Doris went into her "Doris Day's Best Friends" cable show and soon after Rock Hudson passed away.

In 1990, producer Ross Hunter announced plans to make his own "sequel of sorts" to *Pillow Talk*, after there had been 1983 discussions of the same idea. Doris, however, said she could not ever dream of doing a sequel to the film without Rock Hudson (who had died five years earlier). The Hunter sequel was never filmed.

For *Mother*, a film by and starring Albert Brooks which told the story of a grown man moving in with his mother, Brooks reportedly offered Doris the title role, which she turned down. Debbie Reynolds played the part, which earned her a Golden Globe nomination and some of the best reviews of her career.

Perhaps the oddest film idea concerning Doris Day was pairing her in a 1960s musical with none other than the King of rock 'n' roll turned film star, Elvis Presley. The idea did not progress further than the discussion stage.

Day Over the Radio

Her instinct is so correct. Her intonation is flawless. She had a way of being very personal with a song.... Everything she sang was absolutely to one person.
—Rosemary Clooney

She can really make a lyric sound like it's smiling. Or if there's some kind of tear behind it, she can really create a visual effect with an audio art. —Terry Melcher

OVERVIEW

DORIS DAY WAS SUCH a popular actress that many have overlooked her career as a singer. In terms of chart success as a vocalist, Doris Day achieved five #1 songs and 56 Top 40 hit songs in less than 13 years. In terms of longevity and social impact, "Sentimental Journey" was *the* song at the closing of World War II, full of bittersweet memories of what could be, and what may have been. In regard to "Whatever Will Be, Will Be (Qué Será, Será)," fans of Day's rendition have stretched far and wide, including such artists as Sly Stone and Paul McCartney.

Day's admirers encompass a wide variety of people, from private citizens of all classes to entertainers. It was also reported that pop diva Madonna once offered to direct a music video for Doris Day; however, nothing transpired. Decades ago, Motown founder Berry Gordy, Jr., wrote a song as an appreciation of Day. Years later he presented the song in person to his favorite actress and singer.

In his book *An Encyclopedia of Quotations About Music*, Nat Shapiro named Day a strong contender (after Ella Fitzgerald) as a female counterpart to Frank Sinatra, the singer. Shapiro applauded Day:

It is ... with some hesitation that I use "underrated" to preface an enthu-siastic consideration of Doris Day....

When she sings, Doris' charm, sensuality and vivacity are unpretentiously projected in an incipiently husky, readily identifiable voice. She has her very own sound. And happily there's a lot more to her than that. Her natural musicality, her intelligent and sensitive reading of lyrics, her good taste in choice of material and her fine, relaxed sense of time all add up to superior singing.

Partly because she has chosen to remain private and professionally inac-tive, Doris Day is rarely taken seriously by "experts" who write "authorita-tive" books about popular music. I must conclude that they just haven't taken time to listen.

Which brings us right back to the word "underrated." It is this writer's contention that, in the words of Arthur Miller, "attention must be paid."

ALBUMS

Throughout the years, dozens of Day compilations have appeared on vinyl, tape and compact disc. Titles such as *Doris Day Sings Her Great Movie Hits, Day in Hollywood, The Magic of Doris Day, Singin' in the Rain* and *Whatever Will Be, Will Be* are examples of these compilations. These are not included in the list of original albums; however, *Doris Day's Greatest Hits* is listed primarily because it arguably has been her most consistent and best-selling album. *Doris Day It's Magic: Her Early Years at Warner Bros.* is also listed as several of the songs had never been commercially released until this set appeared.

Film Songtrack Albums

Since Warner Bros. owned the dramatic, comedic and vocal performances of its number one actress, Columbia Records was unable to release the songs she sang in her Warner films. When Day's film career succeeded, her label decided to have her re-record the songs she sang in her films. Columbia then released the recordings with the film's title. In many instances, the songs released on vinyl differed from the Day versions on film, especially in the orchestration. One notable difference was the duets, primarily those with Gordon MacRae. Since MacRae was not signed to Columbia Records, the label substituted his vocals in the Day recordings. Thus the Day–MacRae duets can only be heard on the five films they made together.

The following is a listing of Doris Day recordings released throughout her career. These are primarily the original first issue of the recording released as a band singer, in duets, and as a solo artist. The label numbers and charts refer to United States releases.

All of the releases are 33 1/3 rpm 12" releases (unless noted as 10" releases); various other formats of these collections were released with the same song listing. Among them are 78 rpm box sets, 45 rpm box set, cassettes and reel-to-reel. Several have been digitally remastered and are currently available on compact disc.

Young Man with a Horn CL-6106 (10") 1950

"I May Be Wrong," "The Man I Love," "The Very Thought of You," "Pretty Baby," "Melancholy Rhapsody," "Would I Love You," "Too Marvelous for Words," "Get Happy," "I Only Have Eyes for You," "LimeHouse Blues," "With a Song in My Heart," "Lullaby of Broadway" with Harry James and his Orchestra.

Tea for Two Columbia CL-6149 (10") 1950

"Crazy Rhythm," "Here in My Arms," "I Know That You Know," "I Want to Be Happy," "Do Do Do," "I Only Have Eyes for You," "Oh Me! Oh My!," "Tea for Two." Music by Alex Stordahl and his Orchestra with the Ken Lane Singers and the Page Cavanaugh Trio; and Gene Nelson.

Lullaby of Broadway Columbia CL-6168 (10") 1951

"Lullaby of Broadway," "Fine and Dandy," "In a Shanty in Old Shanty Town," "Somebody Loves Me," "Just One of Those Things," "You're Getting to Be a Habit With Me," "I Love the Way You Say Goodnight," "Please Don't Talk About Me When I'm Gone" with the Buddy Cole Quartet. Music by the Norman Luboff Choir. Orchestra under Frank Comstock.

On Moonlight Bay Columbia CL-6186 (10") 1951

"Moonlight Bay," "Tell Me (Why the Nights Are Lonely)," "Till We Meet Again," "Love Ya," "I'm Forever Blowing Bubbles," "Every Little Movement (Has a Meaning All Its Own)," "Cuddle Up a Little Closer," "Christmas Story" with Paul Weston and his Orchestra and the Norman Luboff Choir and Jack Smith.

I'll See You in My Dreams Columbia CL-6198 (10") 1951

"Makin' Whoopee," "The One I Love Belongs to Somebody Else," "It Had to Be You," "I Wish I Had a Girl," "My Buddy," "Nobody's Sweetheart," "Ain't We Got Fun," "I'll See You in My Dreams" with Paul Weston and his Orchestra and the Norman Luboff Choir.

April in Paris Columbia 1581 (10") 1953

"April in Paris," "That's What Makes Paris Paree," "I'm Gonna Ring the Bell

Many of Day's early films were musicals in which she re-recorded the main songs and released on disc. *Young Man with a Horn* (1950) with Kirk Douglas featured many standards and the music of Harry James (Jerry Ohlinger's Movie Material Store, Inc.).

Tonight," "I Know a Place" with Paul Weston and his Orchestra and the Norman Luboff Choir.

By the Light of the Silvery Moon Columbia CL-6248 (10") 1953

"By the Light of the Silvery Moon," "Your Eyes Have Told Me So," "Just One Girl," "Ain't We Got Fun," "If You Were the Only Girl," "Be My Little Bumble Bee," "I'll Forget You," "King Chanticleer" with Paul Weston and his Orchestra and the Norman Luboff Choir.

Calamity Jane Columbia CL-6273 (10") 1954

"Secret Love," "I Can Do Without You," "The Black Hills of Dakota," "The Deadwood Stage," "A Woman's Touch," "'Tis Harry I'm Plannin' to Marry," "Higher Than a Hawk," "Just Blew in From the Windy City." Musical direction by Ray Heindorf.

Young at Heart Columbia CL-6339 (10") 1955

"Hold Me in Your Arms," "Just One of Those Things," "There's a Rising Moon," "Till My Love Comes to Me," "You My Love," "One for My Baby (And One More for the Road)," "Someone to Watch Over Me," "Ready, Willing and Able"+. Musical direction by Percy Faith; Paul Weston (+).

Love Me or Leave Me Columbia CL-710 / CS-8773 1955

"I'll Never Stop Loving You," "Shaking the Blues Away," "Stay on the Right Side Sister," "Sam, the Old Accordion Man," "Never Look Back," "At Sundown," "Mean to Me," "Everybody Loves My Baby (But My Baby Don't Love Nobody But Me)," "It All Depends on You," "Ten Cents a Dance," "You Made Me Love You," "Love Me or Leave Me." Orchestra conducted by Percy Faith.

The Pajama Game Columbia OL-5210 1957

"The Pajama Game (medley)," "Hey There," "There Once Was a Man," "Seven-and-a-Half Cents," "Small Talk," "Once-a-Year Day, "I'm Not at All in Love," "Hernando's Hideaway," "I'll Never Be Jealous Again," "Racing With the Clock (medley)," "Steam Heat," "Finale." Musical direction by Ray Heindorf.

Billy Rose's Jumbo Columbia OS-2260 / OL-5860 1962

"The Circus Is on Parade," "Over and Over Again," "Why Can't I?," "This Can't Be Love," "The Most Beautiful Girl in the World," "My Romance," "The Most Beautiful Girl In the World (version two)," "Little Girl Blue," "Sawdust, Spangles and Dreams" with the MGM Orchestra conducted by George Stoll.

While Day teamed with Frank Sinatra in *Young at Heart*, they had recorded and appeared together on the radio show *Your Hit Parade* (Jerry Ohlinger's Movie Material Store, Inc.).

Original Studio Albums (Non-Soundtrack)
[All 12" unless noted]

You're My Thrill Columbia CL-6071 (10") 1949 [set was reissued along with four additional songs (*) under the title of *Day Dreams* Columbia CL 624 12"]

"You're My Thrill," "Bewitched," "I'm Confessin'," "Sometimes I'm Happy," "I Didn't Know What Time It Was," "You Go to My Head," "When Your Lover Has Gone," "That Old Feeling"; "If I Could Be with You,"* "Darn That Dream,"* "Imagination,"* "I've Only Myself to Blame"* (various conductors).

"For this collection of songs, [Day] has chosen a group of established favorites that are regularly but infrequently heard, songs with a rather more sophisticated touch, both lyrically and musically, than is generally found. In them is some of her finest singing, brilliantly phrased and beautifully keyed to the mood of the song. Here is popular artistry of a high order, applied by Doris Day to popular songs of the first rank."—*from liner notes*

The *Love Me or Leave Me* soundtrack album was number one on the charts for more than four months in 1955, a record for a female singer that held for almost four decades (Jerry Ohlinger's Movie Material Store, Inc.).

Day by Day Columbia CL-942 1957

"Autumn Leaves," "But Beautiful," "But Not for Me," "Day by Day," "Don't Take Your Love from Me," "Gone with the Wind," "Gypsy in My Soul," "Hello, My Lover, Goodbye," "I Hadn't Anyone Till You," "I Remember You," "Song Is You," "There'll Never Be Another You" with Paul Weston and His Music from Hollywood.

"One of the problems that besets an artist like Doris Day when she sits down to plan an album collection is which songs to select, which to discard. She automatically wants to include a few of her own favorites and naturally wants to include those of her fans, and no album is ever long enough to include everything. When Day got together with Paul Weston to plan [the album] they had on hand her own list of favorites and [a list from] Columbia. From the two, Day chose the songs she sings here, and, with Paul Weston, worked out the ideas for appropriate backgrounds for each number. The result is almost literally 'Day' by Day—Doris Day singing songs she personally selected."—*from liner notes*

Preparing to record "Day by Day" (from the collection of Matt Tunia).

Day by Night Columbia CS-8089 / CL-1053 1957

"Under a Blanket of Blue," "I See Your Face Before Me," "Moon Song," "The Lamp Is Low," "You Do Something to Me," "Close Your Eyes," "Dream a Little Dream of Me," "Wrap Your Troubles in Dreams," "Stars Fell on Alabama," "Moonglow," "Soft as a Starlight," "The Night We Called It a Day" with Paul Weston and His Music from Hollywood.

"The songs Doris has chosen are pre-dominantly from the Thirties, an era highly productive of first-rate tunes, and they provide a kind of casual memory book as well as a fine basis for her brilliant interpretations. Even when she is rollicking her way though a novelty tune, Doris Day somehow invariably seems to be singing it for the listener alone. In this program of night songs, the quality is particularly evident, most outstanding in the ballads but even in the handful of songs presented with a jazzier inflection."—*from liner notes*

Hooray for Hollywood Columbia C2L-5 / CS-8066/7 1958

[two record set; later reissued in single record sets as *Day in Hollywood* (Vol. 1 and Vol. 2)]

"Hooray for Hollywood," "Night and Day," "Blues in the Night (My Mama Done Tol' Me)," "Easy to Love," "The Way You Look Tonight," "That Old Black Magic," "Love Is Here to Stay," "Pennies From Heaven," "Over the Rainbow," "I Had the Craziest Dream," "Oh, But I Do," "You'll Never Know," "Cheek to Cheek," "Nice Work If You Can Get It," "Soon," "It's Easy to Remember," "I've Got My Love to Keep Me Warm," "Let's Face the Music and Dance," "In the Still of the Night," "I'll Remember April," "It Might as Well Be Spring," "Three Coins in the Fountain," "A Foggy Day," "It's Magic." Orchestra conducted by Frank DeVol.

"In selecting the twenty-four songs for this collection, Doris Day has aimed at a cross-section of some of the most memorable; some from almost-forgotten films, some from dramatic movies, some among the most popular songs of all time. In design, the collection is a kind of impressionistic souvenir of great songs from the movies, a salute to brilliant craftsmen and the magic that is Hollywood at its best, presented by one of Hollywood's most versatile and accomplished artists."—*from liner notes*

Cuttin' Capers Columbia CS-8078 / CL-1232 1959

"Cuttin' Capers," "Me Too (Ho-Ho! Ha-Ha!)," "Get Out and Get Under the Moon," "Steppin' Out with My Baby," "Fit as a Fiddle (and Ready for Love)," "Let's Take a Walk Around the Block," "The Lady's In Love with You," "Let's Fly Away," "Why Don't We Do This More Often," "Makin' Whoopee," "I Feel Like a Feather in the Breeze," "I'm Sitting on Top of the World." Orchestra under the direction of Frank DeVol.

"It's a long established fact that Doris Day has mighty few peers when it comes to making a popular song sound even better than it has any right to. Her uncommonly persuasive way with a ballad has been celebrated for the whole course of her career, and her treatment of lighter numbers has been equally successful, if perhaps less famous.... This particular collection finds Doris in a distinctly light-hearted frame of mind and voice, offering a sheaf of songs that deal with various euphoric states in various euphoric manners ... here is the incomparable Miss Day, rollicking through a dozen feathery songs, most of them old favorites and some of them sadly forgotten until she revived them."—*from liner notes*

Listen to Day Columbia DDS-1 / DD 1 1960

"Anyway the Wind Blows," "He's So Married," "Oh! What a Lover You'll Be," "Heart Full of Love," "I Enjoy Being a Girl," "Possess Me," "Tunnel of Love," "Love Me in the Daytime," "No," "Pillow Talk,"+ "Inspiration,"+ "Roly Poly"+. Orchestra under the direction of Frank DeVol; Jack Marshall(+).

"'Incomparable' is a word that gets tossed around rather too much these days, but when Doris Day is the subject incomparable is the only word. As a recording star and as a movie actress she has won international success and acclaim, with a consistency of accomplishments that is as rare as it is delightful. This new collection presents Doris Day in some of her most enjoyable performances...."—*from liner notes*

Bob Hope (left) did not believe Doris Day was a big enough attraction for his radio show despite Les Brown's insistence. By the time Hope changed his mind several months later, Day's asking price multiplied (from the collection of Matt Tunia).

What Every Girl Should Know Columbia CS-8234 / CL-1438 1960

"Mood Indigo," "When You're Smiling," "A Fellow Needs a Girl," "My Kinda Love," "What's the Use of Wond'rin," "Something Wonderful," "A Hundred Years from Today," "You Can't Have Everything," "Not Only Should You Love Him," "What Does a Woman Do," "The Everlasting Arms," "What Every Girl Should Know." Orchestra under the direction of Harry Zimmerman.

"What every girl should know (and just possibly every man, too) is that the road of love is not always smooth, but that nevertheless it is still a wonderful journey, well worth the effort. Doris Day lines out this philosophy in a dozen superior songs, some thoughtful, some cheery, and all full of good advice.... But informative as her lyric discourse is, it is even more valuable entertainment, joining fine music and words with fine singing by the lovely, talented and altogether delectable Doris Day."—*from liner notes*

Show Time Columbia CS-8261 / CL-1470 1960

"Ohio," "I Love Paris," "Show Time," "On the Street Where You Live," "The Surrey with the Fringe on Top," "They Say It's Wonderful," "I Got the Sun in the Morning," "The Sound of Music," "I've Grown Accustomed to His Face," "When I'm Not Near the Boy I Love," "People Will Say We're in Love," "A Wonderful Guy." Orchestra conducted by Alex Stordahl.

"From somewhere deep inside, where most girls love or laugh or cry, Doris Day sings. When you listen to the warm, intimate, natural way she has with a tune, memories begin. Her songs seem to touch you, giving voice to unspoken longings. Be it a ballad or rhythm number, her canny knack for projecting the soul of a song is a rare and wonderful gift ... a gift that has made her the world's favorite singing star ... in films ... on records."—*from liner notes*

Bright & Shiny Columbia CS-8414 / CL-1614 1961

"Happy Talk," "Ridin' High," "Stay with the Happy People," "Clap Yo' Hands," "Singin' in the Rain," "I Want to Be Happy," "Make Someone Happy," "On the Sunny Side of the Street," "Twinkle and Shine," "Bright and Shiny," "Gotta Feelin,'" "Keep Smilin', Keep Laughin', Be Happy." Orchestra under the direction of Neal Hefti.

In the studio in the early 1960s (from the collection of Matt Tunia).

"Bright and shiny as a new-minted penny ... the world's best-selling female vocalist combines her high spirits with a warm sensitivity that soars across land and language barriers. A truly versatile artist, Doris illuminates a ballad, lights up a rhythm song. In this collection, she had chosen songs on the sunny side."—*from liner notes*

I Have Dreamed Columbia CS-8460 / CL-1660 1961

"All I Do Is Dream of You," "My Ship," "I Have Dreamed," "Someday I'll Find You," "I Believe in Dreams," "Time to Say Goodnight," "I'll Buy That Dream," "Periwinkle Blues," "Oh What a Beautiful Dream," "We'll Love Again," "When I Grow Too Old to Dream," "You Stepped Out of a Dream." Orchestra under the direction of Jim Harbert.

"Word must have gotten back to a desk at Columbia Records that (with a million other people) I am a Dayniac.... If there's such a thing as cashmere-velvet, it would be [a] description of what she does to these numbers. Either way, new or old, Doris Day makes this material what I'd call 'cuddle-up music for adults.' If she want to she can create a different mood with every song. She can be tender. The next moment throb the beat, the strong, rhythmic drive of her delivery can send you looking for someone to dance with."—*from liner notes by Pete Martin of* The Saturday Evening Post

Duet Doris Day and André Previn (with the André Previn Trio) Columbia CS-8552 / CL-1752 1962

"Remind Me," "Wait Till You See Him," "Who Are We to Say (Obey Your Heart)," "Close Your Eyes," "Falling in Love Again," "Fools Rush In (Where Angels Fear to Tread)," "Give Me Time," "Nobody's Heart," "My One and Only Love," "Control Yourself," "Daydreaming," "Yes" produced by Irving Townsend.

"Doris Day and André Previn had never met before they begun to prepare their album.... At their first meeting, Doris and André discovered many mutual interests—such as sodas, animals and ballads. In fact, that first afternoon Doris sang some of André's songs, three of which—'Yes,' 'Daydreaming' and 'Control Yourself'—with lyrics by Dory Previn, are heard on this album. The Day–Previn duo rehearsed many times after that first encounter. Then, with Red Mitchell, bass, and Frank Capp, drums, they came to Columbia's Hollywood studios where, in a single afternoon, this album was made."—*from liner notes by Irving Townsend*

Doris Day's Greatest Hits Columbia CS-8635 / CL-1210 1962

"Everybody Loves a Lover," "It's Magic," "A Guy Is a Guy," "Secret Love," "Bewitched," "Teacher's Pet," "Whatever Will Be, Will Be (Qué Será, Será)," "If I Give My Heart to You," "(Why Did I Tell You I Was Going to) Shanghai,"

"When I Fall in Love," "Lullaby of Broadway," "Love Me or Leave Me" (various conductors and producers).

This album served as a collection of Day's greatest hits and a few favorites not released as singles. But the album falls short as a true assembling of her "greatest hits." The songs "Love Me or Leave Me" and "Lullaby of Broadway" were not released as singles and therefore did not hit the charts. "Teacher's Pet" was issued as a single; however, it did not crack the top 40 on the national music charts which usually decrees a "hit" song.

Since the collection concentrated on Day's solo recordings, such number one hits as "Sentimental Journey" and "My Dreams Are Getting Better All the Time" with Les Brown, and "Love Somebody" with Buddy Clark, were not included. The top ten hits "My Darling, My Darling" (again with Clark) and "Sugarbush" with Frankie Laine were also bypassed. As for Day's top solo hits, a few were not included including "Again" (a number two hit), the top tens "Would I Love You (Love You, Love You)," "Mister Tap Toe" and the Academy Award–nominated top 20 hit "I'll Never Stop Loving You."

You'll Never Walk Alone Columbia CS-8704 / CL-1904 1962

"Nearer My God to Thee," "I Need Thee Every Hour," "You'll Never Walk Alone," "Abide with Me," "The Lord's Prayer," "Scarlet Ribbons (for Her Hair)," "Bless This House," "Walk with Him," "In the Garden," "The Prodigal Son," "If I Can Help Somebody," "Be Still and Know." Orchestra arranged and conducted by Jim Harbert. Produced by Irv Townsend and Jim Harbert.

"[A]dd one more triumph to the Doris Day story—her first album devoted to spiritual and inspirational songs. This is something that Doris has wanted to do for a long time. A simple and charming person herself, with a joyous philosophy and boundless enthusiasm, she has always felt close to God and to the music that celebrates His glory. With her full-throated voice and intimate approach to music and lyrics, Doris is a 'natural' for the songs on this album."—*from liner notes*

Doris Day and Robert Goulet Sing "Annie Get Your Gun" Columbia OS-2360 / OL-5960 1963

"Overture," "Colonel Buffalo Bill," "I'm a Bad, Bad Man," "Doin' What Comes Natur'lly," "The Girl That I Marry," "You Can't Get a Man with a Gun," "They Say It's Wonderful," "My Defenses Are Down," "Moonshine Lullaby," "I'm an Indian, Too," "I Got Lost in His Arms," "Who Do You Love I Hope?," "I Got the Sun in the Mornin'," "Anything You Can Do," "There's No Business Like Show Business." Orchestra and chorus under the direction of Franz Allers. Produced by Jim Foglesong and Irving Townsend.

"*Annie Get Your Gun* is as American as the redskin chronicles of James Fenimore Cooper. It could have been written only in America by Americans. Ethel

Merman was Annie when she created her. Mary Martin became Annie, a different Annie than Miss Merman's, but essentially an all–American girl. How fitting then to have as the Annie on this recording that most American of today's singing actresses, Doris Day. Her Annie is definitely 'Doin' What Comes Natur'lly.'"—*from liner notes by Leo Lerman*

Love Him! Columbia CS-8931 / CL-2131 1964

"Love Him," "Can't Help Falling in Love," "As Long As He Needs Me," "Funny," "Lollipops and Roses," "Since I Feel for You," "Losing You," "(Now and Then There's) A Fool Such As I," "More," "Night Life," "Softly, As I Leave You." Arranged and conducted by Tommy Oliver. Produced by Terry Melcher.

"While the songs Doris Day has assembled ... are frankly on the sentimental side, Doris sings them all with that special Day urgency implied in the collection's title 'Love Him!' Doris, of course, creates a different mood with each song ... meltingly tender ... scorchingly torchy ... sweetly swinging ... sadly wise. Tommy Oliver's deft orchestral-choral arrangements and conducting—and the versatile lady herself—make 'Love Him!' a *love her* album."—*from liner notes*

The Doris Day Christmas Album Columbia CS-9026 1964

"Silver Bells," "I'll Be Home for Christmas," "Toyland," "Let It Snow! Let It Snow! Let It Snow!" "The Christmas Song," "Winter Wonderland," "Christmas Present," "Have Yourself a Merry Little Christmas," "White Christmas," "Snowfall," "Be a Child at Christmas Time," "The Christmas Waltz" conducted by Dudley C. "Pete" King.

"Let's be honest. Unless you happen to be a very wealthy Californian, Doris Day is not really your girl next door.... The Doris Day who gambols around sound stages—dressed to the caps by Edith Head or Jean Louis—is a far cry from the neighbor who limps flatfooted in corrective shoes and elastic stockings.... The real Doris Day ... always managed to project her innate talent for living and enjoying life. This happiness comes through—sweet and clear—every time she plays a scene or sings a lyric. The sound of her personal happiness gains added tinsel in this tasteful collection of yuletide evergreens."—*from liner notes by Ron Gold*

[Note: reissues and variations of *The Doris Day Christmas Album* throughout the years have included the following songs: "Here Comes Santa Claus," "Ol' Saint Nicholas," both with Les Brown, and "Christmas Present," which she sang in the film *On Moonlight Bay*.]

With a Smile and a Song (with Jimmy Joyce and His Children's Chorus) Columbia CS-9066 / CL-2266 1965

"Whatever Will Be, Will Be (Qué Será, Será)," "Getting to Know You," "Sleepy Baby," "Inchworm," "With a Smile and a Song," "Zip-a-Dee-Doo-Dah," "Give a

Little Whistle," "The Children's Marching Song (Nick Nack Paddy Whack)," "Swinging on a Star," "The Lilac Tree (Perspicacity)," "High Hopes," "Do Re Mi." Arranged and conducted by Allyn Ferguson. Produced by Allen Stanton.

"Doris Day's voice has tenderness and bounce, a mellow glow and sparkling shine all at the same time. It all adds up to brightness, warmth, and a sense of fun in being alive that is a joy to hear. *With a Smile and a Song* is probably the happiest record Doris has made. First of all, there is Doris. Second, she is singing twelve of the brightest, most heartwarming songs of all time.... Last and best of all, Doris is singing in this album with a wonderful group of children.... No one needs to be told about the natural joy and fun in the sound of children singing." —*from liner notes by Dick Maltby, Jr.*

Latin for Lovers Columbia CS-9110 / CL-2310 1965

"Dansero," "How Insensitive (Insensataez)," "Be Mine Tonight (Noche de Ronda)," "Por Favor," "Be True to Me (Savor a Mi)," "Perhaps, Perhaps, Perhaps (Quizas, Quizas, Quizas)," "Our Day Will Come," "Fly Me to the Moon (In Other Words)," "Meditation," "Slightly Out of Tune (Desafinado)," "Summer Has Gone," "Quiet Nights of Quiet Stars (Corcovado)." Arranged and conducted by Mort Garson. Produced by Allen Stanton.

"A singer can't sing without a song, so we should all be grateful to the bossa nova. Not only has this haunting Brazilian rhythm brought a flood of warmly melodic songs in its wake, it has also provided Doris Day with a wonderful opportunity to extend the affinity she showed for Latin music in one of her great hits, 'Que Será, Será.' But there is more to this album than the bossa nova. The Brazilian beat serves merely as an opening wedge around which Doris has gathered a gala array of songs that fit into the meaningful, melodic groove that the bossa nova has established." —*from liner notes by Gordon Barnes*

Doris Day's Sentimental Journey Columbia CS-9160 / CL-2360 1965

"The More I See You," "At Last," "Come to Baby, Do!," "I Had the Craziest Dream/I Don't Want to Walk Without You," "I'll Never Smile Again," "I Remember You," "Serenade in Blue," "I'm Beginning to See the Light," "It Could Happen to You," "It's Been a Long, Long Time," "Sentimental Journey." Arranged and conducted by Mort Garson. Produced by Allen Stanton.

"This record contains many examples of why people still like to listen to Doris Day sing. It's a soft, pleasant, even sometimes sensuous sentimental journey into her past, a past that she doesn't dote on reliving, but one the importance of which she certainly appreciates. Most of the songs come from her Les Brown band singing days, a part of her career that she freely admits helped her tremendously to develop both as a performer and as a person." —*from liner notes by George T. Simon* (The Feeling of Jazz)

Miscellaneous Albums:

Wonderful Day Columbia XTV-82022 1962

"Lover Come Back," "Whatever Will Be, Will Be (Qué Será, Será)," "Pillow Talk," "It's Magic," "Teacher's Pet," "When You're Smiling," "Never Look Back," "Should I Surrender," "Till My Love Comes to Me," "Julie," "Be Prepared," "Possess Me" (various conductors and producers).

This was a limited edition collection of Day's film songs released in 1962 plus two new songs ("Lover Come Back" and "Possess Me") to promote her latest film *Lover Come Back.*

The Love Album 1993 (rediscovered 1967 recordings released in Great Britain)

"Snuggled on Your Shoulder," "Street of Dream," "Life Is Just a Bowl of Cherries," "If I Had My Life to Live Over/Let Me Call You Sweetheart," "Are You Lonesome Tonight," "All Alone," "Sleepy Lagoon," "Faded Summer Love," "Oh, How I Miss You Tonight," "For All We Know," "Wonderful One." Conducted by Sidney H. Feller.

This set of 1967 recordings were considered "lost" for two decades before they were found among Day's boxes in storage. Oddly, this song collection was not released in the United States and was made available only by import. It stands, however, as the final original album released by Doris Day of some of her personal favorite songs.

The Complete Doris Day with Les Brown Sony Music A228298
CCM-029-2 1996

"(I Ain't Hep to That Step But I'll) Dig It," "Let's Be Buddies," "While the Music Plays On," "Three at a Table for Two," "Between Friends," "Broomstreet," "Barbara Allen," "Celery Stalks at Midnight," "Amapola (Pretty Little Poppy)," "Easy as Pie," "Boogie Wooglie Piggy," "Beau Night in Hotchkiss Corners," "Alexander the Swoose (Half Swan-Half Goose)," "Made Up My Mind," "Keep Cool, Fool," "Sentimental Journey," "My Dreams Are Getting Better All the Time," "He's Home for a Little While," "'Tain't Me," "I'll Always Be with You," "A Red Kiss on a Blue Letter," "Till the End of Time," "He'll Have to Cross the Atlantic," "I'd Rather Be with You," "Come to Baby, Do!," "Aren't You Glad You're You?," "The Last Time I Saw You," "We'll Be Together Again," "You Won't Be Satisfied (Until You Break My Heart)," "In the Moon Mist," "Day by Day," "(Ah Yes) There's Good Blues Tonight," "All Through the Day," "The Deevil, Devil, Divil," "I Got the Sun in the Morning," "My Number One Dream Came True," "The Whole World Is Singing My Song," "Are You Still in Love with Me?," "Sooner or Later," "You Should Have Told Me," "The Christmas Song (Merry Christmas to You)," "It Could Happen to You" (various producers).

This anthology contained the songs Day recorded while with Les Brown and His Band of Renown, some of which were true rarities. "I'd Rather Be with You" and "The Deevil, Devil, Divil" were not released until long after Day left the band, and "It Could Happen to You" made its debut almost 50 years later, in 1990. The song "Are You Still in Love With Me?" makes its first appearance with this set, first recorded in 1946. As Joseph F. Laredo wrote in the collection's liner notes: "One of the happiest collaborations to grace the big band era was the pairing of budding vocalist Doris Day with a topflight outfit led by a congenial arranging talent ... named Les Brown. For Doris, the tenure with Brown added a finishing touch of professionalism to her natural singing talent.... For the Brown band, such classic recordings as 'Sentimental Journey' and 'My Dreams Are Getting Better All the Time' lifted what had been a well-respected ensemble of middling notoriety to the very forefront of national popularity."

Doris Day It's Magic: Her Early Years at Warner Bros.
Rhino/TCM R2 75543 1998

"Medley: Romance in High C / Romance on the High Seas," "I'm in Love," "It's Magic," "It's You or No One (with Jazz Trio)," "It's You or No One (ballad)," "Put 'Em in a Box," "Canadian Capers," "My Dream Is Yours," "Tic Tic Tic," "Freddie, Get Ready," "I'll String Along with You," "Someone Like You," "It's a Great Feeling," "Blame My Absent-Minded Heart," "That Was a Big Fat Lie," "There's Nothing Rougher Than Love," "It's Magic (reprise)." Produced by George Feltenstein.

The first official release of Day's film recordings from her first three films. The selections were the actual recordings she made specifically for the films and, until this release, could only be heard on the films themselves. Day had gone into the studio and recorded several of the songs for Columbia Records, which were subsequently released; however, the Columbia arrangements sound different from the film originals, as does Day's interpretation of the songs. Fans welcomed this set and are patiently waiting for future releases, including the many unreleased duets Day sang with other actors in her films.

Golden Girl (The Complete Recordings 1944–1966) Columbia Legacy C2K 65505 1999

"Sentimental Journey," "My Dreams Are Getting Better All the Time," "It's Magic," "Love Somebody," "Tacos, Enchiladas and Beans*," "Put 'Em in a Box, Tie 'Em with a Ribbon (and Throw 'Em in the Deep Blue Sea)," "Someone Like You," "That Old Feeling," "Again," "At the Café Rendezvous," "You Can Have Him," "Cuttin' Capers," "The Very Thought of You," "Too Marvelous for Words," "I Only Have Eyes for You," "Crazy Rhythm," "I've Never Been in Love Before," "It's a Lovely Day Today," "You're Getting to Be a Habit with Me," "In a Shanty

Preparing for a radio broadcast with Les Brown (from the collection of Matt Tunia).

in Old Shanty Town," "Lullaby of Broadway," "On Moonlight Bay," "(Why Did I Tell You I Was Going to) Shanghai," "Baby Doll," "Sugarbush," "A Guy Is a Guy," "April in Paris," "Ain't We Got Fun?" "The Black Hills of Dakota," "Secret Love," "I Speak to the Stars*," "If I Give My Heart to You," "There's a Rising Moon," "Shaking the Blues Away," "I'll Never Stop Loving You," "Whatever Will Be, Will Be (Qué Será, Será)," "There Once Was a Man," "Everybody Loves a Lover," "That Jane from Maine*," "Pillow Talk," "Lover Come Back," "You're Good for Me*," "My Romance," "Doin' What Comes Natur'lly," "Let the Little Girl Limbo*," "Move Over Darling," "Sorry" (various conductors and producers).

Promoted as "The Definitive Collection," this release is far from definitive; it does, however, include many of Day's hit songs and introduced five previously "unreleased" songs (*) in the U.S. One of the songs, "I Speak to the Stars," not only had been issued in the U.S., but was a #16 hit in 1954. The package notes "I'll Never Stop Loving You" was not released as a single although it had been and was a #13 hit in 1955. The collection failed to include ten recordings which were Top Ten hits in the U.S. The notes also misspelled Gordon MacRae's name in the listing of Doris Day's leading men in her films.

Arguably, the 1960s were Day's most inventive recording years, branching out in different music styles and also working with people such as André Previn, Robert Goulet and her own son Terry Melcher. Unfortunately, that era is not represented as well as the 1940s and 1950s. Perhaps this two–CD set should have been expanded to three CDs, which would have been more sensible, especially considering the set sold in the mid–$20 range.

The Bear Family Records Doris Day Collection

In the 1990s, the German Bear Family Records company acquired Doris Day's post–Les Brown Columbia Records catalogue and digitally remastered her recordings into superior compact disc quality. Each set also contained a hardcover book. For complete information, including recording dates and personnel, as well as hearing the vast majority of Day's studio recordings from 1947 through 1967, details can be found in the consummate Bear Family Doris Day box sets.:

> *It's Magic 1947–1950* (six–CD set)
> *Secret Love 1951–1955* (five–CD set)
> *Qué Será 1956–1959* (five–CD set)
> *Move Over Darling 1960–1967* (eight–CD set)

In addition, the Bear Family Records company compiled a two–CD soundtrack to *Pillow Talk* which includes the original songs from the film (including Perry Blackwell's recordings of "I Need No Atmosphere" and "You Lied," as well as her singing "Roly Poly" with Day and Rock Hudson), soundtrack and incidental music by DeVol, and dialogue from the film. In addition to a 64-page book which features the film screenplay and memorabilia accompanying this set, the Columbia recordings by Day are added, as are rare promotional spots originally used exclusively for radio stations to help push the film.

SINGLES

Arguably, the first song Day recorded and pressed on disc was "The Wind and the Rain in Your Hair" in 1939 which was submitted to Bob Crosby when he was seeking a new female vocalist for his band. However, that recording was not made available to the public. The following are recordings that were officially issued on disc to radio stations and record buyers. B-sides with no title are non–Day recordings; numbers 1 through 24 feature Day with Les Brown and His Band of Renown.

1. "(I Ain't Hep to That Step But I'll) Dig It" /
   "While the Music Plays On"
       Okeh 5964
   1940

2. "Let's Be Buddies" /
   "Three at a Table for Two"
       Okeh 5937
   1940

3. "Between Friends" /
   —
       Okeh 6011
   1941

4. "Barbara Allen" /
   "Broomstreet"
       Okeh 6049
   1941

5. "Celery Stalks at Midnight" /
   "Beau Night in Hotchkiss Corners"
       Okeh 6098
   1941

6. "Easy as Pie" /
   "Amapola (Pretty Little Poppy)"
       Okeh 6062
   1941

7. "Booglie Wooglie Piggy" /
   —
       Okeh 6085
   1941

8. "Keep Cool, Fool" /
   "Alexander the Swoose (Half Swan—Half Goose)"
       Okeh 6167
   1941

9. "Made Up My Mind" /
   —
       Okeh 6199
   1941

10. "Sentimental Journey" /
    —
        Columbia 36769
    1944

11. "My Dreams Are Getting Better All the Time" /
    "He's Home for a Little While"
        Columbia 36779
    1945

12. "'Tain't Me" /
    "I'll Always Be with You"
        Columbia 36804
    1945

13. "Till the End of Time" / "He'll Have to Cross the Atlantic (to Get to the Pacific)"
        Columbia 36828
    1945

14. "Aren't You Glad You're You" /
    "The Last Time I Saw You"
        Columbia 36875
    1945

15. "Come to Baby, Do!" / "You Won't Be Satisfied (Until You Break My Heart)"	Columbia 36884 1945
16. "A Red Kiss on a Blue Letter" / "We'll Be Together Again"	Columbia 36896 1945
17. "Day by Day" / —	Columbia 36945 1946
18. "In the Moon Mist" / —	Columbia 36961 1946
19. "(Ah Yes) There's Good Blues Tonight" / —	Columbia 36972 1946
20. "I Got the Sun in the Morning" / —	Columbia 36977 1946
21. "The Whole World Is Singing My Song" / —	Columbia 37066 1946
22. "Sooner or Later" / —	Columbia 37153 1946
23. "The Christmas Song (Merry Christmas to You)" / —	Columbia 37174 1946
24. "You Should Have Told Me" / "My Number One Dream Came True"	Columbia 37208 1946

(THE SOLO YEARS)

25. "It Takes Time" / "Pete"	Columbia 37324 1947
26. "My Young and Foolish Heart" / "Tell Me, Dream Face (What Am I to You?)"	Columbia 37486 1947
27. "When Tonight Is Just a Memory" / "I'm Still Sitting Under the Apple Tree"	Columbia 37568 1947
28. "Just an Old Love of Mine" / "A Chocolate Sundae on a Saturday Night"	Columbia 37821 1947
29. "Papa, Won't You Dance with Me?" / "Say Something Nice About Me Baby"	Columbia 37931 1947
30. "That's the Way He Does It" / "Why Should We Both Be Lonely"	Columbia 38037 1947
31. "Thoughtless" (with the Modernaires) / "I've Only Myself to Blame"	Columbia 38079 1948
32. "It's the Sentimental Things to Do" / "It's a Quiet Town (in Crossbone County)" (with the Modernaires)	Columbia 38159 1948

Mitch Miller oversaw the production of singles and later albums for Columbia Records. He helped convince the label to have Day record original songs rather than remake hits by other performers (from the collection of Matt Tunia).

33.	"Love Somebody" (with Buddy Clark) / "Confess" (with Buddy Clark)	Columbia 38174 1948
34.	"Put 'Em in a Box, Tie It with a Ribbon (and Throw 'Em in the Deep Blue Sea)" / "It's Magic"	Columbia 38188 1948
35.	"It's You or No One" / "I'm in Love" (with Buddy Clark)	Columbia 38290 1948
36.	"It's Magic" / "Pretty Baby"	Columbia 38302 1948
37.	"My Darling, My Darling" (with Buddy Clark) / "That Certain Party" (with Buddy Clark)	Columbia 38353 1949
38.	"Someone Like You" / "My Dream Is Yours"	Columbia 38375 1949
39.	"If You Will Marry Me" (with Buddy Clark) / "You Was" (with Buddy Clark)	Columbia 38392 1949
40.	"Powder Your Face with Sunshine (Smile! Smile! Smile!)" (with Buddy Clark) / "I'll String Along with You" (with Buddy Clark)	Columbia 38394 1949

41. "Don't Gamble with Romance" /   Columbia 38405
    "I'm Beginning to Miss You"   1949

42. "How It Lies, How It Lies, How It Lies" /   Columbia 38453
    "If I Could Be with You One Hour Tonight"   1949

43. "Again" (with the Mellomen) /   Columbia 38467
    "Everywhere You Go" (with the Mellomen)   1949

44. "Blame My Absent Minded Heart" (with the Mellomen) /   Columbia 38507
    "(Where Are You) Now That I Need You" (with   1949
    the Mellomen)

45. "Let's Take an Old-Fashioned Walk" (with   Columbia 38513
    Frank Sinatra) / —   1949

46. "You Can Have Him" (with Dinah Shore) /   Columbia 38514
    —   1949

47. "It's a Great Feeling" (with the Mellomen) /   Columbia 38517
    "At the Café Rendezvous" (with the Mellomen)   1949

48. "That Old Feeling" /   Columbia 38542
    "You're My Thrill" (with the Mellomen)   1949

49. "When Your Lover Has Gone" / "Bewitched   Columbia 38543
    (Bothered and Bewildered)" (with the Mellomen)   1949

50. "I Didn't Know What Time It Was" (with the Mellomen) /   Columbia 38544
    "I'm Confessin' (That I Love You)" (with the Mellomen)   1949

51. "You Go to My Head"/   Columbia 38545
    "Sometimes I'm Happy" (with the Mellomen)   1949

52. "Land of Love (Come My Love, and Live with Me)"   Columbia 38547
    (with the Mellomen) / "The Last Mile Home"   1949

53. "Here Comes Santa Claus" /   Columbia 38584
    "Ol' Saint Nicholas"   1949

54. "Canadian Cutters (Cuttin' Capers)" / "It's Better to   Columbia 38595
    Conceal Than Reveal" (with Dinah Shore)   1949

55. "(There's) A Bluebird on Your Windowsill" /   Columbia 38611
    "The River Seine (La Seine)"   1949

56. "Three Rivers (The Allegheny, Susquehanna and the   Columbia 38614
    Old Monogahela)" / "(It Happened at) The Festival   1950
    of Roses"

57. "The Game of Broken Hearts" /   Columbia 38637
    "I'll Never Slip Around Again"   1950

58. "Quicksilver" (with the Country Cousins) /   Columbia 38638
    "Crocodile Tears"   1950

59. "Save a Little Sunbeam (For a Rainy, Rainy Day)" /   Columbia 38676
    Mama, What'll I Do"   1950

60. "I Don't Wanna Be Kissed by Anyone but You" /   Columbia 38679
    "With You Anywhere You Are"   1950

61. "Bewitched (Bothered and Bewildered)" (with   Columbia 38698
    the Mellomen) / "Imagination"   1950

62. "I Said My Pajamas (and Put on My Prayers)" /   Columbia 38709
    "Enjoy Yourself (It's Later Than You Think)"   1950

63. "I May Be Wrong (But I Think You're Wonderful")" / Columbia 38727
    —   1950

64. "Too Marvelous for Words" /   Columbia 38728
    —   1950

65. "The Very Thought of You" /   Columbia 38729
    —   1950

66. "With a Song in My Heart" /   Columbia 38730
    —   1950

67. "Hoop-Dee-Doo" (with the Mellomen) /   Columbia 38771
    "Marriage Ties" (with the Mellomen)   1950

68. "I Didn't Slip—I Wasn't Pushed—I Fell" (with the   Columbia 38818
    Mellomen) / "Before I Loved You" (with the Mellomen) 1950

69. "I've Forgotten You" /   Columbia 38887
    "Darn That Dream"   1950

70. "Here in My Arms" /   Columbia 38951
    "Crazy Rhythm" (with Gene Nelson)   1950

71. "I Know That You Know" (with Gene Nelson) /   Columbia 38952
    "I Want to Be Happy"   1950

72. "I Only Have Eyes for You" /   Columbia 38953
    "Do Do Do"   1950

73. "Tea for Two" /   Columbia 38954
    "Oh Me! Oh My!" (with Gene Nelson)   1950

74. "Orange Colored Sky" (with the Page Cavanaugh Trio) / Columbia 38980
    "A Load of Hay" (with the Page Cavanaugh Trio)   1950

75. "A Bushel and a Peck" /   Columbia 39008
    "The Best Thing for You"   1950

76. "The Everlasting Arms" (with the Norman Luboff Choir) Columbia 39023
    / "David's Psalm" (with the Norman Luboff Choir)   1950

77. "I've Never Been in Love Before" /   Columbia 39031
    "If I Were a Bell"   1950

78. "Christmas Story" (with the Norman Luboff Choir) / "Silver Bells"

Columbia 39032
1950

79. "It's a Lovely Day Today" / "Nobody's Chasing Me"

Columbia 39055
1950

80. "From This Moment On" / "I Am Loved"

Columbia 39057
1950

81. "You Love Me" / "Ten Thousand Four Hundred Thirty-Two Sheep"

Columbia 39058
1950

82. "The Comb and Paper Polka" / "You Are My Sunshine"

Columbia 39143
1950

83. "Would I Love You (Love You, Love You)" / "Lullaby of Broadway"

Columbia 39159
1951

84. "I'll Be Around" / "I Love the Way You Say Goodnight" (with the Page Cavanaugh Trio)

Columbia 39191
1951

85. "Lullaby of Broadway" (with the Norman Luboff Choir) / "Please Don't Talk About Me When I'm Gone"

Columbia 39197
1951

86. "I Love the Way You Say Goodnight" (with the Norman Luboff Choir) / "Fine and Dandy" (with the Norman Luboff Choir)

Columbia 39198
1951

87. "You're Getting to Be a Habit with Me" / "In a Shanty in Old Shanty Town"

Columbia 39199
1951

88. "Somebody Loves Me" / "Just One of Those Things"

Columbia 39200
1951

89. "I Can't Get Over a Boy (Loving a Girl Like Me" / "Pumpernickel"

Columbia 39255
1951

90. "Something Wonderful" / "We Kiss in a Shadow"

Columbia 39293
1951

91. "It's So Laughable" (with the Four Hits) / "Very Good Advice" (with the Four Hits)

Columbia 39295
1951

92. "(Why Did I Tell You I Was Going to) Shanghai" / "My Life's Desire" (with the Norman Luboff Choir)

Columbia 39423
1951

93. "Tell Me (Why Nights Are Lonely)" / "Moonlight Bay" (with the Norman Luboff Choir)

Columbia 39450
1951

94. "Every Little Movement (Has a Meaning All Its Own)" (with the Norman Luboff Choir) / "Till We Meet Again"

Columbia 39451
1951

95. "Love Ya" (with Jack Smith, the Norman Luboff Choir) / "Cuddle Up a Little Closer"

Columbia 39452
1951

96. "I'm Forever Blowing Bubbles" (with Jack Smith) / — Columbia 39453
1951

97. "Ask Me (Because I'm So in Love)" (with Lee Brothers) / "Lonesome and Sorry" (with Lee Brothers) Columbia 39490
1951

98. "Got Him Off My Hands (But Can't Get Him Off My Mind)" / "Kiss Me Goodbye, Love" (with Lee Brothers) Columbia 39534
1951

99. "Domino" / "If That Doesn't Do It" Columbia 39596
1951

100. "I'll See You in My Dreams" (with the Norman Luboff Choir) / "Ain't We Got Fun" (with Danny Thomas and Lee Brothers) Columbia 39622
1952

101. "The One I Love Belongs to Somebody Else" / "Makin' Whoopee" (with Danny Thomas) Columbia 39623
1952

102. "My Buddy" / "I Wish I Had a Girl" (with the Norman Luboff Choir) Columbia 39624
1952

103. "Nobody's Sweetheart" (with the Norman Luboff Choir) / "It Had to be You" Columbia 39625
1952

104. "Baby Doll" / "Oops" Columbia 39637
1952

105. "A Guy Is a Guy" / "Who Who Who" (with the Starlighters) Columbia 39673
1952

106. "Sugarbush" (with Frankie Laine) / "How Lovely Cooks the Meat" (with Frankie Laine) Columbia 39693
1952

107. "A Little Kiss Goodnight" (with Guy Mitchell) / "Gently Johnny" (with Guy Mitchell) Columbia 39714
1952

108. "A Guy Is a Guy" / — Columbia 39729
1952

109. "It's Magic" — Columbia 39738
1952

110. "When I Fall in Love" (with the Norman Luboff Choir) / "Take Me in Your Arms" Columbia 39786
1952

111. "Make It Soon" / "My Love and Devotion" Columbia 39817
1952

112. "No Two People" (with Donald O'Connor) / "You Can't Lose Me" (with Donald O'Connor) Columbia 39863
1952

113. "April in Paris" (with the Norman Luboff Choir) / "The Cherries" (with the Norman Luboff Choir) Columbia 39881
1952

114. "A Full Time Job" (with Johnnie Ray) /   Columbia 39898
"Ma Says, Pa Says" (with Johnnie Ray)   1952

115. "Mister Tap Toe" (with the Norman Luboff Choir) /   Columbia 39906
"Your Mother and Mine" (with the Four Lads)   1953

116. "The Second Star to the Right" (with the Four Lads) /   Columbia 39913
"You Have My Sympathy"   1953

117. "When the Red, Red Robin Comes Bob, Bob,   Columbia 39970
Bobbin' Along" (with the Norman Luboff Choir) /   1953
"Beautiful Music to Love By"

118. "By the Light of the Silv'ry Moon" /   Columbia 39971
"King Chanticleer" (with the Norman Luboff Choir)   1953

119. "Your Eyes Have Told Me So" /   Columbia 39972
"I'll Forget You"   1953

120. "Be My Little Baby Bumble Bee" (with the Norman   Columbia 39973
Luboff Choir) / "Just One Girl" (with the Norman   1953
Luboff Choir)

121. "Ain't We Got Fun" (with the Norman Luboff Choir) /   Columbia 39974
"If You Were the Only Girl in the World"   1953

122. "Candy Lips" (with Johnnie Ray) /   Columbia 40001
"Let's Walk That-a-Way" (with Johnnie Ray)   1953

123. "Kiss Me Again, Stranger" /   Columbia 40020
"A Purple Cow"   1953

124. "Choo Choo Train" /   Columbia 40063
"This Too Shall Pass"   1953

125. "The Deadwood Stage" /   Columbia 40094
"I Can Do Without You" (with Howard Keel)   1953

126. "The Black Hills of Dakota" /   Columbia 40095
"Just Blew in from the Windy City"   1953

127. "A Woman's Touch" /   Columbia 40096
—   1953

128. "Secret Love" /   Columbia 40097
"'Tis Harry I'm Planning to Marry"   1953

129. "Secret Love" /   Columbia 40108
"The Deadwood Stage"   1954

130. "Lost in Loveliness" /   Columbia 40168
"What Every Girl Should Know"   1954

131. "I Speak to the Stars" /   Columbia 40210
"The Blue Bells of Broadway"   1954

132. "Someone Else's Roses" /
     "Kay Muleta"   Columbia 40234
                                                                     1954

133. "If I Give My Heart to You" (with the Mellomen) /   Columbia 40300
     "Anyone Can Fall in Love"   1954

134. "Ready, Willing and Able" /   Columbia 40371
     "Hold Me in Your Arms"   1954

135. "You My Love" /   Columbia 40372
     —   1954

136. "Ready, Willing and Able" /   Columbia 40373
     —   1954

137. "There's a Moon Rising (For Every Falling Star)   Columbia 40374
     "Hold Me in Your Arms"   1954

138. "'Til My Love Comes to Me" /   Columbia 40408
     "There's a Moon Rising (For Every Falling Star)   1954

139. "Two Hearts, Two Kisses (Make One Love)" (with the   Columbia 40483
     Mellomen) / "Foolishly Yours" (with the Mellomen)   1955

140. "I'll Never Stop Loving You" /   Columbia 40505
     "Never Look Back"   1955

141. "Ooh! Bang! Jiggily! Jang!" /   Columbia 40581
     "Jimmy Unknown"   1955

142. "Love's Little Island" /   Columbia 40618
     "Let It Ring"   1955

143. "Somebody Somewhere" /   Columbia 40673
     "We'll Love Again"   1956

144. "Whatever Will Be, Will Be (Qué Será, Será)" /   Columbia 40704
     "I Gotta Sing Away These Blues"   1956

145. "Julie" /   Columbia 40758
     "Love in a Home"   1956

146. "The Party's Over" /   Columbia 40798
     "Whad'ja Put in That Kiss"   1956

147. "Twelve O'Clock Tonight" /   Columbia 40870
     "Today Will Be Yesterday Tomorrow"   1957

148. "Through the Eyes of Love" /   Columbia 40952
     "Nothing in the World"   1957

149. "The Man Who Invented Love" /   Columbia 41015
     "Rickety Rackety Rendezvous"   1957

150. "Walk a Chalk Line" /   Columbia 41071
     "Soft as a Starlight"   1957

151. "Teacher's Pet" /
"Blues in the Night (My Mama Done Tol' Me)" Columbia 41103
1957

152. "A Very Precious Love" /
"Teacher's Pet" Columbia 41123
1957

153. "Everybody Loves a Lover" /
"Instant Love" Columbia 41195
1958

154. "The Tunnel of Love" /
"Run Away Skidaddle, Skidoo" Columbia 41252
1958

155. "I Enjoy Being a Girl" /
"Kissin' My Honey" Columbia 41307
1958

156. "Love Me in the Daytime" /
"He's So Married" Columbia 41354
1959

157. "It Happened to Jane" /
"Be Prepared" Columbia 41391
1959

158. "Possess Me" /
"Roly Poly" Columbia 41450
1959

159. "Pillow Talk" /
"Inspiration" Columbia 41463
1959

160. "Anyway the Wind Blows" /
"Soft as a Starlight" Columbia 41569
1959

161. "The Sound of Music" /
"Heart Full of Love" Columbia 41542
1960

162. "Please Don't Eat the Daisies" /
"Here We Go Again" Columbia 41630
1960

163. "The Blue Train" /
"A Perfect Understanding" Columbia 41703
1960

164. "What Does a Woman Do" /
"Daffa Down Dilly" Columbia 41791
1960

165. "Make Someone Happy" /
"Bright and Shiny" Columbia 41944
1961

166. "Twinkle and Shine" /
"Gotta Feelin'" Columbia 41993
1961

167. "Who Knows What Might Have Been" /
"Should I Surrender" Columbia 42260
1961

168. "Lover Come Back" /
"Falling" Columbia 42295
1962

169. "Move Over Darling" /
"Twinkle Lullaby" Columbia 42912
1963

170. "Rainbow's End" / "Send Me No Flowers"	Columbia 43153 1964
171. "Be a Child at Christmastime" / "Christmas Present"	Columbia 43174 1964
172. "Meditation" / "How Insensitive"	Columbia 43278 1964
173. "Summer Has Gone" / "Catch the Bouquet"	Columbia 43314 1965
174. "Another Go Around" / "Not Only Should You Love Him"	Columbia 43440 1965
175. "Do Not Disturb" / "Au Revoir Is Goodbye with a Smile"	Columbia 43459 1965
176. "Every Now and Then (You Come Around)"/ "There They Are"	Columbia 43606 1966
177. "The Glass Bottom Boat"/ "Soft as a Starlight"	Columbia 43688 1966
178. "Sorry" / "Caprice"	Columbia 44150 1967

RELEASED SONGS

The following listed songs are noted as the earliest versions, although Day had re-recorded a few songs at times throughout her career. For example, Day's lead vocal on "Sentimental Journey" was first recorded with Les Brown and His Band of Renown. Almost 20 years later, Day recorded it as a solo for her album *Doris Day's Sentimental Journey*. Also, a few of the earlier versions were duets and are listed with the singer; years refer to song release and/or recorded.

This list includes Day's recordings with Les Brown; her post–Brown songs on Columbia Records from 1947 through 1967; the 1967 Arwin sessions later issued as *The Love Album* in 1993; and previously unreleased cuts issued for the first time with the Bear Family box sets in the 1990s.

A
"Abide with Me" 1962
"Again" 1949
"Ain't We Got Fun" (with Danny Thomas) 1952
"Alexander the Swoose (Half Swan—Half Goose)" (with Les Brown) 1941
"All Alone" 1967

"All I Do Is Dream of You" 1961
"All Through the Day" (with Les Brown) 1946
"Amapola (Pretty Little Poppy)" (with Les Brown) 1941
"Another Go Around" 1965
"Anyone Can Fall in Love" 1954
"Anything You Can Do" (with Robert Goulet) 1962
"Anyway the Wind Blows" 1959
"April in Paris" 1952
"Are You Lonesome Tonight" 1967
"Are You Still in Love with Me?" (with Les Brown) 1946
"Aren't You Glad You're You" (with Les Brown) 1945
"As a Child" 1961
"As Long As He Needs Me" 1963
"Ask Me (Because I'm So in Love)" 1951
"At Last" 1964
"At Sundown" 1955
"At the Café Rendezvous" 1949
"Au Revoir Is Goodbye with a Smile" 1965
"Autumn Leaves" 1956

B
"Baby Doll" 1952
"Barbara Allen" (with Les Brown) 1946
"Be a Child at Christmas Time" 1964
"Be Mine Tonight" 1964
"Be My Little Baby Bumble Bee" 1953
"Be Prepared" 1959
"Be Still and Know" 1962
"Be True to Me" 1964
"Beau Night in Hotchkiss Corners" (with Les Brown) 1941
"Beautiful Music to Love By" 1953
"Before I Loved You" 1950
"The Best Thing for You" 1950
"Between Friends" (with Les Brown) 1941
"Bewitched (Bothered and Bewildered)" 1949
"The Black Hills of Dakota" 1953
"Blame My Absent Minded Heart" 1949
"Bless This House" 1962
"The Blue Bells of Broadway" 1954
"The Blue Train" 1960
"(There's) A Bluebird on Your Windowsill" 1949
"Blues in the Night (My Mama Done Tol' Me)" 1958

"Booglie Wooglie Piggy" (with Les Brown) 1941
"Bright and Shiny" 1961
"Broomstreet" (with Les Brown) 1941
"A Bushel and a Peck" 1950
"But Beautiful" 1956
"But Not for Me" 1956
"By the Light of the Silv'ry Moon" 1953

C
"Canadian Capers (Cuttin' Capers)" 1949
"Candy Lips" 1953
"Can't Help Falling in Love" 1963
"Caprice" 1966
"Catch the Bouquet" 1965
"Celery Stalks at Midnight" (with Les Brown) 1941
"Cheek to Cheek" 1958
"The Cherries" 1952
"The Children's Marching Song (Nick Nack Paddy Whack)" 1964
"A Chocolate Sundae on a Saturday Night" 1947
"Choo Choo Train" 1953
"Christmas Present" 1964
"The Christmas Song (Merry Christmas to You)" (with Les Brown) 1946
"Christmas Story" 1950
"The Christmas Waltz" 1964
"The Circus Is on Parade" (with Martha Raye & Jimmy Durante) 1962
"Clap Yo' Hands" 1961
"Close Your Eyes" 1957
"The Comb and Paper Polka" 1951
"Come to Baby, Do!" (with Les Brown) 1945
"Confess" (with Buddy Clark) 1948
"Control Yourself" 1962
"Crazy Rhythm" 1950
"Crocodile Tears" 1949
"Cuddle Up a Little Bit Closer" 1951
"Cuttin' Capers" 1959

D
"Daffa Down Dilly" 1960
"Dansero" 1964
"Darn That Dream" 1950
"David's Psalm" 1950
"Day by Day" (with Les Brown) 1946
"Day Dreaming" 1962

"The Deadwood Stage" 1953
"Deck the Halls with Boughs of Holly" 1959
"The Deevil, Devil, Divil" (with Les Brown) 1946
"(I Ain't Hep to That Step but I'll) Dig It" (with Les Brown) 1940
"Do Do Do" 1950
"Do Not Disturb" 1965
"Do Re Mi" 1964
"Doin' What Comes Natur'lly" 1962
"Domino" 1951
"Don't Gamble with Romance" 1949
"Don't Take Your Love from Me" 1956
"Dream a Little Dream of Me" 1957

E
"Easy as Pie" (with Les Brown) 1941
"Easy to Love" 1958
"Enjoy Yourself (It's Later Than You Think)" 1950
"The Everlasting Arms" 1950
"Every Little Movement (Has a Meaning All Its Own)" 1951
"Every Now and Then (You Come Around)" 1966
"Everybody Loves a Lover" 1958
"Everybody Loves My Baby (But My Baby Don't Love Nobody but Me)" 1955
"Everywhere You Go" 1949

F
"Faded Summer Love" 1967
"Falling" 1960
"Falling in Love Again" 1962
"A Fellow Needs a Girl" 1960
"(It Happened at the) Festival of Roses" 1949
"Fine and Dandy" 1951
"Fit as a Fiddle (And Ready for Love)" 1959
"Fly Me to the Moon (In Other Words)" 1964
"A Foggy Day" 1958
"(Now and Then There's) A Fool Such as I" 1963
"Foolishly Yours" 1955
"Fools Rush In" 1962
"For All We Know" 1967
"Freddie, Get Ready" 1949
"From This Moment On" 1950
"A Full Time Job" (with Johnny Ray) 1952
"Funny" 1963

G

"The Game of Broken Hearts" 1949
"Gently Johnny" (with Guy Mitchell) 1952
"Get Out and Get Under the Moon" 1959
"Getting to Know You" 1964
"Give a Little Whistle" 1964
"Give Me Time" 1962
"The Glass Bottom Boat" 1966
"Gone with the Wind" 1956
"Got Him Off My Hands (But I Can't Get Him Off My Mind)" 1951
"Gotta Feelin'" 1961
"A Guy Is a Guy" 1952
"The Gypsy in My Soul" 1956

H

"Happy Talk" 1961
"Have Yourself a Merry Little Christmas" 1964
"Heart Full of Love" 1959
"Hello, My Lover, Goodbye" 1956
"He'll Have to Cross the Atlantic (to Get to the Pacific)" (with Les Brown) 1945
"He's Home for a Little While" (with Les Brown) 1945
"He's So Married" 1959
"He's Such a Gentleman" 1950
"Here Comes Santa Claus" 1949
"Here in My Arms" 1950
"Here We Go Again" 1960
"High Hopes" 1964
"His Fraternity Pin" (with Buddy Clark) 1948
"Hold Me in Your Arms" 1954
"Hoop Dee Do" 1950
"Hooray for Hollywood" 1958
"How Insensitive" 1964
"How It Lies, How It Lies, How It Lies" 1949
"How Lovely Cooks the Meat" (with Frankie Laine) 1952
"A Hundred Years from Today" 1960

I

"I Am Loved" 1950
"I Believe in Dreams" 1961
"I Can Do Without You" (with Howard Keel) 1953
"I Can't Get Over a Boy Like You (Loving a Girl Like Me)" 1951
"I Didn't Know What Time It Was" 1949

"I Didn't Slip, I Wasn't Pushed, I Fell" 1950
"I Don't Want to Be Kissed by Anyone but You" 1950
"I Don't Want to Walk Without You" 1964
"I Enjoy Being a Girl" 1958
"I Feel Like a Feather in the Breeze" 1959
"I Got Lost in His Arms" 1962
"I Got the Sun in the Morning" (with Les Brown) 1946
"I Gotta Sing Away These Blues" 1955
"I Had the Craziest Dream" 1958
"I Hadn't Anyone Till You" 1956
"I Have Dreamed" 1961
"I Know a Place" 1952
"I Know That You Know" 1950
"I Love Paris" 1960
"I Love the Way You Say Goodnight" 1950
"I May Be Wrong (But I Think You're Wonderful)" 1950
"I Need Thee Every Hour" 1962
"I Only Have Eyes for You" 1950
"I Remember You" 1956
"I Said My Pajamas (and Put on My Prayers)" 1950
"I See Your Face Before Me" 1957
"I Speak to the Stars" 1954
"I Want to Be Happy" 1950
"I Went a Wooing" 1950
"I Wish I Had a Girl" 1952
"I'd Rather Be with You" (with Les Brown) 1945
"If I Can Help Somebody" 1962
"If I Could Be with You One Hour Tonight" 1949
"If I Give My Heart to You" 1954
"If I Had to Live My Life Over" 1967
"If I Were a Bell" 1950
"If That Doesn't Do It" 1951
"If You Were the Only Girl in the World" 1953
"If You Will Marry Me" (with Buddy Clark) 1949
"I'll Always Be with You" (with Les Brown) 1945
"I'll Be Around" 1951
"I'll Be Home for Christmas" 1964
"I'll Buy That Dream" 1961
"I'll Forget You" 1953
"I'll Never Slip Around Again" 1949
"I'll Never Smile Again" 1964
"I'll Never Stop Loving You" 1955

"I'll Remember April" 1958

"I'll See You in My Dreams" 1952

"I'll String Along with You" (with Buddy Clark) 1949

"I'm a Big Girl Now" 1955

"I'm an Indian, Too" 1962

"I'm Beginning to Miss You" 1949

"I'm Beginning to See the Light" 1964

"I'm Confessin' (That I Love You)" 1949

"I'm Forever Blowing Bubbles" (with Jack Smith) 1951

"I'm Gonna Ring the Bell Tonight" 1952

"I'm in Love" (with Buddy Clark) 1948

"I'm Not at All in Love" (with *The Pajama Game* cast) 1957

"I'm Sittin' on Top of the World" 1959

"I'm Still Sitting Under the Apple Tree" 1947

"I've Forgotten You" 1950

"I've Got My Love to Keep Me Warm" 1958

"I've Grown Accustomed to His Face" 1960

"I've Never Been in Love Before" 1950

"I've Only Myself to Blame" 1948

"Imagination" 1950

"In a Shanty in Old Shanty Town" 1951

"In Love in Vain" 1962

"In the Garden" 1962

"In the Moon Mist" (with Les Brown) 1946

"In the Secret Place" 1961

"In the Still of the Night" 1958

"Inchworm" 1964

"Inspiration" 1959

"Instant Love" 1958

"It All Depends on You" 1955

"It Could Happen to You" (with Les Brown) 1945

"It Had to Be You" 1952

"It Happened to Jane" 1959

"It Might as Well Be Spring" 1958

"It Takes Time" 1947

"It a Quiet Town (In Crossbone Country)" 1948

"It's a Great Feeling" 1949

"It's a Lovely Day Today" 1950

"It's Been a Long, Long Time" 1964

"It's Better to Conceal Than Reveal" (with Dinah Shore) 1949

"It's Easy to Remember" 1958

"It's Magic" 1948

"It's on the Tip of My Tongue" 1949
"It's So Laughable" 1951
"It's the Sentimental Thing to Do" 1948
"It's You or No One" 1948

J
"Jimmy Unknown" 1954
"Julie" 1956
"Just an Old Love of Mine" 1947
"Just Blew in from the Windy City" 1953
"Just Imagine" 1948
"Just One Girl" 1953
"Just One of Those Things" 1951

K
"Kay Muleta" 1954
"Keep Cool, Fool" (with Les Brown) 1941
"Keep Smilin', Keep Laughin', Be Happy" 1961
"King Chanticleer" 1953
"Kiss Me Again, Stranger" 1953
"Kiss Me Goodbye, Love" 1951
"Kissin' My Honey" 1958

L
"The Lady's in Love with You" 1958
"The Lamp Is Low" 1957
"Land of Love (Come My Love, and Live with Me)" 1949
"The Last Mile Home" 1949
"The Last Time I Saw You" (with Les Brown) 1945
"Let It Ring" 1956
"Let It Snow! Let It Snow! Let It Snow!" 1964
"Let Me Call You Sweetheart" 1967
"Let No Walls Divide" 1961
"Let the Little Girl Limbo" 1963
"Let's Be Buddies" (with Les Brown) 1940
"Let's Face the Music and Dance" 1958
"Let's Fly Away" 1959
"Let's Take a Walk Around the Block" 1959
"Let's Take an Old-Fashioned Walk" (with Frank Sinatra) 1949
"Let's Walk That-Away" (with Johnnie Ray) 1953
"Life Is Just a Bowl of Cherries" 1967
"The Lilac Tree" 1964
"Little Girl Blue" 1962

"A Little Kiss Goodnight" (with Guy Mitchell) 1952
"Live It Up" 1955
"A Load of Hay" 1950
"Lollipops and Roses" 1963
"Lonesome and Sorry" 1951
"Look All Around" 1961
"The Lord's Prayer" 1962
"Losing You" 1963
"Lost in Loveliness" 1954
"Love Him" 1963
"Love in a Home" 1956
"Love Is Here to Stay" 1958
"Love Me in the Daytime" 1959
"Love Me or Leave Me" 1955
"Love Somebody" (with Buddy Clark) 1948
"Love Ya" (with Jack Smith) 1951
"Love You Dearly" 1954
"Love's Little Island" 1956
"Lover Come Back" 1961
"Lullaby of Broadway" 1951

M
"Ma Says, Pa Says" (with Johnnie Ray) 1952
"Made Up My Mind" (with Les Brown) 1941
"Make It Soon" 1952
"Make Someone Happy" 1961
"Makin' Whoopee" 1959 (with Danny Thomas) 1952
"Mama, What'll I Do" 1950
"The Man Who Invented Love" 1957
"Marriage Ties" 1950
"Me Too (Ho-Ho! Ha-Ha)" 1959
"Mean to Me" 1955
"Meditation" 1964
"Mister Tap Toe" 1952
"Mood Indigo" 1960
"Moon Song" 1957
"Moonglow" 1957
"Moonlight Bay" 1951
"Moonlight Lover" 1963
"Moonshine Lullaby" 1962
"More" 1963
"The More I See You" 1964

"Move Over, Darling" 1963
"My Buddy" 1952
"My Darling, My Darling" (with Buddy Clark) 1948
"My Dream Is Yours" 1949
"My Dreams Are Getting Better All the Time" (with Les Brown) 1945
"My Life's Desire" 1951
"My Kinda Love" 1960
"My Love and Devotion" 1952
"My Number One Dream Came True" (with Les Brown) 1946
"My One and Only Love" 1962
"My Romance" 1962
"My Ship" 1961
"My Young and Foolish Heart" 1947

N

"Nearer My God to Thee" 1962
"Never Look Back" 1955
"Nice Work If You Can Get It" 1958
"Night and Day" 1958
"Night Life" 1963
"The Night We Called It a Day" 1957
"No" 1959
"No Moon at All" 1948
"No Two People" (with Donald O'Connor) 1952
"Nobody's Chasing Me" 1950
"Nobody's Heart" 1962
"Nobody's Sweetheart" 1952
"Not Only Should You Love Him" 1960
"Nothing in the World" 1956
"(Where Are You) Now That I Need You" 1949

O

"Oh, but I Do" 1958
"Oh, How I Miss You Tonight" 1967
"Oh Me! Oh My!" (with Gene Nelson) 1950
"Oh What a Beautiful Dream" 1961
"Oh! What a Lover You'll Be" 1959
"Ohio" 1960
"Ol' Saint Nicholas" 1949
"On the Street Where You Live" 1960
"On the Sunny Side of the Street" 1961
"Once a Year Day!" (with *The Pajama Game* cast) 1957
"The One I Love Belongs to Somebody Else" 1952

"Oo-Wee Baby" 1964
"Ooh! Bang! Jiggily! Jang!" 1955
"Oops" 1952
"Orange Colored Sky" 1950
"Our Day Will Come" 1964
"Over and Over Again" 1962
"Over the Rainbow" 1958

P

"Papa, Won't You Dance with Me?" 1947
"The Party's Over" 1956
"Pennies from Heaven" 1958
"People Will Say We're in Love" 1960
"A Perfect Understanding" 1959
"Perhaps, Perhaps, Perhaps" 1964
"Periwinkle Blue" 1961
"Pete" 1947
"Pillow Talk" 1959
"Please Don't Eat the Daisies" 1960
"Please Don't Talk About Me When I'm Gone" 1951
"Por Favor" 1964
"Possess Me" 1958
"Powder Your Face with Sunshine" 1949
"Pretty Baby" 1948
"The Prodigal Son" 1962
"Pumpernickel" 1951
"A Purple Cow" 1953
"Put 'Em in a Box, Tie 'Em with a Ribbon (and Throw 'Em in the Deep Blue
  Sea)" 1948

Q

"Quicksilver" 1949
"Quiet Nights of Quiet Stars" 1964

R

"Rainbow's End" 1964
"Ready, Willing and Able" 1954
"A Red Kiss on a Blue Letter" (with Les Brown) 1945
"Remind Me" 1962
"Rickety Rackety Rendezvous" 1957
"Ridin' High" 1961
"The River Seine (La Seine)" 1949
"Roly Poly" 1959
"Run Away, Skidaddle Skidoo" 1958

S

"Sam, the Old Accordion Man" 1955

"Save a Little Sunbeam (For a Rainy, Rainy Day)" 1950

"Sawdust, Spangles and Dreams" (with the *Jumbo* cast) 1962

"Say Something Nice About Me Baby" 1947

"Scarlet Ribbons (For Her Hair)" 1962

"The Second Star to the Right" 1952

"Secret Love" 1953

"Send Me No Flowers" 1964

"Sentimental Journey" (with Les Brown) 1944

"Serenade in Blue" 1964

"Seven and a Half Cents" (with *The Pajama Game* cast) 1957

"Shaking the Blues Away" 1955

"(Why Did I Tell You I Was Going to) Shanghai" 1951

"Should I Surrender" 1961

"Show Time" (Parts I and II) 1960

"Silver Bells" 1950

"Since I Fell for You" 1963

"Singin' in the Rain" 1961

"Sleepy Baby" 1964

"Sleepy Lagoon" 1967

"Slightly Out of Tune" 1964

"Small Talk" (with John Raitt) 1957

"Snowfall" 1964

"Snuggled on Your Shoulder" 1967

"Soft as the Starlight" 1957

"Softly as I Leave You" 1963

"Somebody Loves Me" 1951

"Somebody Somewhere" 1956

"Someday I'll Find You" 1961

"Someone Else's Roses" 1954

"Someone Like You" 1949

"Something Wonderful" 1951

"Sometimes, I'm Happy" 1949

"The Song Is You" 1956

"Soon" 1958

"Sooner or Later" (with Les Brown) 1946

"Sorry" 1967

"The Sound of Music" 1959

"Spesh'lly You" 1949

"Stars Fell on Alabama" 1957

"Stay on the Right Side, Sister" 1955

"Stay with the Happy People" 1961
"Steppin' Out with My Baby" 1958
"Street of Dreams" 1967
"Sugarbush" (with Frankie Laine) 1952
"Summer Has Gone" 1964
"The Surrey with the Fringe on Top" 1960
"Swinging on a Star" 1964

T

"Tacos, Enchiladas and Beans" 1948
"'Tain't Me" (with Les Brown) 1945
"Take Me in Your Arms" 1952
"Tea for Two" 1950
"Teacher's Pet" 1957
"Tell Me, Dream Face (What Am I to You?)" 1947
"Tell Me (Why the Nights Are So Lonely)" 1951
"Ten Cents a Dance" 1955
"Ten Thousand Four Hundred Thirty Two Sheep" 1950
"That Certain Party" (with Buddy Clark) 1948
"That Jane from Maine" 1958
"That Old Black Magic" 1958
"That Old Feeling" 1949
"That Was a Big Fat Lie" 1949
"That's the Way He Does It" 1947
"That's What Makes Paris Paree" 1952
"There Once Was a Man" (with John Raitt) 1957
"There They Are" 1966
"There Will Never Be Another You" 1956
"There's a Rising Moon (For Every Falling Star)" 1954
"(Ah Yes) There's Good Blues Tonight" (with Les Brown) 1946
"There's Nothing Rougher Than Love" 1949
"These Days" (harmony on Terry Melcher song) 1974
"They Say It's Wonderful" 1960
"This Can't Be Love" 1962
"This Too Shall Pass Away" 1953
"Thoughtless" 1948
"Three at a Table for Two" (with Les Brown) 1940
"Three Coins in the Fountain" 1958
"The Three Rivers (The Allegheny, Susquehanna and the Old Monongahela)"
    1949
"Through the Eyes of Love" 1957
"Tic Tic Tic" 1949

"Til My Love Comes to Me" 1954
"Till the End of Time" (with Les Brown) 1945
"Till We Meet Again" 1951
"Time to Say Goodnight" 1961
"'Tis Harry I'm Planning to Marry" 1953
"Today Will Be Yesterday Tomorrow" 1956
"Too Marvelous for Words" 1950
"Toyland" 1964
"The Tunnel of Love" 1958
"Twelve O'Clock Tonight" 1957
"Twinkle and Shine" 1961
"Twinkle Lullaby" 1963
"Two Hearts, Two Kisses (Make One Love)" 1955

U

"Under a Blanket of Blue" 1957

V

"Very Good Advice" 1951
"A Very Precious Love" 1958
"The Very Thought of You" 1950

W

"Wait Till You See Him" 1962
"Walk a Chalk Line" 1957
"Walk with Him" 1962
"The Way You Look Tonight" 1958
"We Kiss in a Shadow" 1951
"We'll Be Together Again" (with Les Brown) 1945
"We'll Love Again" 1956
"Whad'ja Put in That Kiss" 1956
"What Does a Woman Do?" 1960
"What Every Girl Should Know" 1954
"Whatever Will Be, Will Be (Qué Será, Será)" 1955
"What's the Use of Wond'rin'" 1960
"When I Fall in Love" 1952
"When I Grow Too Old to Dream" 1961
"When I'm Happy" 1955
"When I'm Not Near the Boy I Love" 1960
"When the Red, Red Robin Comes Bob, Bob Bobbin' Along" 1953
"When Tonight Is Just a Memory" 1947
"When Your Lover Has Gone" 1949

"When You're Smilin'" 1960
"White Christmas" 1964
"While the Music Plays On" (with Les Brown) 1940
"A Whisper Away" 1965
"Who Are We to Say" 1962
"Who Knows What Might Have Been" 1961
"Who Who Who" 1952
"The Whole World Is Singing My Song" (with Les Brown) 1946
"Why Can't I?" (with Martha Raye) 1962
"Why Don't We Do This More Often" 1959
"Why Should We Both Be Lonely?" 1947
"Winter Wonderland" 1964
"With a Smile and a Song" 1964
"With a Song in My Heart" 1950
"With You Anywhere You Are" 1950
"A Woman's Touch" 1953
"A Wonderful Guy" 1960
"Wonderful One" 1967
"Would I Love You (Love You, Love You)" 1951
"Wrap Your Troubles in Dreams" 1957

Y
"Yes" 1962
"You Are My Sunshine" 1951
"You Can Have Him" (with Dinah Shore) 1949
"You Can't Get a Man with a Gun" 1962
"You Can't Have Everything" 1960
"You Can't Lose Me" 1952
"You Do Something to Me" 1957
"You Go to My Head" 1949
"You Have My Sympathy" 1953
"You Love Me" 1950
"You Made Me Love You (I Didn't Want to Do It)" 1955
"You My Love" 1954
"You Should Have Told Me" (with Les Brown) 1946
"You Stepped Out of a Dream" 1961
"You Was" (with Buddy Clark) 1949
"You Won't Be Satisfied (Until You Break My Heart)" (with Les Brown) 1945
"You'll Never Know" 1958
"You'll Never Walk Alone" 1962
"You're Driving Me Crazy (What Did I Do?)" 1959
"You're Getting to Be a Habit with Me" 1951

"You're Good for Me" 1961
"You're My Thrill" 1949
"Your Eyes Have Told Me So" 1953
"Your Mother and Mine" 1952

Z
"Zip-a-Dee-Doo-Dah" 1964

UNRELEASED SONGS

It is rumored that Doris Day recorded over 1,000 songs in her life. Officially, more than 600 songs have been legitimately released for public purchase. Whether there remains a few hundred unreleased songs sitting in a vault at Columbia or are in Day's possession (or both) is debatable.

While several of her film songs were later re-recorded for public consumption, many of the original recordings are available only on videos of the films. These are primarily the Warner Bros. movies including her duets with Gordon MacRae (including *On Moonlight Bay* and *By the Light of the Silvery Moon*), as well as Howard Keel with the *Calamity Jane* duets. Although the original soundtrack recordings from Day's first three films were belatedly issued in 1998 (see *Doris Day: It's Magic*), the others remain unreleased in audio form.

Also, there are a few dozen songs that were heard publicly but have never been properly issued to music buyers, most of which were presented on Day's television appearances. Unfortunately, none of her television appearance have been legitimately released on video, but less than pristine copies are available in the underground market.

While some of the songs she sang were selections she had previously recorded, there are a few that she presented for the first time. Most are full-length versions while a handful are a few lyrics from the songs. The following are Day renditions of songs that were never legitimately released in the United States:

"Ain't We Got Fun" with Gordon MacRae from *By the Light of the Silvery Moon*

"Anything Goes" with John Denver, Rich Little and Tim Conway from *Doris day toDay*

"Be My Little Bumble Bee" with Gordon MacRae and Russell Arms from *By the Light of the Silvery Moon*

"Best Friend" theme song from *Doris Day's Best Friends*

"The Black Hills of Dakota" with Howard Keel from *Calamity Jane*

"The Bluebells of Broadway" with cast of *Lucky Me*

"Both Sides Now" from *The Doris Mary Anne Kapplehoff Special*

"By the Kissing Rock" with Gordon MacRae from *The West Point Story*

"By the Light of the Silvery Moon" with Gordon MacRae and cast from *By the Light of the Silvery Moon*

"By the Light of the Silvery Moon" with John Denver from *The John Denver Show*

"By the Old Mill Stream" from "The Antique" (*The Doris Day Show*)

"Christmas Story" with Gordon MacRae from *On Moonlight Bay*

"Crocodile Rock" from *Doris Day's Best Friends* episode 1

"Daydream" from *Doris Day's Best Friends* episode 11

"Disney Girls" from *Doris Day's Best Friends* episode 21

"Do Do Do" with Gordon MacRae from *Tea for Two*

"Everybody Loves a Lover" / "Meditation" / "Quiet Nights of Quiet Stars" (medley) with Perry Como from *The Doris Mary Anne Kapplehoff Special*

"Everybody Loves a Lover" / "Young at Heart" / "Teacher's Pet" / "There Are Such Things" / "Love Me or Leave Me" / "Secret Love" / "With a Song in My Heart" / "Whatever Will Be, Will Be" / "Everybody Loves a Lover" (medley) with Rich Little from *Doris day toDay*

"Everyone's Gone to the Moon" from *Doris Day's Best Friends* episode 13

"Exactly Like You" with John Denver from *Doris day toDay*

"Follow Me" with John Denver from *Doris day toDay*

"For He's a Jolly Good Fellow" from "The Gift" (*The Doris Day Show*)

"The Girl Who Invented Rock and Roll" from *Teacher's Pet*

"High Hopes" with cast from *Lucky Me*

"Hurry! It's Lovely Up Here" from *The Doris Mary Anne Kapplehoff Special*

"I Can Do Without You" with Howard Keel from *Calamity Jane*

"I Know That You Know" with Gordon MacRae from *Tea for Two*

"I Left My Heart in San Francisco" with Tony Bennett from "Tony Bennett Is Eating Here" (*The Doris Day Show*)

"I Love the Way You Say Goodnight" with Gene Nelson from *Lullaby of Broadway*

"I Want to Be Happy" with Gordon MacRae from *Tea for Two*

"I'll See You in My Dreams" with John Denver from *The John Denver Show*

"I'm Just a Caboose on Your Train of Thought" from "The Songwriter" (*The Doris Day Show*)

"If You Were the Only Girl in the World" with Gordon MacRae from *By the Light of the Silvery Moon*

"In the Summertime" / "You Don't Want My Love" / "If I Had to Live My Life Over" / "Let Me Call You Sweetheart" (medley) with Perry Como from *The Doris Mary Anne Kapplehoff Special*

"Is This Love" with Les Brown

"Isn't Love Wonderful" with Ray Bolger and Claude Dauphin from *April in Paris*

"It Must Be Good" with cast from *April in Paris*

"It's All Happening at the Zoo" from *Doris Day's Best Friends* episode 22

"It's Magic"/"Sentimental Journey" (medley) from *The Doris Mary Anne Kapplehoff Special*

"Jingle Bells" from "It's Christmas Time in the City" (*The Doris Day Show*)

"Kima Kimo" from "The Uniform" (*The Doris Day Show*)

"Love You Dearly" with Robert Cummings from *Lucky Me*

"Men" with Phil Silvers from *Lucky Me*

"Midnight at the Oasis" with John Denver, Rich Little and Tim Conway from *Doris day toDay*

"Military Polka" with Gordon MacRae and cast from *The West Point Story*

"My Baby Makes Me Proud" with Tim Conway from *Doris day toDay*

"My Heart" from *Doris Day's Best Friends* episode 6

"My Lost Horizon" with Les Brown

"No No Nanette" with cast from *Tea for Two*

"No No Nora" from *I'll See You in My Dreams*

"Octopus's Garden" from *Doris Day's Best Friends*

"(On) Moonlight Bay" with Gordon MacRae from *On Moonlight Bay*

"(On) Moonlight Bay" with John Denver from *The John Denver Show*

"Parisian Pretties" with cast from *Lucky Me*

"The Place You Hold in My Heart" from *April in Paris*

"Row, Row, Row Your Boat" from "The Songwriter" (*The Doris Day Show*)

"Rescue Me" from *Doris Day's Best Friends* episode 5

"Ryan" from *Doris Day's Best Friends* episode 8

"Secret Love" / "Who Will Buy?"/ "The 59th Street Song (Feelin' Groovy)"/ "Ob-la-di, Ob-la-da" (medley) from *The Doris Mary Anne Kapplehoff Special*

"Shine on Harvest Moon" from "Duke the Performer" (*The Doris Day Show*)

"Sing a Sunshine Song"/ "You Are the Sunshine of My Life"/ "Sunshine and Lollipops"/ "You Are My Sunshine"/ "Sunshine on My Shoulders"/ "Sing a Sunshine Song" (medley) with John Denver from *Doris day toDay*

"Somebody Loves Me" with Gene Nelson from *Lullaby of Broadway*

"Stew Beau" from *Doris Day's Best Friends* episode 7

"The Superstition Song" from *Lucky Me*

"Swingin' Down the Lane" with Danny Thomas and cast from *I'll See You in My Dreams*

"Tea for Two" with Gordon MacRae from *Tea for Two*

"Tea for Two"/ "Did You Ever See a Dream Walking?"/ "Give Me a Little Kiss"/ "On the Atchison, Topeka and Santa Fe"/ "Put on a Happy Face"/ "Follow Me" (medley/different lyrics) with John Denver from *Doris day toDay*

"That's What Makes Paris Paree" with Claude Dauphin from *April in Paris*

"Them Was the Good Old Days" from *The Doris Mary Anne Kapplehoff Special*

"Till We Meet Again" with Gordon MacRae from *On Moonlight Bay*

"Toot Toot Tootsie Goodbye" from *I'll See You in My Dreams*

"Wanna Sing Like an Angel" from *Lucky Me*

"The Way We Were" from *Doris day toDay*

"Weeds in the Garden of My Heart" from "The Songwriter" (*The Doris Day Show*)

"When You Were Sweet Sixteen" / "Everybody Loves a Lover" / "Meditation" / "Quiet Nights of Quiet Stars" / "Summertime (In the Summertime)" / "You Don't Want My Love" / "If I Had to Live My Life Over" / "Let Me Call You Sweetheart" (medley) with Perry Como from *The Doris Mary Anne Kapplehoff Special*

"Wildfire" from *Doris Day's Best Friends* episode 10

"A Woman's Touch" with Allyn McLerie from *Calamity Jane*

"Yes Sir, That's My Baby" with Danny Thomas and cast from *I'll See You in My Dreams*

"You Are So Beautiful" from *Doris Day's Best Friends* episode 4

"You Can Make It Big" from *Doris Day's Best Friends* episode 3

"You Love Me" with Gordon MacRae from *the West Point Story*

"You Must've Been a Beautiful Baby" from *The Doris Mary Anne Kapplehoff Special*

"You, My Love" with Frank Sinatra from *Young at Heart*

"Your Eyes Have Told Me So" with Gordon MacRae from *By the Light of the Silvery Moon*

"Your Love is Like Butter Gone Rancid" from "The Songwriter" (*The Doris Day Show*)

"You're Gonna Lose Your Gal" with Gordon MacRae from *Starlift*

LIVE RECORDINGS

Aside from formal recordings, there were many songs recorded of Doris Day singing live in concert that were broadcast on radio, as well as on radio shows which were not covered in a studio. Many of these were of Day and the Page Cavanaugh Trio dating from the late 1940s and early 1950s, and of her with Les Brown and His Band of Renown. Although these songs were not considered official releases (i.e., Columbia Records), several have been made available in various formats by small companies. Among the songs recorded include:

"Ain't Misbehavin'" (with Les Brown)
"Along the Navajo Trail" (with Les Brown)
"Amore" (with Les Brown)
"An Apple Blossom Wedding"
"Baby It's Cold Outside" (with Les Brown)
"Be Anything, but Be Mine" (with The Page Cavanaugh Trio)
"Because You're Mine"
"Blue Music" (with Les Brown)
"Blue Skies" (with The Page Cavanaugh Trio)
"Coffee, Cigarettes and Memories"
"The Coffee Song"
"Crazy Rhythm"
"Crying My Heart Out for You" (with The Page Cavanaugh Trio)
"Don't Worry 'Bout Me" (with The Page Cavanaugh Trio)
"Don't You Know That I Care" (with Les Brown)
"Dream" (with Les Brown)
"Easy Street" (with Les Brown)
"Embraceable You" (with Les Brown)
"Every Day I Love You Just a Little Bit More"
"Everything I Have Is Yours"
"Feudin' and Fightin'"
"Goodnight, Wherever You Are" (with Les Brown)
"Growing Pains" (with Les Brown)
"I Can't Give You Anything but Love" (with The Page Cavanaugh Trio)
"I Can't Help It" (with Les Brown)
"I Could Write a Book" (with The Page Cavanaugh Trio)
"I Didn't Know About You" (with Les Brown)
"I Dream of You" (with Les Brown)
"I Know a Little Bit About a Lot of Things"
"I Wish I Didn't Love You So"

"I Wish I Knew" (with Les Brown)

"I Won't Dance"

"If You Were There" (with Les Brown)

"I'm Glad I Waited for You" (with Les Brown)

"I'm Happy About the Whole Thing" (with Barney Rapp)

"I'm Having a Wonderful Wish"

"I'm in the Mood for Love" (with The Page Cavanaugh Trio)

"I'm Making Believe" (with Les Brown)

"I've Got a Feeling You're Fooling"

"I've Got It Bad and That Ain't Good" (with The Page Cavanaugh Trio)

"I've Never Forgotten" (with Les Brown)

"Invitation to the Blues" (with Les Brown)

"It's a Crying Shame" (with Les Brown)

"It's Love, Love, Love" (with Les Brown)

"It's Too Soon to Know"

"The Joint Is Really Jumping Down at Carnegie Hall"

"Just You, Just Me" (with The Page Cavanaugh Trio)

"A Kiss to Remember" (with Les Brown)

"The Lady from Twenty-Nine Psalms"

"Land of Dreams" (with Les Brown)

"The Last Time I Saw You" (with Les Brown)

"Life Can Be Beautiful"

"Light Your Lamp" (with The Page Cavanaugh Trio)

"Like Someone in Love" (with Les Brown)

"Little Sir Echo" (with Barney Rapp)

"Long Ago and Far Away" (with Les Brown)

"Love Letters" (with Les Brown)

"Love to Be with You"

"Lucky Us" (with Bob Hope)

"Mad About That Man" (with Bob Hope and Jimmy Durante)

"The Man I Love" (with Les Brown)

"Maybe" (with Les Brown)

"Melancholy Baby" (with Al Jolson)

"Moon on My Pillow" (with Les Brown)

"More Than You Know"

"My Blue Heaven" (with Al Jolson)

"My Sugar Is So Refined"

"Near You"

"Oh, What It Seemed to Be" (with Les Brown)

"Please Mr. Sun"

"Put Your Arms Around Me" (with Al Jolson)

"Red Hot Henry Brown" (with Kirk Douglas)

"'S Wonderful" (with The Page Cavanaugh Trio)
"Salt Water Cowboys" (with Les Brown)
"San Fernando Valley" (with Les Brown)
"Saturday Night" (with Les Brown)
"September in the Rain" (with The Page Cavanaugh Trio)
"September Song"
"Silent Night"
"Sleigh Ride in July" (with Les Brown)
"Slowpoke"
"Some Sunday Morning" (with Les Brown)
"Somewhere in the Night" (with Les Brown)
"S'posin'" (with The Page Cavanaugh Trio)
"Stardust" (with The Page Cavanaugh Trio)
"A Stranger in Town" (with Les Brown)
"Sweet Evening Breeze"
"Take Me Out to the Ball Game" (with Frank Sinatra)
"That's for Me" (with Les Brown)
"That's My Desire"
"There I Go" (with Les Brown)
"There, I've Said It Again" (with Les Brown)
"There'll Be Some Changes Made"
"There's No Business Like Show Business" (with Frank Sinatra)
"There's No You" (with Les Brown)
"This Heart of Mine" (with Les Brown)
"Tomorrow Is Forever" (with Les Brown)
"Two Heavens" (with Les Brown)
"Welcome to My Dream" (with Les Brown)
"What Are You Going to Do?" (with Les Brown)
"What Is Love?" (with Broderick Crawford)
"Wonder"
"A Wonderful Winter" (with Les Brown)
"You Brought a New Kind of Love to Me" (with The Page Cavanaugh Trio)
"You Do"
"You May Not Love Me" (with Les Brown)
"You Oughta Be in Pictures" (with The Page Cavanaugh Trio)

RADIO SHOWS

Doris Day began her career in entertainment at Cincinnati's WLW-AM radio station. From 1934 to 1939, WLW was the most powerful station in the United

States, broadcasting on half a million watts. As a result, WLW was dubbed "the Nation's Station," and the station's programs were heard around the nation.

Day's first appearance on WLW was singing on the variety show *Carlin's Carnival* in 1939. The show was a two-hour Saturday morning variety show that included students from area schools who wanted to perform on the air. Andre Carlin announced each student with their name, where they lived, what school they attended, and their teacher's name. Accompanied by a piano, Day sang "Day After Day," and continued making appearances on the show.

Following a gig at Charlie Yee's Shanghai Inn, Day became the lead vocalist with Barney Rapp and his New Englanders. She returned to the radio waves while singing live with Rapp at his club The Sign of the Drum. It was not until the next decade that she came back to the WLW studios as a regular performer. After stints with Rapp, followed by Bob Crosby and his Bobcats, Fred Waring and then Les Brown and his Band of Renown, as well as a disastrous first marriage, Day returned to Cincinnati and to WLW.

While weekends at WLW were spent singing in a beer-sponsored show whose title Day herself doesn't recall, she became a regular on the 15-minute program *Moon River*, the biggest syndicated show WLW had at the time. *Moon River* featured Day singing four nights a week, and an organist who played "Clair de Lune" in the background while poetry was read by, as Day recalled, "a sexy-voiced announcer."

Day also served as the hostess of MGM's *The Lion's Roar* in which she introduced the latest movies in release from MGM and sang with the studio band. *The Lion's Roar* was also 15 minutes in length, but five times a week. Ironically, almost a dozen years later, Day found herself starring in her first MGM movie, *Love Me or Leave Me*. Thirty years later, Day portrayed a radio announcer in a television episode of *The Doris Day Show*. In "Just a Miss Understanding," however, she was neither a hostess nor a singer, but an advice commentator for a late night radio talk show.

Day left WLW again after Les Brown convinced her to rejoin him and his band in 1944. Between recording and personal appearances, the group also made radio appearances on *Guest Star Radio* and *Spotlight Bands* from 1944 through 1946. One radio program in which Les Brown and His Band of Renown was often heard was *One Night Stand*. These were primarily live broadcasts from whatever venue where they were performing. A glimpse into the broadcast history of the program gives some insight as to the band's cross-country travels and appearances:

May 23, 1944: "It's Love, Love, Love" at White Sulphur, West Virginia
October 7, 1944: "It Had to Be You" at Bowman Field, Kentucky
January 15, 1945: "This Heart of Mine," "Don't You Know I Care," "Saturday Night" and February 6: "A Wonderful Winter," "Sleighride in July" at Café Rouge, Hotel Pennsylvania, New York City

July 24, 1945: "I Wish I Knew" and July 26 "Growing Pains," "There's No You" at the Hollywood Palladium, Los Angeles

August 9, 1945: "Along the Navajo Trail," "Blue Music" at the Peacock Room, Dallas, Texas

August 23, 1945: "A Stranger in Town" at the Hollywood Palladium, Los Angeles

December 28, 1945: "Let It Snow! Let It Snow! Let It Snow!" at Café Rouge, Hotel Pennsylvania, New York City

When Day moved to Los Angeles with her second husband in 1946, she returned to radio as a singer on Bob Sweeny and Hal March's radio show on CBS. Day worked for 13 weeks at $89 a week before being dropped because the network felt she had no future in radio—despite the

With bandleader Bob Crosby, 1939 (Jerry Ohlinger's Movie Material Store, Inc.).

fact her years with Les Brown yielded several radio appearances and hit songs.

This move to Los Angeles eventually resulted in an onslaught of professional forays beginning in 1947. Day was selected as the lead in the Warner Bros. movie *Romance on the High Seas*; she continued recording as a solo performer with Columbia Records; and several radio show performances followed. These included *The Rudy Vallee Show* where she sang "Easy Street" and "The Coffee Song" on January 4, 1947, and a September 1947 appearance on *Mail Call* with Chili Williams, Frank Nelson and Frank Sinatra, with whom she duetted "Tea for Two." Day was also on "I Am an American" with Perry Como, aired live from the Hollywood Bowl, and guested on CBS's *Club 15*, which reunited her with Bob Crosby, host of the radio show.

Day joined *Your Hit Parade* in the last months of 1947 on a regular basis. *Your Hit Parade* was a 30-minute weekly show in which Frank Sinatra hosted with Day as a featured singer. Day usually sang solos including the rarely heard "You Do" and "Feudin' and Fightin'" (both from October 11); "An Apple Blossom Wedding"; "That's My Desire," "I Wish I Didn't Love You So" (all from the September 27 broadcast); "I Won't Dance" (November 1); and "Near You" (November 22). At times, Day and Sinatra duetted on songs like "Take Me Out to the Ball Game" (September 27) and "There's No Business Like Show Business" (October 4). The pair also appeared on *Command Performance USA!* for Armed Force Radio in the fall of 1947.

After fulfilling her 20-week contract on *Your Hit Parade*, Day was dropped from the show because the sponsors, the American Tobacco Company, believed her singing style was too similar to Sinatra's. She continued making appearances on shows including "Here's to Veterans," again with Sinatra, followed by the Philco Radio Show *New Swan Show* on November 7, 1948, with Bing Crosby and Bob Hope; and Kraft Music Hall's *The Al Jolson Show* on December 30, 1948, when she sang "My Blue Heaven," which she later sang in the film *Love Me or Leave Me*, and duetted with Jolson on "Melancholy Baby." Day returned to the show on April 28, 1949, and sang "Put Your Arms Around Me" with Jolson.

In the autumn of 1948, Day signed on as the featured singer on *The Bob Hope Show*. Inasmuch as Day was beginning to dislike singing in front of a live studio audience, it was preferable over traveling for live performances as she did with Hope. There were 50 shows in 50 days, sometimes two shows in a day. More than once the small plane that Day, Hope and the troupe rode was caught in bad weather, from snowstorms to fog, rocking back and forth with a few close calls, including a near-crash in Pittsburgh. This resulted in her rarely taking any trip by air, which continues to the present day.

During one stop at Little Rock, Arkansas, the group was asked to perform at a hospital before their regular show. Hope agreed, but when he did his comedy routine, the patients did not react. He then realized they were in a mental hospital. Hope cut his act short and introduced Day with the feeling that if anyone could lift an audience, she could. After she sung a couple songs, Hope recalled, the patients were smiling and applauding.

While she sang on *The Bob Hope Show*, Day also performed in skits, although she personally felt most of them were sophomoric, saved only through Hope's delivery skill. One on going joke was Hope referring to his co-star as J.B. The audience never knew the initials stood for "jut butt." This was in reference to Day's figure and the fact that Hope kidded her that, "One could play a nice game of bridge on your ass."

The show featured guest appearances by some of the great radio stars of that era including Jack Benny, Jimmy Durante, Bing Crosby and Fred Allen. Some of the songs Day sang included "Everyday I Love You Just a Little Bit More" (November 9, 1948); "My Darling, My Darling" (December 7, 1948); "I'm Having a Wonderful Wish" (May 31, 1949); "(There's) A Bluebird on Your Window-sill" and "Where Are You (Now That I Need You)" (January 17, 1950).

Day made guest appearances on other radio shows. One was *The Dean Martin–Jerry Lewis Show* broadcast on May 31, 1949, with not only the famed duo, but also Lucille Ball; *The Buddy Clark Melody Hour* on June 6 and July 26, 1949; and *Railroad Hour* with Gordon MacRae on November 21, 1949, on which the pair performed *No, No Nanette*, which was also the basis of their musical film *Tea for Two*, released the following year. The pair also performed *Girl Crazy* on another broadcast of the show.

Day appeared on *The Bob Hope Show* through April 1950, by which time her agent and soon-to-be third husband Marty Melcher requested to Hope that his client was not to sing ballads but only bouncy songs. Hope agreed, much to his dismay. He considered Day one of the great singers, especially with ballads because she had a sense of timing. "It broke my heart," Hope admitted years later. "She was so great with ballads."

Day returned to radio with a regular show in 1952, *The Doris Day Show*, which had her visiting and performing skits with guests and singing such rarities as "I'm in the Mood for Love," "Just You, Just Me," "I Could Write a Book" and "Crying My Heart Out for You." This 25-minute program was aired on CBS radio with Johnny Jacobs and Roy Rowan serving as announcers. The show was broadcast from 1952 to 1953 and guest star appearances included Danny Thomas (March 28, 1952) and Kirk Douglas, with whom she performed the song "Red Hot Henry Brown" (November 25, 1952).

Throughout her career, several of Day's performances on the radio did not originate from a radio station, but on location. These include her four appearances at the Academy Awards. On March 24, 1949, she sang the Oscar-nominated song "It's Magic" live at the ceremony, but Day's remaining Oscar shows consisted of the presentation of awards. These were broadcast simultaneously on radio and television.

After the run of her self-titled show ended, Day made few appearances on radio. She concentrated on her film and recording careers which were not only more financially lucrative, but time-consuming. It was simply not possible to juggle the three careers. Although she performed in person, from the Hollywood Palladium to Carnegie Hall and Madison Square Garden and countless venues in between, it was the radio airwaves which served to introduce Doris Day to many listeners around the world.

MUSIC AWARDS AND CHARTS

In the twelve and a half years between her first and last *Billboard* Top 40 singles chart entry (from "Sentimental Journey" in 1946 through 1958's "Everybody Loves a Lover"), Doris Day spent a total of 26 weeks at number one, and 460 weeks in the Top 40 with 56 charting singles. Combining these figures results in that every week for almost nine years there was a Doris Day song in the Top 40, and for half a year there was a Doris Day song at number one. In that same time frame, Day also appeared in dozens of radio telecasts and starred in 23 films.

U.S. Top 200 Charted Albums

(peak positions according to *Billboard* magazine):

1949 *You're My Thrill* #5	1955 *Love Me or Leave Me* #1 (17 wks)
1950 *Young Man with a Horn* #1 (11 wks)	1956 *Day by Day* #11
	1957 *The Pajama Game* #9
1951 *Lullaby of Broadway* #1	1960 *Listen to Day* #26
1951 *On Moonlight Bay* #2	1961 *I Have Dreamed* #97
1951 *I'll See You in My Dreams* #1	1963 *Love Him!* #102
1953 *By the Light of the Silvery Moon* #3	1964 *The Doris Day Christmas Album* #92
1953 *Calamity Jane* #2	
1954 *Young at Heart* #15	

Doris Day was ranked as the sixteenth most popular album artist of the 1950s. Frank Sinatra, Johnny Mathis and Elvis Presley held the top three spots, respectively. Doris was not only the top ranking female artist, but the only female in the Top 20 for the decade.

More impressive is her *Love Me or Leave Me* soundtrack album, which spent 17 weeks at number one on the album charts, and was the third most successful album of the 1950s (behind the *South Pacific* soundtrack and Harry Belafonte's *Calypso*). More than 40 years since its release, *Love Me or Leave Me* still ranked in the Top 20 of the most successful albums of all time, a testament to Doris Day the singer. Only one other female artist placed in the Top 20 (Whitney Houston and *The Bodyguard* film soundtrack).

Your Hit Parade

Your Hit Parade was an American weekly survey of the best-selling sheet music and records, the songs receiving most radio airplay and those songs played most on "automatic coin machines" (juke boxes). The show counted down the top seven hit songs and began as a radio show in 1935. It was then televised from 1950 through 1959, at which time the chart tabulation was drawn from *Billboard* magazine. *Your Hit Parade* was presented by Lucky Strike cigarettes, and Doris Day appeared as a regular on the radio show with Frank Sinatra. The following are her popular recordings that charted:

Year	Title	Peak	Weeks on Chart
1945	"Sentimental Journey"	1	16
1945	"My Dream Are Getting Better All the Time"	1	15
1945	"'Till the End of Time"	1	19
1946	"The Whole World Is Singing My Song"	2	13
1946	"You Won't Be Satisfied"	2	8
1946	"Day by Day"	2	13

Year	Title	Peak	Weeks on Chart
1946	"Aren't You Glad You're You?"	3	10
1948	"It's Magic"	1	16
1948	"My Darling, My Darling"	2	13
1949	"Again"	1	20
1949	"Powder Your Face with Sunshine"	1	15
1950	"Bewitched (Bothered and Bewildered)"	1	16
1950	"I Said My Pajamas"	2	6
1950	"Hoop-Dee-Doo"	3	11
1951	"Shanghai"	3	14
1952	"A Guy Is a Guy"	2	8
1954	"Secret Love"	1	16
1954	"If I Give My Heart to You"	1	12

U.S. Top 40 Charted Singles

(according to *Billboard* [BB] magazine; post–1949 include *Cash Box* [CB] magazine rankings;* signifies *Cash Box* ranking the song's popularity rather than the recording by individual artists; songs that hit the Top 10 are highlighted)

"Again" #2 1949

"Aren't You Glad You're You?" #11 1945

"Anyone Can Fall in Love" #27 1954 (B-side of "If I Give My Heart to You")

"Baby Doll" #34 CB 1952

"Bewitched (Bothered and Bewildered)" #9 BB, #1 CB* 1950

"(There's) A Bluebird on Your Windowsill" #19 1949

"A Bushel and a Peck" #16 1950

"Canadian Capers (Cuttin' Capers)" #15 1949 (from the film *My Dream Is Yours*)

"Candy Lips" #17 BB, #18 CB 1953

"The Cherries" #39 CB 1952

"Choo-Choo Train (Ch-Ch-Foo)" #20 1952

"The Christmas Song (Merry Christmas to You)" #12 1947

"Come to Baby, Do!" #13 1945

"Confess" #16 1948 (B-side of "Love Somebody")

"Crocodile Tears" #25 CB 1950 (B-side of "Quicksilver")

"Day by Day" #15 1946

"Domino" #21 1951

"Enjoy Yourself (It's Later Than You Think)" #24 1950

"Everybody Loves a Lover" #6 BB, #6 CB 1958

"Everywhere You Go" #22 1949 (B-side of "Again")

"Foolishly Yours" #25 CB 1955

"A Full Time Job" #20 BB, #21 CB 1952

"A Game of Broken Hearts" #26 CB 1950

"Gently Johnny" #31 1952 (B-side of "A Little Kiss Goodnight")

"A Guy Is a Guy" #1 BB, #1 CB 1952

"Hold Me in Your Arms" #39 CB 1954

"Hoop-Dee-Doo" #17 BB, #4 CB* 1950

"How Lovely Cooks the Meat" #32 CB 1952 (B-side of "Sugarbush")

"I Didn't Slip—I Wasn't Pushed—I Fell" #19 BB, #15 CB 1950

"I Got the Sun in the Morning" #10 1946

"I Said My Pajamas (and Put on My Prayers)" #21 1950

"I Speak to the Stars" #16 BB, #17 CB 1954 (from the film *Lucky Me*)

"I'll Never Stop Loving You" #13 BB, #14 CB 1955 (from the film *Love Me or Leave Me*)

"If I Give My Heart to You" #3 BB, #1 CB 1954

"It's a Lovely Day Today" #30 1951

"It's Magic" #2 1948 (original B-side of "Put 'Em in a Box, Tie It with a Ribbon (and Throw 'Em in the Deep Blue Sea)" from the film *Romance on the High Seas*)

"Julie" #40 CB 1956 (from the film *Julie*)

"Kiss Me Again, Stranger" #30 1953

"Let's Take an Old Fashioned Walk" #17 1949

"Let's Walk That-a-Way" #31 CB 1953 (B-side of "Candy Lips")

"A Little Kiss Goodnight" #20 CB 1952

"Lost in Loveliness" #25 CB 1954

"Love Somebody" #1 1948

"Lullaby of Broadway" #22 CB 1951

"Ma Says, Pa Says" #23 BB, #28 CB 1952 (B-side of "A Full Time Job")

"Mister Tap Toe" #10 BB, #11 CB 1953

"My Darling, My Darling" #7 1948

"My Dreams Are Getting Better All the Time" #1 1945

"My Life's Desire" #23 CB 1951 (B-side of "Shanghai")

"My Love and Devotion" #31 CB 1952

"No Two People" #25 1953

"Now That I Need You" #20 1949

"Papa, Won't You Dance with Me?" #21 1947

"Powder Your Face with Sunshine (Smile! Smile! Smile!)" #16 1949

"A Purple Cow" #25 1953 (B-side of "Kiss Me Again, Stranger")

"Put 'Em in a Box, Tie It with a Ribbon (and Throw 'Em in the Deep Blue Sea)" #27 1948 (from the film *Romance On the High Seas*)

"Quicksilver" #20 1950

"Ready, Willing and Able" #31 CB 1954

"The River Seine" #37 CB 1950 (B-side of "(There's) A Bluebird on Your Windowsill")

"Secret Love" #1 BB, #1 CB 1954 (from the film *Calamity Jane*)
"Sentimental Journey" #1 1945
"Shanghai" #7 BB, #9 CB 1951
"Someone Else's Roses" #32 CB 1954
"Sooner or Later" #13 1947
"Sugarbush" #7 BB, #13 CB 1952
"'Tain't Me" #10 1945
"Teacher's Pet" #36 CB 1958 (from the film *Teacher's Pet*)
"Tell Me" #26 CB 1951
"Thoughtless" #24 1948
"Till the End of Time" #3 1945
"Whatever Will Be, Will Be (Qué Será, Será)" #2 BB, #3 CB 1956 (from the
    film *The Man Who Knew Too Much*)
"When I Fall in Love" #20 BB, #36 CB 1952
"When the Red, Red Robin Comes Bob-Bob-Bobbin' Along" #29 BB 1953
"The Whole World Is Singing My Song" #6 1946
"Would I Love You (Love You, Love You)" #10 BB 1951
"You Won't Be Satisfied (Until You Break My Heart)" #4 1946 (B-side of "Come
    to Baby, Do!")

U.S. #1 Songs

"Sentimental Journey" (9 weeks at #1 BB)
"My Dreams Are Getting Better All the Time" (7 weeks BB)
"Love Somebody" (5 weeks BB)
"Secret Love" (4 weeks BB; 5 weeks CB)
"Bewitched" (4 weeks CB*)
"If I Give My Heart to You" (2 weeks CB)
"A Guy Is a Guy" (1 week BB; 1 week CB)

Surprisingly, two of Day's more popular and enduring songs did not hit the top spot on either music magazine: "It's Magic," from Day's film debut, peaked at number two for one week on *Billboard*. Nineteen fifty-six's "Whatever Will Be, Will Be (Qué Será, Será)" held at #2 for three weeks on *Billboard* and spent more than a couple months in the top five on *Cash Box*. It was primarily kept from hitting number one by that year's latest sensation, Elvis Presley and his "Don't Be Cruel" / "Hound Dog" single.

Longest Charting U.S. Top 40 Songs [12 weeks or more]

"Sentimental Journey" 28 weeks BB
"Secret Love" 28 weeks CB; 22 weeks BB

"Bewitched (Bothered and Bewildered)" 26 weeks CB*; 15 weeks BB
"Whatever Will Be, Will Be (Qué Será, Será)" 24 weeks CB; 22 weeks BB
"Love Somebody" 24 weeks BB
"If I Give My Heart to You" 24 weeks CB; 17 weeks BB
"Hoop-Dee-Doo" 22 weeks CB*; 12 weeks BB
"It's Magic" 21 weeks BB
"A Guy Is a Guy" 20 weeks CB; 19 weeks BB
"Shanghai" 20 weeks CB; 17 weeks BB
"I'll Never Stop Loving You" 19 weeks CB
"Again" 19 weeks BB
"Sugarbush" 18 weeks CB; 14 weeks BB
"My Dreams Are Getting Better All the Time" 16 weeks BB
"You Won't Be Satisfied (Until You Break My Heart)" 15 weeks BB
"I Didn't Slip—I Wasn't Pushed—I Fell" 14 weeks CB
"My Darling, My Darling" 13 weeks BB
"'Till the End of Time" 13 weeks BB
"Everybody Loves a Lover" 13 weeks CB; 12 weeks BB

U.K. Top 30 Songs [from 1952-on when charting began]

"Sugarbush"	August 1952	#8
"My Love and Devotion"	September 1952	#10
"Ma Says, Pa Says"	March 1953	#12
"A Full Time Job"	March 1953	#11
"Let's Walk That-Away"	June 1953	#4
"Secret Love"	February 1954	#1
"The Black Hills of Dakota"	June 1954	#7
"If I Give My Heart to You"	September 1954	#4
"Ready, Willing and Able"	February 1955	#7
"Love Me or Leave Me"	July 1955	#20
"I'll Never Stop Loving You"	September 1955	#17
"Whatever Will Be, Will Be (Qué Será, Será)"	May 1956	#1
"A Very Precious Love"	March 1958	#16
"Everybody Loves a Lover"	August 1958	#25
"Move Over, Darling"	February 1964	#8

["Move Over, Darling" was reissued in 1987 and re-entered the U.K. charts, peaking at #45. By then the charts had expanded its number of songs listed in the weekly survey.]

Gold Record Awards

The following records sold more than one million copies and were awarded a Gold Record Award from the Recording Industry Association of America (RIAA):

SINGLES:

"A Guy Is a Guy"
"It's Magic"
"Love Somebody"
"Secret Love"
"Sentimental Journey"
"Sugarbush"
"Whatever Will Be, Will Be (Qué Será, Será)"

ALBUMS:

Doris Day's Greatest Hits

The Grammy Awards

The Grammy Awards, given out annually by the National Academy of Recording Arts and Sciences (NARAS), honors the top artists in their respective recording fields. The awards began in 1958 and are the oldest honor in the United States for recording artists. Surprisingly to many, Doris Day never won a Grammy Award. She was, however, nominated twice for Best Vocal Performance Female—and lost on both occasions to Ella Fitzgerald, one of her all-time favorite singers:

1958 BEST VOCAL PERFORMANCE, FEMALE NOMINEES:

Doris Day, "Everybody Loves a Lover" (single)
Ella Fitzgerald, *Ella Fitzgerald Sings the Irving Berlin Songbook* (album)
Edie Gormé, *Edie in Love* (album)
Peggy Lee, "Fever" (single)
Keely Smith, "I Wish You Love" (single)

1960 BEST VOCAL PERFORMANCE, SINGLE RECORD OR TRACK, FEMALE NOMINEES:

Doris Day, "The Sound of Music"
Eileen Farrell, "I've Gotta Right to Sing the Blues"
Ella Fitzgerald, "Mack the Knife"
Brenda Lee, "I'm Sorry"
Peggy Lee, "I'm Gonna Go Fishin'"

Although "Sentimental Journey" was nominated to the NARAS Hall of Fame in 1975, it was not until 1998 that the song was finally admitted. In 1999, "Secret Love" was also honored with induction into the Grammy Hall of Fame.

The Best Song Academy Award

Perhaps more than any other female vocalist, the joining of music and film that Doris Day experienced was a perfectly matched combination. In many of her films, Day sang the title song, and most of the songs have become classics in their own right.

Although Day was nominated only once for her acting skills (Best Actress for *Pillow Talk*), six original songs which she not only sang, but introduced to the film and radio public, were nominated for Best Song Academy Awards. Only Barbra Streisand has surpassed this record; however, it took more than 20 years to achieve this. Day's were amassed in only eight years, including a double nomination in 1956:

1948: "It's Magic" from *Romance on the High Seas*
1949: "It's a Great Feeling" from *It's a Great Feeling*
1954: "Secret Love" from *Calamity Jane* (winner)
1955: "I'll Never Stop Loving You" from *Love Me or Leave Me*
1956: "Julie" from *Julie*
1956: "Whatever Will Be, Will Be (Qué Será, Será)" from *The Man Who Knew Too Much* (winner)

Day on the Television

"Hollywood and the networks so often say, 'We are giving the public what it wants.' ...It seems to me it is up to Hollywood and the networks to lead rather than follow."—Doris Day, 1975

OVERVIEW

BECAUSE OF DORIS DAY'S consistent draw as a film personality, there was no need for her to work in television. Her films, as well as her recordings, ensured a paying audience without Day appearing on television talk shows to promote each product she had in release. Nor did she have any desire to work in television, especially a series. She knew from her friends in the industry that a television series was more difficult and demanding than making a film, primarily due to the rush in assembling a finished product. In terms of running time, one full television season of two dozen 30-minute episodes is the equivalent of six full-length theatrical films.

When Day discovered her husband Marty Melcher signed her to a five-season, two-film deal with CBS-TV without her knowledge or consent, she honored the agreement. As a result, the television series took precedence over film offers. Day's personal obligation and concentration to make *The Doris Day Show* succeed left little time or interest in making a motion picture.

CBS was so confident that *The Doris Day Show* was destined to succeed that the network offered a five-season run. This was a gamble because there was no assurance the series would be a hit, despite Day's involvement. A majority of television

225

programs were then and are now given a probationary period of a few weeks in order for the networks to measure its degree of success (or failure). In the event a series has the potential of garnering good ratings, a full season or multiple seasons will be ordered by the network. If a series falls below expectations, the network usually cancels it. When the first season of *The Doris Day Show* did not garner huge ratings, Day reworked it and made it more appealing to the television audience while CBS moved it to a more ideal time slot which made it a ratings winner.

The two films with the network were later negotiated to a pair of variety specials instead, a format Day enjoyed. Both specials featured her in comedy sketches and singing. Since she had stopped singing professionally, Day chose to retrain her voice to ensure a professional delivery rather than muddle through or lip synch with earlier recordings. It was a wise decision as many who had forgotten Day the singer commented on her unique vocal quality in the specials.

Both *The Doris Mary Anne Kapplehoff Special* in 1971 and *Doris day toDay* in 1975 were ratings winners. While the 1970s provided a banquet of innumerable specials of this genre which at times developed into weekly series, from Sonny and Cher to Tony Orlando and Dawn, Day chose not to make any more despite the success she had with the pair.

Day returned to television a decade later with *Doris Day's Best Friends* in 1985, a limited informational series about animals for cable television. The weekly half-hour programs featured Day with several of her former co-workers from music (Les Brown and His Band of Renown), films (Tony Randall, Howard Keel), television (Kaye Ballard, Denver Pyle), and industry friends (Joan Fontaine, Robert Wagner, Loni Anderson). Most episodes included Day in music videos of newly recorded songs.

In her television years, Day consented to several appearances on various talk shows and specials, including three times on NBC's *The Tonight Show*. Aside from those and a handful of showings at industry fetes, Day never made guest appearances on sitcoms or played supporting characters on series like many of her contemporaries. Her reasoning behind this is not that she has anything against such roles, but because none of the several offered have interested her. There have been many fans who have thought a cameo in any of her former co-star's television series would have been a welcome surprise, especially in the 1970s. Perhaps a nosy neighbor in Tony Randall's *The Odd Couple*; an heiress accused of murder in Rock Hudson's *McMillan and Wife*; a former girlfriend in James Garner's *The Rockford Files*; or even a visiting nurse in McLean Stevenson's *M*A*S*H*...

THE DORIS DAY SHOW

CBS-Television / 1968–73 / 30 minutes

TELEVISED:

September 1968 to September 1969 Tuesdays 9:30–10 P.M. (Eastern Standard Time)

September 1969 to September 1973 Mondays 9:30–10 P.M. (EST)

(Includes the first run of episodes and reruns during regular prime time)

CREDITS:

Executive Producers: Martin Melcher, Terry Melcher, Don Genson, Doris Day; *Producers:* Jack Elinson, Norman Paul, Edward H. Feldman, George Turpin, Bob Sweeney, Richard Dorso; *Associate Producers:* Jerry London, George Turpin; *Music:* Jimmie Haskell, William Loose; *Theme Song:* "Qué Será, Será" by Jay Livingston & Ray Evans, performed by Doris Day; *Theme Score:* Bob Mersey; *Creator:* James Fritzell; *Art Direction:* Perry Ferguson II; *Supervising Film Editor:* Howard French, A.C.E.; *Film Editor:* Michael Kahn; *Director of Photography:* Richard L. Rawlings; *Production Manager:* Abby Singer; *Set Decorator:* James Hassinger; *Sound Mixer:* William M. Ford, Woodruff Clark; *Assistant Director:* Robert Daley, Louis B. Appleton; *Story Editor:* Sid Morse; *Script Supervisor:* Maggie Lawrence; *Dialogue Coach:* Kay Stewart; *Makeup:* Harry Maret; *Hairstyles:* Barbara Lampson; Ms. Day's *Costumes:* Connie Edney; *Women's Costumes:* Joy Turney; *Men's Costumes:* Leonard F. Mann; *Property Master:* Sam Loreno, V.E. "Ted" Ross; *Wardrobe Furnished by:* Joseph Magnin.

The Doris Day Show has been regarded by television historians as the series with the most format changes. Of course there were cast and location changes, but these were not far-fetched considering the series lasted five seasons over six years. What critics and historians have failed to note was that the character of Doris Martin evolved during the course of the series, not unlike real life but unlike most television shows.

Following the death of her husband, Doris Martin and her two sons moved from New York to her father's farm in Mill Valley, California. In order to help with expenses and, perhaps, as a personal fulfillment, she took a job as a secretary for *Today's World* magazine in nearby San Francisco. Later she moved to the city, closer to her job, because the commute was time-consuming. Office personnel changed, as did her bosses. Doris Martin climbed the corporate ladder to become a reporter and associate editor at the magazine, despite the fact she had been a respected reporter in New York years earlier. Perhaps critics were not accustomed to seeing character growth which resulted in change.

The show became a respectful hit in the United States, garnering a 22.8 Nielsen rating high in its second season, and peaking as high as number six among

Publicity shot, 1970 (Jerry Ohlinger's Movie Material Store, Inc.).

all weekly shows. It consistently won its time slot, and usually landed in the Top 20 in the weekly ratings.

While television shows either build a large audience over time then diminish or are huge hits from the beginning and then decline, *The Doris Day Show* experienced an erratic audience share throughout its run in the United States. The premiere season garnered less than a 21.0 share. The second year, viewership jumped to a 22.8 average, placing at #10 for the year. The next season, the show dropped to a 20.7 share and #20 among all shows, while in its fourth year the program's viewers increased to a 21.2 average audience share. In its final outing, *The Doris Day Show* averaged less than 20.0 and did not make the top 25 popular shows of 1972–73. Oddly, *The Doris Day Show* was shown intermittently and only regionally in Great Britain, despite the fact Day had as large a following as in the United States. In France and French Canada the series was known as *Qué Será, Será*.

Strangely, the series did not receive a single Emmy nomination throughout its entire run. Day herself deserved a nomination, if not the award itself, for the episode "The Woman Hater" (season two), in which she ad-libbed more than one-fourth of this memorable and humorous episode. Day was, however, nominated for a Golden Globe by the Hollywood Foreign Press for Best Actress in a Television Series in 1969. The series itself also received a nod that same year. Neither won.

The show has not been largely shown in syndication, but was a staple for a few years on cable's CBN (The Family Channel) in the mid 1980s. Still, memories of the show prevailed because in 1995, *Vanity Fair* called the character of Doris Martin "one of the best working women in television."

The Doris Day Show's success as a comedy is credited to the ensemble of its writers, cast, directors, producers and crew. Day preferred situation comedy for her character and encouraged the writers to give the spoken jokes to other characters. Day successfully translated Doris Martin's antics and predicaments into humor, much as she had done in her films. In comparing with today's television comedies which primarily rely on a character's lines, one can see a void with the lack of character situations, and an unbalanced mix of verbal and non-verbal comedy.

Day also retained her sense of humor with the series. In the episode "How Can I Ignore the Man Next Door?" with Billy DeWolfe as Mr. Jarvis, Doris Martin has fixed his television set and he turns it on. On the screen is Doris Day (though really a scene from the show's "The Fly Boy" episode). No words are spoken, just an image of her. Mr. Jarvis remarks, "Can't stand that woman!" before the set blows up.

In "Doris' House Guest," DeWolfe as Mr. Jarvis again expresses his dislike for the entertainer. While speaking with Doris Martin, he complains that the neighbor has *The Doris Day Show* playing on their television set. Again, he says he can't stand her. In reality, Day and DeWolfe were great friends.

In 1971's "Whodunit, Doris," Doris Martin and her boss Mr. Bennett are watching television, and he asks her who the woman is. She answers, "Doris Day." He erroneously remembers her as being a very good ice skater. Smoke emits from the television set, at which time Doris Martin remarks, "She's really hot stuff!" Other episodes made reference to Day's films and her co-stars, most frequently Rock Hudson.

The series' theme song featured the voice of Day singing her signature song, "Whatever Will Be, Will Be (Qué Será, Será)." Throughout the course of the show's run, three different versions of the song appeared over the opening credits. In the pilot episode, "Dinner for Mom," Day sang the song off-camera during a scene, and it was played in a restaurant scene in the episode "Doris Meets a Prince." This from a woman who originally felt its appeal was limited when she first recorded the song in 1956.

The series contains some of Doris Day's funniest work, with seasons two through five providing the bulk of the show's best-written and -acted episodes. Although the first year includes a majority of the series' worst episodes—a statement Doris Day does not dispute—there are many humorous moments and several good episodes from the season.

Season One: 1968-69
Tuesdays, 9:30 P.M. EST

Average Nielsen rating: less than 21.0 (placed #30 for the season among all shows on television)

CBS Tuesday night line-up: *The Red Skelton Show, The Doris Day Show, 60 Minutes* / Specials

NBC aired a movie of the week to compete with *The Doris Day Show*, while the short-lived series *N.Y.P.D.* was shown on ABC.

CAST:

Doris Day (Doris Martin); Denver Pyle (Buck Webb); Fran Ryan (Aggie Thompson); James Hampton (LeRoy B. Simpson); Naomi Stevens (Juanita); Philip Brown (Billy Martin); Tod Starke (Toby Martin); Lord Nelson (Nelson).

REVIEWS:

"*The Doris Day Show* makes *Family Affair* look like a meeting of the Mafia."— *Los Angeles Times*

"As in films, Miss Day here displays her usual talent for somehow squeezing the corn juice out of a square role. She is evocative and believable and, in fact, the whole show is well cast. The locale ... [however] would seem to be somewhere between *Green Acres* and *Petticoat Junction*."—*Variety*, September 25, 1968

"When the show hit the air, it was everything you knew it would be—pure, unadulterated, wall-to-wall freckle, Doris-Daysies-in-my-garden-type Doris Day, a real throwback to the good old days when there was no problem that goodness couldn't solve."—*TV Guide*, December 28, 1968

When *The Doris Day Show* premiered in September 1968, Day was cast as Doris Martin (nee Webb), who had worked for *Ladies' World* magazine in New York while having a family with her husband Steve. After Steve's death, Doris and the boys moved in with her father on the family ranch near Cotina, Mill Valley, California. There she adjusted to rural life and helped on the ranch along with her father Buck, LeRoy the hired hand and Aggie the housekeeper. In December 1968, Aggie was replaced by Juanita.

The beautifully shot, serene, opening credits of the first year's programs showed Doris and the cast in the sun-sparkled outdoors while a new arrangement of "Qué Será, Será" with Doris and a choir of children played on the soundtrack.

The ranch, complete with cows, pigs, horses and sheepdog Nelson, was located near Cotina in Mill Valley, outside of San Francisco. The sprawling house had four bedrooms, two stairways (a main one and another located in the kitchen) and a huge living room filled with antiques.

"I was not prepared to go into television, and I didn't know a thing about it," she later told Barbara Walters. "I was not really ready for it, and I did not like the first year." The first year was largely panned by critics; however, the public welcomed Doris Day into their homes and it was the season's highest-rated new show.

EPISODES: [as originally scheduled]

Dinner for Mom (September 24, 1968)

Billy and Toby take Doris out to dinner for her birthday with money they earned. While eating, Doris discovers the boys removed her money from her purse and the bill is larger than the amount they have.

Featuring: Norm Alden as the Road House Manager, Leonard Stone as the Waiter; *Writers:* Dick Bensfield, Perry Grant; *Director:* Bob Sweeney.

The Uniform (October 1, 1968)

After seeing Billy's Little League uniform, Toby lies that he also has a uniform, which is for the school choir. When the tone-deaf Toby doesn't get a place in the choir, he's ashamed to tell the family the truth, but eventually confesses.

Featuring: Woodrow Parfrey as Maxwell Digby, Scott Crawford as Ben; *Writer:* Sid Morse; *Director:* Bruce Bilson.

The Antique (October 8, 1968)

Billy and Toby sell lemonade to earn money and instead sell an old table which is a family heirloom to two old ladies. The antique hunters later return for a pot belly stove, but Doris has it switched with a worthless one to get the table back.

Featuring: Estelle Winwood as Gertrude, Maudie Prickett as Bertie; *Writer:* Dorothy Cooper Foote; *Director:* Bob Sweeney.

The Matchmakers (October 22, 1968)

When Billy, Toby and Buck come in last place in every event at a father-son competition, the boys suggest Doris should marry again. They plot to get local sports hero Deputy Puckum interested in Doris.

Featuring: Frank Maxwell as Sheriff Ben Anders, Carl Byrd as Deputy Dan Case, Noam Pitlik as Deputy Ubbie Puckum; *Writer:* Richard Baer; *Director:* Bruce Bilson.

The Songwriter (October 29, 1968)

Doris discovers that LeRoy is caught in a phony song publishing scheme. She exposes the business with her song "Your Love Is Like Butter Gone Rancid," which is also accepted by the publisher.

Featuring: Jerry Hausner as the Mailman; *Writer:* Joseph Bonaduce; *Director:* Gary Nelson.

LeRoy B. Simpson (November 19, 1968)

In a flashback episode, Doris and Aggie recall how LeRoy came into the family. Shortly after LeRoy arrives, pieces of jewelry are missing and Buck and

Aggie believe LeRoy is the thief. But LeRoy discovers the true thieves crows who like shiny objects.

     Writer: Sid Morse; *Director:* Bob Sweeney.

The Black Eye (November 26, 1968)

Billy comes home from school with a black eye, but won't tell Doris who gave it to him. Buck thinks his grandson is a coward, but it's discovered the bully is a neighbor girl who likes Billy.

     Featuring: Lisa Gerritsen as Jackie, Woodrow Parfrey as Mr. Digby; *Writer:* Ray Singer; *Director:* Bob Sweeney.

The Librarian (December 3, 1968)

LeRoy becomes entranced with the town librarian and decides to recite a poem in her poetry group. But when another speaker has chosen the same poem, LeRoy delivers a simple poem among suppressed laughter. The librarian confronts LeRoy and tells him admires what he's done and they begin dating.

     Featuring: Ryan MacDonald as Dr. Travis Peabody, Kelly Jean Peters as Winifred Proxmire, Keith Taylor as Carl; *Writer:* Harry Winkler; *Director:* Bob Sweeney.

The Camping Trip (December 10, 1968)

While the boys continually talk about the legends they've been told by Native American Joe Whitecloud, Buck becomes jealous. When Joe "dirties" the name of John Wayne, Buck cancels a camping trip. He later makes amends with Joe after LeRoy attempts to take the boys on the trip.

     Featuring: Harry Corden as Joe Whitecloud; *Writer:* Jerry Devine; *Director:* Bruce Bilson.

Love a Duck (December 17, 1968)

Billy finds a duck that has been injured from a poacher's shotgun. Using a duck caller, Doris plans to catch the poacher, Tyrone Lovey. But Lovey also has a duck caller, and as he nears Doris's call, he falls into an abandoned well. After Lovey promises not to do any more poaching, Doris helps him out.

     Featuring: Strother Martin as Tyrone Lovey; *Writer:* Jerry Devine; *Director:* Gary Nelson.

Buck's Girl (December 24, 1968)

Buck and Doc Carpenter, the local veterinarian, both fall for the town's new manicurist, Verna McIntosh. When each discovers the other has been seeing Verna, a wedge is driven into their friendship.

     Featuring: Walter Sande as Doc Carpenter, Kay Stewart as Verna McIntosh, Paul Barselow as the Barber; *Writer:* Carl Kleinschmitt; *Director:* Gary Nelson.

The Date (December 31, 1968)

Juanita and Frank, the owner of the sporting goods store, go on a date but he gets cold feet when Buck talks about marriage.

From the 1969-70 season: Day, Philip Brown, Tod Starke and Denver Pyle (Jerry Ohlinger's Movie Material Store, Inc.).

Featuring: Joe De Santis as Frank Gorian; *Writer:* E. Duke Vincent, Bruce Johnson; *Director:* Bruce Bilson.

The Job (January 7, 1969)

Doris' former boss, Maggie Wells, convinces Doris to help with a magazine article in New York. Maggie returns with Doris to the farm and attempts to convince the family that Doris should return to New York for good.

Featuring: Linda Watkins as Maggie, Jo Miya as Jo; *Written by:* James L. Brooks; *Directed by:* Bob Sweeney.

Let Them Out of the Nest (January 14, 1969)

When Billy and Toby get a job delivering eggs, Doris intervenes, thinking the boys are not responsible. They fake being sick and Doris ends up delivering the eggs herself with Billy's bicycle since none of the vehicles on the farm are working.

Featuring: Hal Smith as the Drunk, Barbara Pepper as the Woman, Raymond Kark as the Police Officer, Keith Huntley as the Newsboy, Robert Graham as Arthur; *Writers:* Peggy Elliott, Ed Scharlach; *Director:* Bruce Bilson.

The Friend (January 21, 1969)

A local milk company agrees to give the school free milk in exchange for models for an advertisement. Doris and the boys and two of their friends agree to pose in the ad, but the girl Toby asks to appear with them is black, which is unacceptable to the company.

Featuring: Woodrow Parfrey as Maxwell Digby, Peggy Rea as Grace Henley, George Morgan as Brig Mitchell, Lisa Gerritsen as Jackie Clements, Cheri Grant as Patty, Raymond Kark as Harvey Miller, R. G. Armstrong as Henry R. Pritchart; *Writers:* E. Duke Vincent, Bruce Johnson; *Director:* Bob Sweeney.

The Clock (January 28, 1969)

LeRoy buys an antique clock for Doris, but the clock bongs so loudly that she can't sleep. Buck takes the clock and sells it. But it is returned to Doris, and continues to strike as before.

Featuring: Strother Martin as Tyrone Lovey, Peggy Rea as Grace Henley; *Writer:* Joe Bonaduce; *Director:* Bruce Bilson.

The Buddy (February 4, 1969)

Major Emma Flood, an old marine friend of Buck's, visits while Doris is out of town. Recently retired, Emma helps out on the farm and puts the family on a military regime.

Featuring: Mary Wickes as Emma Flood, Willis Bouchey as Col. Forsythe; *Writer:* Harry Winkler; *Director:* Gary Nelson.

The Fly Boy (February 11, 1969)

When sonic booms cause damage to the farm, an Air Force colonel visits to apologize—and asks Doris for a date. When she learns his intention is to add her to his list of conquests, Doris goes on the date, acting like a seductress and then tells the colonel that she knows his game.

Featuring: Frank Aletter as Col. Carson, Al Travis as Ben, Tom Curry as Charlie, James Truesdell as Al, Tom Falk as the Sergeant; *Writer:* Howard Leeds; *Director:* Gary Nelson.

The Tournament (February 18, 1969)

When LeRoy accidentally injures Doc's pitching hand, he becomes Buck's partner in a horseshoe contest. But LeRoy develops a case of stage fright and can't pitch.

Featuring: Walter Sande as "Doc" Carpenter; *Writer:* Perry Grant, Dick Bensfield; *Director:* Gary Nelson.

Love Thy Neighbor (March 4, 1969)

When Buck can't afford a new tractor, Doris confronts neighbor Tugwell, who owes Buck for two horses. But Tugwell plots for his son to marry Doris in order to avoid paying the debt.

Featuring: J. Pat O'Malley as Zeno Tugwell, Read Morgan as Stonewall Tugwell; *Writer:* Sid Morse; *Director:* Harry Falk.

The Con Man (March 11, 1969)

While fundraising for a new convention center, Doris welcomes architect Roger Flanders. When Doris discovers that Flanders is about to leave them with the money they raised, she convinces him to stay and see his project realized.

Featuring: Joseph Campanella as Roger Flanders, Madge Blake as Mrs. Hardy, Bard Stevens as Committeeman, Peter Brocco as Jed Anslinger, James Millhollin as Horace Burkhart, Kay Stewart as Committeewoman #1, Evelyn King as Committeewoman #2, Dodie Warren as Committeewoman #3; *Writer:* Si Rose; *Director:* Bruce Bilson.

The Musical (March 18, 1969)

Doris directs a school musical but the principal refuses the show after the students are performing in a modern way. Doris revamps the program to the 1920s to illustrate how backward the principal's thinking is.

Featuring: Ray Teal as Mr. Ekstrom, Gary Dubin as Freddie, Michele Tobin as Gloria; *Writer:* Sid Morse; *Director:* Bruce Bilson.

The Baby Sitter (March 25, 1969)

Doris watches the Bensons' unruly children while Hal and Dorothy are at the hospital waiting for the arrival of another child. She accidentally locks herself in the linen closet and is later found when Hal returns after the baby is delivered.

Featuring: Paul Smith as Hal Benson, Peggy Rea as Dorothy Benson, Julie

Reese as Elizabeth Benson, Jodie Foster as Jenny Benson, Ted Foulkes as Adam Benson, Lynnel Atkins as Rachel Benson, Hal Smith as Mr. Pebee; *Writer:* Bruce Howard; *Director:* Harry Falk.

The Still (April 1, 1969)

Doris collects evidence from two elderly moonshiners but is caught by two government agents and jailed. When LeRoy strikes a match, the moonshine explodes, thus destroying the evidence.

Featuring: Barney Phillips as Sheriff Ben Anders, Jesslyn Fax as Lydia, Florence Lake as Adelaide, Jeff DeBenning as Agent Bronson, Tom Falk as Agent Willoughby; *Writers:* Lloyd Turner, Whitey Mitchell; *Director:* Gary Nelson.

The Gift (April 8, 1969)

The family plans to send LeRoy on a trip to see his grandmother, and prepares a list of how the chores will be divided while he's away. LeRoy mistakenly believes he's going to be fired.

Writers: Arthur Alsberg, Don Nelson; *Director:* Harry Falk.

The Tiger (April 15, 1969)

An escaped tiger stows away in the back of Doris' truck but LeRoy accidentally sets the animal free before the sheriff arrives to claim it. A posse goes into the woods to get the tiger, but Doris and LeRoy find it first before anyone can harm it.

Featuring: Barney Phillips as Sheriff Ben Anders, Bard Stevens as Deputy Sheriff; *Writer:* Norman Katkov; *Director:* Gary Nelson.

The Five-Dollar Bill (April 29, 1969)

Billy returns a lost wallet to neighbor Mrs. Loomis, but she accuses him of stealing $5 from it. Doris discovers that Mrs. Loomis' son took the money.

Featuring: Shirley Mitchell as Mrs. Loomis, Stuart Lee as Alfred Loomis, Jerry Hausner as Mr. Kibbler; *Writer:* John McGreevey; *Director:* Gary Nelson.

The Relatives (May 6, 1969)

Doris plans to paint and wallpaper while the family is gone for the weekend. She and Juanita, however, run into problems when three of LeRoy's cousins visit and attempt to help, but they do more harm than good.

Featuring: Alan Sues as Edgar Simpson, Dennis Fimple as Herman Simpson, Robert Easton as Albert Simpson, J. P. Cranshaw and Ernie, Bard Stevens as Ben; *Writer:* Bruce Howard; *Director:* Harry Falk.

Season Two 1969-70
Mondays, 9:30 P.M. EST
(CBS moved the series from Tuesday to Monday nights for the remainder of the run)

Average Nielsen rating: 22.8 (placed #10 for the season among all shows on television)

CBS Monday night line-up: *Gunsmoke, Here's Lucy, Mayberry RFD, The Doris Day Show, The Carol Burnett Show*

Competing against *The Doris Day Show* was a movie of the week on NBC. ABC aired *The Survivors*, which ultimately died.

CAST:

Doris Day (Doris Martin); Denver Pyle (Buck Webb); Philip Brown (Billy Martin); Tod Starke (Toby Martin); McLean Stevenson (Michael Nicholson); Rose Marie (Myrna Gibbons).

REVIEWS:

"On the first day, [Doris] gets the job [as a secretary].... Her experiences in seeking out a job are genuinely amusing, and ... a viewer even shares a sense of anticipation after she nabs her new job.... One does hope for, if not always expect, a few laughs and a sense of involvement. Judged by the season opener, Miss Day and family, plus Rose Marie and her new boss do achieve this sort of communication with the audience. That's the kind of appeal on which successful sitcoms are built, and so the 'new improved' Doris Day show shapes up as a Nielsen favorite." —*Variety*, September 24, 1969

"Doris is an enormously natural and personable performer, but she's neither old or ugly, so why, I'd like to ask, must all of her close-ups be shot with so many filters over the screen that she looks like she's being photographed through Vaseline?"—Rex Reed, *Big Screen, Little Screen*

The first season's ratings started out extremely well, but fell as the year continued. CBS decided to move the show to its strong Monday night line up, while Day and the show's creative staff made changes in the show itself.

The second season brought a change in format for *The Doris Day Show*. Feeling she should help with expenses on the ranch, Doris Martin finds a job in nearby San Francisco and begins a new life as a commuter, working at *Today's World* magazine. The season's episodes alternated between both locations.

Doris Martin's job at *Today's World* was as executive secretary to managing editor Michael Nicholson, played by McLean Stevenson. Paul Smith as Assistant Editor Ron Harvey was added as was Rose Marie, who played single gal Myrna Gibbons, Mr. Harvey's secretary.

A new, hipper title credit opening was made for the second season, with Doris saying goodbye to her family on the ranch, then driving her red convertible into San Francisco. The theme song "Qué Será, Será" was replaced with a new version that was performed more upbeat and as a solo by Day.

EPISODES:

Doris Gets a Job (September 22, 1969)

Doris secures a job as executive secretary at *Today's World* magazine in San Francisco. Co-worker Myrna advises Doris to hide the fact that she has children as it may interfere with work.

Featuring: Paul Smith as Ron Harvey, Carol Worthington as Miss Bennington, Eldon Quick as Mr. Willoughby, Joel Mell as Man #1, Larry Gelman as Man #2; *Writers:* Jack Elinson, Norman Paul; *Director:* Coby Ruskin.

A Frog Called Harold (October 6, 1969)

Toby's frog Harold escapes and jumps into Doris' purse. At the office, bank officials are visiting and the frog stows away to the bank where Doris retrieves it. She later learns that the frog in her purse was not Harold after all.

Featuring: Paul Smith as Ron Harvey, Parley Baer as Mr. Thornby, David Manzy as Dave, Jack Garner as the Aide, Issa Arnal as Office Girl, Ralph Neff as Bank Guard, Ed McReady as Man in Restaurant; *Writer:* Budd Grossman; *Director:* Coby Ruskin.

The Woman Hater (October 13, 1969)

When *Today's World* publishes a series of articles by woman hater Alex Rhinehart, Doris changes the writer's negative opinion. She then goes on a date with him to reinforces his conception of a stereotypical female. Rhinehart catches on and allows the magazine to publish the original article, followed by a positive piece on the importance of women.

McLean Stevenson played Doris Martin's boss in seasons two and three (Jerry Ohlinger's Movie Material Store, Inc.).

Featuring: Anthony Eisley as Alex Rhinehart, Luis de Cordova as Head Waiter, Johnny Collins III as Dave, Pete Kellett as Husband, Judy March as Wife, Julius Johnsen as Bartender; *Writer:* Budd Grossman; *Director:* Coby Ruskin.

The Chocolate Bar War (October 20, 1969)

Doris helps Billy sell candy bars at a supermarket for a fundraiser-contest and confronts an overly aggressive mother whose son is also selling. That evening, she attends a party with Mr. Nicholson, and discovers the hostess of the party is the woman from the supermarket.

Featuring: Max Showalter as Mr. Fletcher, Amzie Strickland as Mrs. Fletcher, Jane Aull as Woman #1 at Market, Howard Culver as Man #1 at Market, Brad Trumball as Man #2 at Market, Marshall Kent as Elderly Man at Market, Walter Mathews as Man #1 at Party, Tim Weldon as Jonathan Fletcher, Jan Arvan as Man #2 at Party, Lynn Wood as Woman at Party, Don G. Ross as Charlie; *Writers:* Jack Elinson, Norman Paul; *Director:* Harry Falk.

Married for a Day (October 27, 1969)

Mr. Nicholson introduces Doris as his wife in a scheme to convince the husband-hunting Karen that he's unavailable.

Featuring: Julie Adams as Karen Carruthers, Paul Smith as Ron Harvey; *Writers:* Norman Paul, Jack Elinson; *Director:* Earl Bellamy.

Buck's Portrait (November 11, 1969)

Famous artist Amanda Merriwether is commissioned to paint a *Today's World* cover. She finds Buck is the perfect model. But when Buck discovers the cover is an abstract, Doris explains that the cover isn't his physical self, but his spiritual inner being.

Featuring: Mabel Albertson as Amanda Merriwether, Hal Smith as Merle, Charles Wagenheim as Edgar, Bob Jellison as Smokey, Issa Arnal as Receptionist, J.P. Cranshaw as Farmer, Riza Royce as Woman Farmer, Woodrow Parfrey as Barton Durston; *Writer:* Doug Tibbles; *Director:* Earl Bellamy.

The Health King (November 10, 1969)

Mr. Nicholson asks Doris to convince health writer Bruce Saunders to give *Today's World* the serialization rights of his book. When Doris and Saunders are caught in a downpour, she stays at his apartment while her clothes dry. Mr. Nicholson barges in to fight him for Doris' honor.

Featuring: Michael Forest as Bruce Saunders, Ernest Harada as Ling, Lavina Dawson as Waitress, Joan Lemmo as Woman #1, Bunny Summers as Woman #2; *Writer:* Budd Grossman; *Director:* Coby Ruskin.

Doris the Model (November 17, 1969)

Today's World obtains the exclusive showing of Paris designer Montagne's fashion collection. But when the models sneak out and get married, Doris fills in to model the designs.

Featuring: Johnny Haymer as Montagne, Paul Smith as Ron Harvey, Gail Stevens as Yvette, Arlyn Genson as Simone, Paul Marin as Hal, Larry Gelman as Nat, Sam Javis as the Waiter, Jerry Fitzpatrick as the Valet; *Writers:* Norman Paul, Jack Elinson; *Director:* Hal Cooper.

Doris Strikes Out (November 24, 1969)

Doris is mesmerized when a handsome French movie star, Claude LeMaire, visits the magazine and invites her to his film premiere. Doris spends the day preparing for the date and then umpires her son's little league game. The game lasts for hours, so Doris calls strikes to finish it, then ends up sleeping through LeMaire's entire film.

Featuring: Jacques Bergerac as Claude LeMaire, James Chandler as Dr. Parker, Gordon Jump as Little League Manager, Darrell Rice as Joey, Alan DeWitt as the Hairdresser; *Writers:* Norman Paul, Jack Elinson; *Director:* Coby Ruskin.

Singles Only (December 8, 1969)

Myrna signs a lease for an apartment at a "swinging singles" complex. But she is disappointed when she sees the one-room apartment and the male tenants in the building. When the manager refuses to break the lease, she and Doris plot to change his mind.

Featuring: Sid Melton as Lou Lester, Ed Fury as Chet, Michael Lerner as the Fat Man, Joseph Perry as Harry Dumbrowski, Joe Ross as Virgil Praskins, Alice Backes as Agnes Albright, Ben Young as Second Handsome Man, Carol Worthington as Girl; *Writers:* William Raynor, Myles Wilder; *Director:* William Wiard.

Rose Marie with Doris in season two (Jerry Ohlinger's Movie Material Store, Inc.).

Togetherness (December 15, 1969)

Doris plans a weekend to spend quality time with Buck and her sons. After learning that the boys were invited to a stay-over, Doris tells them to go and then calls Ron Harvey to accept an invitation to a play she had declined earlier. But their plans are cut short when the boys return home with upset stomachs after eating too many chili dogs.

Featuring: Paul Smith as Ron Harvey, Karen Arthur as Gloria; *Writers:* William Raynor, Myles Wilder; *Director:* Alan Rafkin.

A Two Family Christmas (December 22, 1969)

Doris invites Mr. Nicholson, Myrna and Ron to spend Christmas with her on the ranch, but they have plans and decline. After a few drinks, Ron berates Mr. Nicholson, and Myrna insults others with her Jimmy Durante impersonation. Later that evening, the trio have a change of heart and go to the ranch to celebrate Christmas.

Featuring: Paul Smith as Ron Harvey, David Manzy as Dave, Carleen Frans as Eileen, J. B. Douglas as Mr. Singer; *Writers:* Jack Elinson, Norman Paul; *Director:* Lawrence Dobkin.

You're as Old as You Feel (December 29, 1969)

When Doris drags him to the dentist to have the tooth fixed, Buck believes he is falling apart. In order to get Buck out of his rut, Doris hires bumbling neighbor Merle to run the farm. But only when Buck sees Merle trying to teach Billy and Toby how to throw a football, does Buck return to his old self.

Featuring: Hal Smith as Merle, Herb Vigran as the Dentist; *Writers:* Norman Paul, Jack Elinson; *Director:* Larry Dobkin.

The Prizefighter and the Lady (January 5, 1970)

In her first writing assignment, Doris tries to interview fighter Duke Farentino, but he'd rather dance than talk with her. Doris is later brought to a fight that Duke is losing. When Duke sees that she now has short hair (she had been wearing a wig), his opponent knocks him out.

Featuring: Larry Storch as Duke Farentino, Buddy Lester as Eddie, Jim Cross as Larry, Sidney Clute as Howard, Chick Casey as Herman, Gerald York as Pete, Lauro Salas as Garcia, Frankie Van as Referee, Paul Smith as Ron Harvey; *Writer:* Budd Grossman; *Director:* Denver Pyle.

Doris vs. the Computer (January 12, 1970)

The electric company threatens to cut off the power at the ranch when its computer indicates that Doris hasn't paid her bill. After Doris issues another personal check, she receives a refund—for $214,000.

Featuring: Billy De Wolfe as Mr. Jarvis, Frank Corsentino as Hippie #1, Christina Dean as Hippie #2, Gregg Jakobson as Hippie #3, Jerry Jones as Policeman; *Writers:* Arthur Alsberg, Don Nelson; *Director:* Denver Pyle.

Hot Dogs (January 19, 1970)

Doris and Myrna discover a locked automobile containing six dogs with its windows rolled up. They retrieve the canines, but the dog's sitter tracks Doris down and she is arrested for taking the animals.

Featuring: James Millhollin as Paul, Jerome Cowan as Justice William Forester, Paul Smith as Ron Harvey, Issa Arnal as Helen, Charles Lane as Judge Carter, Owen Bush as Locksmith; *Writers:* Jack Elinson, Norman Paul, Don Genson; *Director:* Coby Ruskin.

Today's World Catches Measles (January 26, 1970)

Doris invites Mr. Nicholson and Ron Harvey to the farm for a relaxing weekend but the pair are exposed to measles and need to be quarantined. Mr. Nicholson reads Dr. Wagner's writings about being a country doctor and decides to run them as the lead story.

Featuring: Edward Andrews as Col. Fairburn, Walter Sande as Dr. Wagner, Paul Smith as Ron Harvey, Joe Hoover as Jack, Breland Rice as Phil, Issa Arnal as Helen, Geri Ewing as Secretary; *Writers:* Jack Elinson, Norman Paul; *Director:* Fred de Cordova.

The Gas Station (February 2, 1970)

Doris and Myrna run LeRoy's gas station so that he can join his wife, who is having their baby at the hospital. The station is on a bypass and is overrun with customers, one of whom robs the place.

Featuring: Jim Hampton as LeRoy B. Simpson, Tina Holland as Terry Tidy, John Carter as Hold Up Man, Bob Jellison as Smokey, Herman Griffith as Man #1, Herb Weil as Sporty Guy, Virgil Frye as Motorcyclist, Charles Dugdale as Man #2, Martin Ashe as Man #3, Jon Kowal as Truck Driver, Eddie Quillan as Man #4, Eric Scott as Boy; *Writers:* Jack Elinson, Norman Paul, Don Genson; *Director:* Hal Cooper.

Kidnapped (February 9, 1970)

Doris is kidnapped while working on an expose on gangster Barney Moore. She befriends Moore's abused wife, who helps Doris escape, but her cover is blown when Ron and Myrna see Doris leaving the hideout.

Featuring: Bruce Gordon as Barney Moore, Kaye Ballard as Flossie Moore, Avery Schreiber as Warren Coleman, Paul Smith as Ron Harvey, Hagen Smith as Lefty Watson, Gene Dynarski as Lefty Kretch, Scott Perry as Detective, Ricco Cattani as Bartender; *Writer:* Doug Tibbles; *Director:* Coby Ruskin.

Doris Hires a Millionaire (two-part episode, February 23 and March 2, 1970)

Doris mistakes publicity-shy billionaire William Tyler for a bum and gives him a job on the farm. Meanwhile, *Today's World* is attempting to locate Tyler and take his picture, which has not been published in more than 30 years. Doris and Buck discover his true identity as Ron Harvey snaps his picture. Doris convinces Mr. Nicholson not to publish Tyler's photograph.

Featuring: Lew Ayres as William Tyler, Paul Smith as Ron Harvey, Ross Elliott as Mr. Clark, John Stuart as Mr. Bradford, Issa Arnal as Helen, John Lawrence as Policeman; *Writers:* Budd Grossman (part 1), Norman Paul and Jack Elinson (part 2); *Director:* Fred de Cordova.

A Woman's Intuition (March 9, 1970)

Doris and Mr. Nicholson plan for an exclusive interview with Ed King, owner of a hamburger chain. At the airport, Doris has a premonition, so the pair takes a different flight which ends up being hijacked to Cuba.

Featuring: Bernie Kopell as Major Laguinita, Sandy Kenyon as Zeke Kraley, Carol Worthington as Stewardess, Gordon Jump as Ticket Agent, Ricco Cattani as Waiter, Perla Walter as Girl Soldier; *Writer:* Rick Mittleman; *Director:* Denver Pyle.

Doris Meets a Prince (March 16, 1970)

A visiting prince asks Doris to marry him. Before Doris can decline, the prince withdraws the proposal as a revolution in his country has abolished the throne, leaving him penniless. He then opens a restaurant in San Francisco.

Featuring: Cesare Danova as Prince Carlos, Eric Mason as The Aide, Roy Roberts as Mr. Gilby, Luis de Cordova as Prime Minister, Paul Smith as Ron Harvey; *Writer:* Budd Grossman; *Director:* Fred de Cordova.

The Duke Returns (March 23, 1970)

Duke Farentino has retired from the ring to open his own dance studio and asks Doris, Myrna and Ron to give dance lessons. Mr. Nicholson asks Doris to accompany him to a dancing party, then learns of her moonlighting when he goes to Duke's studio for lessons.

Featuring: Larry Storch as Duke Farentino, Michael Lerner as Mr. Murray, Paul Smith as Ron Harvey, George Dunn as Hillbilly, Margaret Wheeler as Mrs. Forbush; *Writers:* Norman Paul, Jack Elinson; *Director:* Denver Pyle.

The Office Troubleshooter (March 30, 1970)

Col. Fairburn hires Mr. Jarvis as the magazine's new efficiency expert. Doris, Ron and Myrna plot to have him fired and put vodka in his drinking water. After Mr. Jarvis tells Col. Fairburn off, he is fired and the workers are allowed to continue as before.

Featuring: Billy De Wolfe as Mr. Jarvis, Edward Andrews as Col. Fairburn, Paul Smith as Ron Harvey; *Writer:* Budd Grossman; *Director:* Coby Ruskin.

Col. Fairburn Takes Over (April 6, 1970)

Col. Fairburn assumes control of the office staff and develops a special interest in Doris. She senses he is going to propose so she takes him to a discotheque, where he sees his daughter and son-in-law, who have just eloped.

Featuring: Edward Andrews as Col. Fairburn, Fredericka Myers as Sharon Fairburn, Paul Smith as Ron Harvey, Scott Perry as Jim, De De Young as Helen, Titus Moody as Messanger; *Writers:* Rick Mittleman, Don Genson; *Director:* Coby Ruskin.

Third Season 1970-71
Mondays, 9:30 P.M. EST

Average Nielsen rating: 20.7 (placed #20 for the season among all shows on television)

CBS Monday night line-up: *Gunsmoke, Here's Lucy, Mayberry RFD, The Doris Day Show, The Carol Burnett Show*

Competing against *The Doris Day Show* was a movie of the week on NBC, while ABC premiered *NFL Monday Night Football*.

CAST:

Doris Day (Doris Martin); Rose Marie (Myrna Gibbons); Paul Smith (Ron Harvey); McLean Stevenson (Michael Nicholson); Philip Brown (Billy Martin); Tod Starke (Toby Martin).

REVIEWS:

"*The Doris Day Show* should get the nod for sheer grit if for nothing else. [I]t has survived two theme changes and now places the star in an urban setting.

"The preemer struck no bright sparks with the exception of Kaye Ballard's florid portrayal as Miss Day's new Italian landlady. Miss Day is still a one-note (poignancy) actress, and producer-writers Elinson and Paul did very little to enlarge upon her talents.... Miss Day could use stronger character support."—*Variety*, September 23, 1970

Publicity shot, 1971 (Jerry Ohlinger's Movie Material Store, Inc.).

The third season found Doris Martin and her sons moving off the ranch and into an apartment above Pallucci's Italian Restaurant in San Francisco. The Palluccis (played by Kaye Ballard and Bernie Kopell), as well as nemesis Mr. Jarvis (Billy DeWolfe, Day's co-star in *Tea for Two* and *Lullaby of Broadway*), joined the cast as her neighbors. Doris continued working at *Today's World*.

Yet another opening credits sequence was made for the new season, retaining the "Qué Será, Será" theme song. Doris ran down the spiral stairway of her apartment in the first shot, while scenes of her in San Francisco and the main cast were featured. The opening was stylish with quick, split-second, zoom-in repeat cuts unlike anything from that era.

Another item of interest was the arrival of ABC's *Monday Night Football*. Scheduled opposite *The Doris Day Show*, it was arguably the series' strongest competition during its run. "Pro Football Tackles Doris Day," *TV Guide* predicted prematurely in September 1970. While *Monday Night Football* drew a large audience, *The Doris Day Show* prevailed and placed higher than its rival in this and next season's year-end Nielsen ratings.

EPISODES:

Doris Finds an Apartment (September 14, 1970)

Doris decides to move into San Francisco and finds an apartment over Pallucci's Italian Restaurant. Moving day turns into an unplanned party and Mr. Pallucci cancels the lease. He changes his mind after the boys compliment him that he makes the best pizza.

Featuring: Kaye Ballard as Angie Pallucci, Bernie Kopell as Louie Pallucci, Gene Dynarski as Moving Man #1, Jon Kowal as Moving Man #2, Carol Worthington as the Welcome Lady, Gordon Jump as the Captain, Joe Hoover as Co-Pilot; *Writers:* Jack Elinson, Norman Paul; *Director:* Denver Pyle.

The Feminist (September 21, 1970)

Ron is attacked by a feminist after trying to secure the serialization rights to her book. Doris attempts to get them by passing off as a feminist. But when the author is wooed by the male editor of *Newsmonth*, she changes her feelings toward men.

Featuring: Jason Evers as David Cowley, Elvia Allman as Harriet Henderson, Lavina Dawson as Clara, Robert Shayne as Andrew McIntyre, Ralph Montgomery as Waiter; *Writers:* Norman Paul, Jack Elinson; *Director:* Denver Pyle.

How Can I Ignore the Man Next Door? (September 28, 1970)

Mr. Jarvis unknowingly moves in next door to Doris. When she invites Jarvis in for tea, he slips on a skateboard, throwing his back out. While he is recuperating, Doris tries to adjust his bed, but he gets caught in it. After he squeezes out, his back realigns.

Featuring: Billy De Wolfe as Mr. Jarvis; *Writer:* Budd Grossman; *Director:* Denver Pyle.

Dinner for One (October 5, 1970)

Doris tries to help the Palluccis' slow business by convincing food critic Dudley Grey to dine there. Grey, however, makes his visits incognito. The group caters to a man they believe is the food critic while Grey is ignored.

Featuring: Kaye Ballard as Angie Pallucci, Bernie Kopell as Louie Pallucci,

Stubby Kaye as the Panhandler, Robert Emhardt as Dudley Grey, Eldon Quick as Perry Ferguson, Martin Ashe as the Chauffeur; *Writers:* Jack Elinson, Norman Paul; *Director:* Denver Pyle.

Doris Leaves Today's World (two-part episode, October 12 and October 19, 1970)

William Tyler returns and lures Doris away from the magazine to be his personal secretary. Several times Tyler calls and asks Doris to join him at meetings in different parts of the world. But it's when Toby is missing at home while Doris is in Greece that she decides to quit and return to her job at *Today's World*.

Featuring: Lew Ayres as William Tyler, Teru Shimada as Mr. Orokumu, Richard Angarola as Mr. Constantine, John Stuart as Jameson, J. Pat Cranshaw as Fred, Rob Hathaway as Tom Roberts, Tamara Mosahid as Dancer; *Writers:* Jack Elinson, Norman Paul; *Director:* Reza Badiyi.

The Fashion Show (October 26, 1970)

Doris agrees to model a new line of fashions by designer Montagne that the magazine is covering. Myrna unknowingly invites a spy from another fashion house, who steals the final piece. Montagne quickly concocts a gown out of a garment bag, and receives raves for his collection.

Featuring: Johnny Haymer as Montagne, Miguel Landa as Jacques Giroux, Harriet Medin as Marie; *Writers:* Jack Elinson, Norman Paul; *Director:* Reza Badiyi.

Lost and Found (November 2, 1970)

When Myrna realizes she must have left a news article at a club, she and Doris try to find it. The club is open only for go-go dancer auditions, so Doris tries out while Myrna attempts to finds the article. They later locate it in a dumpster.

Featuring: Buddy Lewis as Mr. Vincent, Jerry Crews as Stage Manager, Jade Manhatten as Girl #1, Kitty Malone as Girl #2; *Writers:* Norman Paul, Jack Elinson; *Director:* William Wiard.

Duke the Performer (November 9, 1970)

Duke decides to become a nightclub performer and asks Doris for help. The nightclub owner sees the pair rehearsing and asks both of them to bring their act to the club. On their opening night, Doris fakes laryngitis to prove Duke can do the act on his own.

Featuring: Larry Storch as Duke Farentino, Norman Alden as Nicky Burke, Marie Roe as Duchess #1, Dean Myles as Duchess #2, Chick Casey as Waiter; *Writers:* Fred S. Fox, Seaman Jacobs; *Director:* William Wiard.

Doris the Spy (November 16, 1970)

Doris arrives at the airport after collecting recipes for an article. She mistakenly takes another person's valise containing top secret government plans. Doris is then taken into custody by federal agents who believe she is a spy.

Featuring: John Mc-Giver as Chief, Estelle Winwood as Mrs. McDougal, Carol Worthington as Ethel, James Sikking as Bowers, John Kroger as Nelson, B.J. Mason as Foster, Bernie Kuby as Lab Man, Kaye Stewart as Emma; *Writer:* Budd Grossman; *Director:* Reza Badiyi.

Tony Bennett Is Eating Here (November 23, 1970)

A nervous Doris interviews singer Tony Bennett and then arranges for him to dine at Pallucci's so that he can enjoy a meal without in-

Tony Bennett appeared as himself in a 1970 episode (from the collection of Matt Tunia).

terruption from fans. But Angie tells a few friends and Bennett ends up being overwhelmed by autograph seekers.

Featuring: Tony Bennett as Himself, Kaye Ballard as Angie Pallucci, Bernie Kopell as Louie Pallucci, Jerome Guardino as Man, Joan Lemmo as Woman #1, Bunny Summers as Woman #2, Lou Massad as Waiter; *Writers:* Jack Elinson, Norman Paul; *Director:* Reza Badiyi.

Cousin Charlie (November 30, 1970)

Doris' content vagabond cousin Charlie stops in for a visit. She arranges for Charlie to work as a salesman for the magazine where he becomes a driven, power-hungry businessman. When he realizes he isn't truly happy, he quits and returns to his drifting lifestyle.

Featuring: Van Johnson as Charlie Webb, Read Morgan as the Policeman, Peter Hobbs as Mr. Donovan, Henry Hunter as Mr. Williams; *Writer:* Budd Grossman; *Director:* William Wiard.

Love Makes the Pizza Go 'Round (December 7, 1970)

Doris learns Angie and Louie have been so busy that the romance in their marriage is fizzling. She attempts to put some spice into the marriage by fixing up Angie, but Louie thinks Angie is having an affair.

Featuring: Kaye Ballard as Angie Pallucci, Bernie Kopell as Louie Pallucci, Charles Circillo as Mario, Paula Victor as the Fortune Teller; *Writer:* Budd Grossman; *Director:* William Wiard.

Buck Visits the Big City (December 14, 1970)

While on a weekend visit, Doris persuades Buck to retire to San Francisco.

She arranges a party for him and Buck meets a retired man who is equally bored. Buck hires the man to help him on the farm and returns to the country.

Featuring: Denver Pyle as Buck, King Moody as Policeman, John Gallaudet as George Stoner, Iris Adrian as Roxie, Sylvia Hayes as Woman, Geraldine Ewing as Helen; *Writer:* Bud Grossman; *Director:* William Wiard.

It's Christmas Time in the City (December 21, 1970)

When Doris invites Mr. Jarvis to her Christmas party, he declines, and threatens to report her to the police if it gets too noisy. However, when he hears Christmas carols coming from the party, he has a change of heart and asks Doris if he can join them.

Featuring: Kaye Ballard as Angie Pallucci, Billy DeWolfe as Mr. Jarvis, Denver Pyle as Buck, Bernie Kopell as Louie Pallucci, Carol Worthington as Ethel, John Lawrence as Santa Claus; *Writers:* Jack Elinson, Norman Paul; *Director:* Denver Pyle.

Doris vs. Pollution (December 28, 1970)

Doris writes an article against air pollution emitting from a chemical plant in which Col. Fairburn is chairman. After his prized fish begin dying, Col. Fairburn not only approves the story, but orders changes at the plant.

Featuring: Edward Andrews as Col. Fairburn, Carol Worthington as Ethel, James Sikking as Mr. Sutton, Kay Kuter as Nursery Man, Jerome Guardino as Cab Driver, Owen Bush as Serviceman, Eddie Baker as Driver, Donald Newsome as Man; *Writers:* Jack Elinson, Norman Paul; *Director:* Denver Pyle.

The Forward Pass (January 11, 1971)

Ron uses Doris to obtain an interview with famous quarterback Joe Garrison. The football player postpones the interview with Ron, leaving him alone with Doris in his apartment. He chases Doris and ends up breaking his leg.

Featuring: Dick Gautier as Joe Garrison, Gordon Jump as Man #2, Tony Giorgio as Maitre d', Gavin Mooney as First Reporter, Tom Stewart as Second Reporter, Vern Rowe as Hawker, Michael Michaelian as Man #1, Paula Warner as First Girl, Beverly Ralston as Second Girl, Marty Koppenhafer as Third Girl, Karen Bouchard as Fourth Girl, Carollyn DeVore as Fifth Girl; *Writer:* Budd Grossman; *Director:* William Wiard.

Duke's Girlfriend (January 18, 1971)

Duke tells Doris he is going to marry socialite Alison Otis Peabody, but Doris believes she is really a gold-digging phony. Ron poses as a wealthy bachelor to woo Alison. When the pair are on a date, Duke sees them and discovers the truth.

Featuring: Larry Storch as Duke Farentino, Charlene Polite as Alison Otis Peabody, Alan DeWitt as Salesman, Lou Massad as Waiter, Karen Bouchard as Cigarette Girl; *Writers:* Jack Elinson, Norman Paul; *Director:* Peter Baldwin.

Jarvis' Uncle (January 25, 1971)

Mr. Jarvis' Uncle Randolph visits, and Doris is delighted to learn he is not like his nephew. Mr. Jarvis mistakenly thinks Randolph and Doris are planning to marry. Randolph lectures his nephew and Mr. Jarvis soon displays a relaxed side of himself.

Featuring: Billy DeWolfe as Mr. Jarvis and as Uncle Randolph "Randy" Jarvis, Sylvia Hayes as the Waitress; *Writer:* Budd Grossman; *Director:* Reza Badiyi.

Lassoin' LeRoy (February 1, 1971)

After LeRoy wins $20,000 at a rodeo, he begins spending it carelessly. Doris takes action by hiding the cash in her broken toaster until she can get a cashier's check from the bank. Unfortunately, the boys give Ethel the toaster for a library fund drive.

Featuring: Jim Hampton as LeRoy B. Simpson, Carol Worthington as Ethel, Paul Sorenson as John Wilkinson, Winifred Coffin as Clara Bixby, Dan Scott as Tex Bradshaw, Vern Rowe as Waiter, Roland "Rusty" Loudermilk as Red Davis, Jane Aull as Woman, De De Young as Girl Photographer, Kitty Malone as Souvenir Girl; *Writers:* Jack Elinson, Norman Paul; *Director:* Peter Baldwin.

Colonel Fairburn, Jr. (February 8, 1971)

When Mr. Nicholson leaves for a convention, Col. Fairburn's son, Clifford, is named managing editor. But the clean-cut young man is really a hippie who tries to turn the magazine into a liberal, hip publication for the younger generation.

Featuring: Edward Andrews as Col. Fairburn, Rick Ely as Clifford Fairburn, Larry Gelman as Terry Madden, Nancy Kerby as Girl #1, Karen Specht as Girl #2, Annette Molen as Girl #3, Murray Polluck as Man, Louise Lane as Woman; *Writers:* Budd Grossman, Don Genson; *Director:* Lee Philips.

Billy's First Date (February 15, 1971)

Billy plans to go to the school dance with the prettiest girl in his class. The two parents decide they both will chaperone. At the dance, the youngsters find they have nothing in common, unlike their parents.

Featuring: Ricardo Montalban as Richard Cordavan, Lisa Gerritsen as Sue Ann Cordavan, Alene Towne as Mrs. Gessford, Carol Worthington as Ethel, Ceil Cabot as Hostess; *Writers:* Jack Elinson, Norman Paul; *Director:* Reza Badiyi.

Doris Goes to Hollywood (February 22, 1971)

Doris wins a Doris Day look alike contest and is mistaken for Day at the studio by many people, including Henry Fonda. His biggest fan, Doris tries to peek at Fonda but she falls into a water trough. At that time, Day arrives to meet her drenched look-alike.

Featuring: Henry Fonda as Himself, Oscar Beregi as Otto Von Braunstein, Joey Forman as Harry Maret, Paula Victor as Secretary, William Tregoe as Mr.

Kaye Ballard (middle) and Bernie Kopell were Angie and Louie Pallucci, owners of Doris Martin's apartment in seasons three and four (Jerry Ohlinger's Movie Material Store, Inc.).

Conroy, Ralph Montgomery as Security Policeman, Bill Martel as Guard, Eddie Baker as Indian; *Writers:* Jack Elinson, Norman Paul, Don Genson; *Director:* William Wiard.

Skiing Anyone? (March 1, 1971)

Myrna sprains her ankle while on a skiing weekend with Doris. Her treating physician and Doris start going out, but Doris feels guilty not staying with Myrna. The doctor then arranges for a group of guys to keep Myrna company.

Featuring: John Gavin as Dr. Jeffrey Forbes, Miguel Landa as Jacques Dubois, Bob Kenneally as Room Clerk, Robert Shayne as Mr. Gilroy, Michael Sterns as Bellhop, Scott Perry as Bill Walley, Harper Carter as Jerry Clark; *Writers:* Jack Elinson, Norman Paul; *Director:* Reza Badiyi.

The Father-Son Weekend (March 8, 1971)

After Buck has to bow out of bringing Toby on a father-son weekend camp-out, Doris takes his place, despite her gender. The pair forge on and wins races and fishing competitions and finally the father-son trophy.

Featuring: John Astin as Jim Keatley, John Lupton as Charles Rogers, Richard

Steele as Bradley Keatley, Ted Foulkes as Dean Rogers, H.M. Wynant as Gary Hansen, Billy McMickle as Chris Hansen; *Writer:* Budd Grossman; *Director:* Reza Badiyi.

Young Love (March 15, 1971)

Doris' young niece April believes she may be pregnant. At a party, her boyfriend makes a joke about April's condition which she takes wrongly. She learns she isn't pregnant, but is unsure of her relationship with Peter. After talking to Doris, April returns to Peter.

Featuring: Meredith Baxter as April, Michael Burns as Peter, Bobby Griffin as Coleman, Brenda Sykes as Dulcie, Abbi Henderson as Erica, Dick Van Patton as April's Father; *Writers:* Bob Sand, Bruce Bilson; *Director:* Norman Tokar.

(This episode was an unused pilot for a spin-off series starring Meredith Baxter.)

Fourth Season 1971-72
Mondays, 9:30 P.M. EST

Average Nielsen rating: 21.2 (placed #23 for the season among all shows on television)

CBS Monday night line-up: *Gunsmoke, Here's Lucy, The Doris Day Show, My Three Sons, Arnie*

Airing opposite *The Doris Day Show* was a movie of the week on NBC; ABC showed *NFL Monday Night Football.*

CAST:

Doris Day (Doris Martin); John Dehner (Cy Bennett); Jackie Joseph (Jackie Parker).

REVIEWS:

"During the off-season *The Doris Day Show* shucked its old format for a new one…. The preem show made one wonder why. The new alignment has star Day (looking marvelous, incidentally) as a career girl—associate editor of a magazine— and seems to be seeking a format somewhat akin to the Mary Tyler Moore skein…. [Based on the premiere episode], the show has no place to go but up. Dehner is no [Ed] Asner—and adjustments in the concept of the role are immediately in order. More to the point, the writing level needs upgrading to get some basically funny relations going between the principals—or else Miss Day could be in trouble."—*Variety*, September 22, 1971

The fourth season saw the fourth and final format change in the series. Doris Martin was promoted to associate editor at *Today's World*, working for city editor

Cyril (Cy) Bennett (played by John Dehner). Jackie Joseph came aboard the show as Mr. Bennett's secretary, Jackie Parker. Doris became a single working woman without children; gone were the characters Ron Harvey, Michael Nicholson, and Myrna Gibbons.

As for the unresolved dismissal of characters, one answer is the possibility that the series moved ahead several years between seasons three and four. In that time span, several things may have happened which explains the show's format change: Doris' father passed away; the boys have grown up and are living on their own; Ron Harvey and Myrna Gibbons either left the magazine on their own or were fired for their inefficiency; and Mr. Nicholson moved to another job in the journalism field.

Some critics felt this modification was to make the series similar to CBS's *The Mary Tyler Moore Show*, which featured a working woman with no husband or children. While the Moore series debuted in 1970, it ranked lower in the Nielsen ratings than *The Doris Day Show*. In fact, it only became a hit in the 1972-73 season—the same year *The Doris Day Show* changed its format.

EPISODES:

And Here's ... Doris (September 13, 1971)

Mr. Bennett pressures Doris into getting him an appearance on TV's popular late-night talk show. Mr. Bennett appears with a case of stage fright and accidentally destroys the show's set, but awards Doris with her own office.

Featuring: Bob Crane as Bob Carter, Jack Wells as Jim, Joseph Mell as Jacob Berns, Alan DeWitt as Prof. Frisbee; *Writer:* Laurence Marks; *Director:* Norman Tokar.

Mr. and Mrs. Raffles (September 20, 1971)

When stolen jewels are planted on Mr. Jarvis, he and Doris are caught returning them to the store. While in jail, they are confronted by a couple who are the real jewel thieves and are asked to take part in a heist. Doris and Mr. Jarvis agree and are cleared when the police arrive to arrest the real thieves.

Featuring: Billy De Wolfe as Mr. Jarvis, Ken Lynch as Detective Broder, H.M. Wynant as Rodney, Lynnette Mettey as Dolly; *Writer:* Arthur Julian; *Director:* Norman Tokar.

When in Rome, Don't (September 27, 1971)

While in Rome with Jackie, Doris falls in love with Carlo and is heartbroken when her opinion of some paintings by famed artist Benadetti destroys the romance. When Doris and Jackie are on the return flight home, Doris not only discovers Mr. Bennett on the same flight, but that Carlo is also Benadetti.

Featuring: Cesare Danova as Carlo Benadetti, Dick Patterson as Albert, Lew Palter as Pietro, Ryan MacDonald as Clerk; *Writer:* Richard M. Powell; *Director:* Jerry London.

Charity Begins in the Office
(October 4, 1971)

Mr. Bennett volunteers Doris's help to Mrs. Fairburn with a charity ball. Doris discovers that consultant Roger Sidney is overcharging services, then pocketing the difference. She exposes Roger, who pays the money he embezzled and resigns from future fund raising.

Featuring: Elvia Allman as Mrs. Fairburn, Joey Forman as Roger Sidney, Estelle Winwood as Rhoda, Will B. Abel as Gordon, Winifred Coffin as Agnes; *Writer:* Phil Sharp; *Director:* William Wiard.

A Weighty Problem (October 11, 1971)

Doris and Angie go to a health spa to watch Mrs. Miggins, the wife of a soon-to-be-released convict who stole $2,000,000 that was never

John Dehner and Jackie Joseph (right) joined *The Doris Day Show* in its fourth season (Jerry Ohlinger's Movie Material Store, Inc.).

recovered. Angie sniffs out a pizza she saw Mrs. Miggins buy, hidden in a corner stone of the building—along with the money.

Featuring: Kaye Ballard as Angie Pallucci, Iris Adrian as Mrs. Miggins, Rob Hathaway as Bellboy; *Writer:* Arthur Julian; *Director:* Bruce Bilson.

The People's Choice (October 18, 1971)

After Doris discovers councilman Sam Appleton has an illegal bookmaking ring in her neighborhood laundromat, she and Mr. Bennett convince Mr. Jarvis to run for a seat on the city council in the upcoming election.

Featuring: Billy De Wolfe as Mr. Jarvis, Harold Peary as Sam Appleton, June Wilkinson as Laura, Russell Gossett as Man; *Writer:* Arthur Julian; *Director:* Jerry London.

A Fine Romance (October 25, 1971)

While researching a story on computer dating, Doris befriends a lonely man sent by the service. However, he feels Doris is out for his money and reports her to the police. To investigate Doris, Sgt. Bill Winston goes undercover, posing as a man sent by the agency, and the two begin dating.

Featuring: Robert Lansing as Sgt. Bill Winston, John Fiedler as Harvey Krantz, Bunny Summers as Lucy, Michael Fox as Capt. Mallory, Gordon Jump as Mr. Robinson, David Frank as Harry, Larry McCormick as Jim; *Writer:* Laurence Marks; *Director:* Norman Tokar.

The Albatross (November 1, 1971)

Cousin Charlie returns and learns that Doris has given a small elephant to Mr. Bennett. Acting as a courier, Charlie had hidden microfilm in it that he was to deliver to government agents. They retrieve the elephant but are confronted by spies who take the elephant from them. A wall hanging falls to end the theft.

Featuring: Van Johnson as Charlie Webb, Felice Orlandi as Antoine, Ricco Cattani as Boris, Sabrina Scharf as Valerie Becker, Howard Curtis as Hans, Paul Sorenson as Bartender; *Writer:* Arthur Julian; *Director:* Irving J. Moore.

Have I Got a Fellow For You (November 8, 1971)

Angie plays cupid, first fixing Doris up with Charlie, a practical joker plumber from Mason City, Iowa, then with a handsome airline pilot. Doris and the pilot get together but are interrupted when Charlie stops by to tell Doris about the plumber's convention.

Featuring: Kaye Ballard as Angie Pallucci, Alan Hale, Jr. as Charlie, Nico Minardos as Nico, John Stephenson as Tim, Barbara Nichols as Mrs. Hollister, with Tony Cristino; *Writer:* Arthur Julian; *Director:* William Wiard.

Publicity shot, 1972.

To England with Doris (November 15, 1971)

Doris travels to England to acquire the magazine rights to Sir Robert Kingsley's book. He declines the offer but asks Doris out. The two began spending time together, and Sir Robert proposes marriage.

Featuring: Jon Cypher as Sir Robert Kingsley, Diana Chesney as Mother, Laurie Main as Father, Dick Wilson as Callahan, Towyna Thomas as Maid; *Writer:* Laurence Marks; *Director:* Lee Philips.

The Sheik of Araby (November 22, 1971)

Doris is mistakenly kidnapped by rebels who threaten to kill her if their king doesn't abdicate and return their land to its people. When the rebels ask her to leave, Doris refuses, having sided with them. The king abdicates and the country becomes a democracy.

Featuring: Dick Gautier as Omar, Richard Angarola as Ben Ali, Vanda Barra as the Queen, Henry Corden as the King, James Lemp as Guard #2, Joe Lo Presti as Guard #1; *Writer:* Arthur Julian; *Director:* Richard Kinon.

Doris and the Doctor (November 29, 1971)

After receiving a medical bill, Mr. Bennett orders Doris to investigate Dr. Peter Lawrence while writing an article on the high cost

Peter Lawford played Doris Martin's love interest when she wasn't dating others—namely Patrick O'Neal (Jerry Ohlinger's Movie Material Store, Inc.).

of medical treatment. But after spending much time with him, Doris concludes that Dr. Lawrence earns every penny he charges.

Featuring: Peter Lawford as Dr. Peter Lawrence, Paula Victor as Lady Patient, Lew Palter as Luigi; *Writer:* Laurence Marks; *Director:* William Wiard.

Happiness Is Not Being Fired (December 6, 1971)

Doris is fired for exposing a housing development scandal in which Col. Fairburn was a major investor. Angie gains access for Doris to preview an exhibit given by her cousin Vito. There they botch an attempted robbery and Mr. Bennett is forced to rehire Doris to acquire the story.

Featuring: Kaye Ballard as Angie Pallucci, Bruce Kirby as Vito, Joe Ruskin as Harry, Lou Krugman as Phony Vito, Richard Hurst as Mechanic, Donald Newsome as Policeman; *Writer:* Arthur Julian; *Director:* Irving J. Moore.

Whodunit, Doris (December 13, 1971)

Harry Miller, disguised as Santa Claus, is found holding a gun next to a murder victim. He denies committing the murder, but when the police learn the victim owed Miller money, he is charged. Doris discovers that the victim's cousin, Ralph, committed the murder.

Featuring: Charles Nelson Reilly as Ralph Mantley, Cliff Norton as Harry Miller, Ken Lynch as Detective Broder, Kennedy W. Gordy as Boy, Walter Sande as Head Santa; *Writer:* Gary Belkin; *Director:* Marc Daniels.

The Wings of an Angel (December 27, 1971)

Doris receives a fan letter from jailed notorious mobster Frankie Fury. When Frankie is pardoned, he gives Doris his story so that it may help the kids of this generation. But she discovers the taped confession is him rambling about a dog.

Featuring: Marc Lawrence as Frankie Fury, David Doyle as Warden McPherson, Jack Griffin as Guard, Dick Patterson as Albert; *Writer:* Richard M. Powell; *Director:* Richard Kinon.

Doris at Sea (January 3, 1972)

After Dr. Lawrence performs an emergency operation on a famous Greek billionaire, Doris cares for the patient, trying to get an interview. But the Greek falls in love with Doris and tries to win her over, not knowing about her relationship with Dr. Lawrence.

Featuring: Peter Lawford as Dr. Peter Lawrence, Karl Bruck as Captain, Anthony Caruso as Nicholas Kavros, Ben Wrigley as First Reporter, Larry McCormick as Jim, David Frank as Harry, Gavin James as Pilot, Vern Rowe as Messenger, Tom Stewart as Second Reporter; *Writer:* Laurence Marks; *Director:* Marc Daniels.

The Sorrow of Sangapur (January 10, 1972)

While on a train ride, a group of rebels and a shady inspector attempt to steal the Sorrow of Sangapur jewel from the Maharajah and his wife. Doris and Mr. Bennett end up with the jewel, which the Maharajah gives back to the people of India.

Featuring: Lloyd Bochner as Stephen, Henry Corden as Maharajah, Larry Hovis as Hassan, Arlene Martel as Maharani, Ben Wright as Medoc; *Writer:* Richard Powell; *Director:* William Wiard.

The Blessed Event (January 17, 1972)

When Angie and Louie leave on a trip, Doris watches their expectant dog Sophie. She takes her to the office where Sophie tears Mr. Bennett's pants, and this results in him losing a new job offer.

Featuring: Kaye Ballard as Angie Pallucci, Bernie Kopell as Louie Pallucci, Henry Hunter as Randolph Chandler, Paula Victor as Nina, Joan Lemmo as Stella Nordimi; *Writer:* Arthur Julian; *Director:* Bruce Bilson.

Who's Got the Trenchcoat (January 24, 1972)

Jackie buys Mr. Bennett a new trenchcoat for his birthday and donates his old one to a mission thrift shop. Mr. Bennett tries to retrieve his old coat and discovers the man wearing it was once a respected newspaperman.

Featuring: Regis Toomey as Charley Smith, Charles Wagenheim as Milt Schnitzer, Paula Victor as Sister Clara, Ben Wrigley as Harry, Larry McCormick as Jim, Louise Lane as First Secretary, Geraldine Ewing as Second Secretary; *Writer:* Don Genson; *Director:* William Wiard.

Doris' House Guest (January 31, 1972)

Thelma, a relation of Col. Fairburn, stays at Doris's place while mending a broken heart. Thelma's fiancé Henry attempts to make up with her, but she ignores him. To make Thelma jealous, Doris and Henry pretend they are dating.

Featuring: Billy De Wolfe as Mr. Jarvis, Barbara Hale as Thelma King, Jack Dodson as Henry Thurston; *Writer:* Arthur Julian; *Director:* Bruce Bilson.

The Crapshooter Who Would Be King (February 7, 1972)

Doris and Mr. Bennett travel to the Mediterranean to interview the ruler of a small principality. But Doris is misled when a butler, Bruno, poses as the prince's distant cousin. Doris and Bruno go to the casino, where he breaks the bank playing craps.

Featuring: John Banner as Bruno, Lee Bergere as Rupert, Henry Corden as Emile, Richard Angarola as Antoine, Lou Massad as Ricardo, Sid Conrad as Man; *Writer:* Richard M. Powell; *Director:* Edward H. Feldman.

Cover Girl (February 21, 1972)

Doris persuades Carlo Benadetti to design a cover for *Today's World* to increase circulation. But Carlo is much too busy entertaining Doris and sightseeing to paint the cover. When Doris and co-worker Matt act as they are lovers to force Carlo into finishing the work, it nearly backfires. Carlo forgives her and delivers a masterpiece.

Featuring: Cesare Danova as Carlo Benadetti, Rory Calhoun as Matt, Norman Stuart as Dr. Backschneider, Larry McCormick as Reporter; *Writer:* Laurence Marks; *Director:* Bill Wiard.

Gowns by Louie (February 28, 1972)

Doris persuades snobbish French designer Jacques Moreau to allow her couturier's creations in an international fashion show; however, Doris' designer, Louie, is really a tailor and dry cleaner. Impressed with the collection, Jacques asks Louie to be his partner.

Featuring: Werner Klemperer as Jacques Moreau, Joseph Mell as Louie Salkawitz, Lester Fletcher as Claude, Charles Cirillo as Vito; *Writer:* Arthur Julian; *Director:* William Wiard.

There's a Horse Thief in Every Family Tree (March 6, 1972)

When a horse thief written about by Doris turns out to be the ancestor of a prominent San Francisco family, she finds her job in jeopardy. Doris tries to speak to the family, but she is mistaken as the newly hired maid.

Featuring: Harriet E. MacGibbon as Mrs. Townsend, Robert Emhardt as Mr. Townsend, Sandy Kenyon as Randolph, Ceil Cabot as Cook; *Writer:* Phil Sharp; *Director:* Norman Tokar.

Fifth Season 1972–73
Mondays, 9:30 P.M. EST

Average Nielsen rating: under 20.0; did not rank in the year's Top 25 shows.

CBS Monday night line-up: *Gunsmoke, Here's Lucy, The Doris Day Show, The New Bill Cosby Show*

Airing opposite *The Doris Day Show* was a movie of the week on NBC while ABC showed *NFL Monday Night Football.*

CAST:

Doris Day (Doris Martin); John Dehner (Cy Bennett); Jackie Joseph (Jackie Parker)

REVIEWS:

"This premiere show was a hark-back to those days when Miss Day labored in the Hollywood vineyards with Rock Hudson. There was in the show the veiled implication that [Peter] Lawford might be bedding the liberated Miss Day, but it was handled with the sly caution of a 1930's society comedy.

"It is indicative of the febrile plotting that Miss Day's ambiguous virginity looms important at all in these times."—*Variety,* September 20, 1972

The previous season's format continued unchanged into the fifth and final season of *The Doris Day Show.* Another opening credit was made (the series' fourth), with Doris Martin walking down her spiral stairway in a black dress to open her front door, and scenes from the fashion show episode replaced the previous credit montage.

After the Palluccis sold the apartment building to concentrate on their restaurant business, Mr. Jarvis eventually purchased the building to become Doris's landlord this season. Doris Martin's main romantic involvements included Dr. Peter Lawrence (Peter Lawford) and Jonathan Rusk (Patrick O'Neal, who co-starred with Doris in *Where Were You When the Lights Went Out?*), a foreign correspondent. Throughout the season, viewers wondered which—or if—she would chose between the two. By the end of the season, Doris and Jonathan announced their marriage plans.

EPISODES:

No More Advice ... Please (September 11, 1972)

Dr. Peter Lawrence mistakenly discovers that the seemingly solid romance between him and Doris is shattered by an anthropology professor who has written a best-selling novel. Mr. Bennett encourages Peter to make Doris jealous by going on a date with another woman.

Featuring: Peter Lawford as Dr. Peter Lawrence, Don Chastain as Eric Stewart, Luis de Cordova as Jules, Melissa Whittaker as Melissa; *Writer:* Laurence Marks; *Director:* Marc Daniels.

The Great Talent Raid (September 18, 1972)

After becoming the women's editor of *Prestige* magazine, Doris yearns for *Today's World* and attempts to return. She plots to have various *Prestige* employees defect to *Today's World* and vice versa, causing turmoil within the magazines.

Featuring: Billy De Wolfe as Himself, Ralph Story as John Scott, Glynn Turman as Al Davis, Luis de Cordova as Jules, De De Young as Ellen, John Kroger as Jim, Tom Stewart as Harry; *Writers:* William Raynor, Myles Wilder; *Director:* William Wiard.

Just a Miss Understanding (September 25, 1972)

Doris can't afford a custom made valise for Peter when her work bonus is less than expected. She quietly moonlight a job as the radio advice announcer Miss Understanding from midnight to five in the morning.

Featuring: Peter Lawford as Dr. Peter Lawrence, Joe Hoover as Jim, Jack DeMave as Dave Genson; *Writer:* Charlotte Brown; *Director:* Lee Philips.

The Press Secretary (October 2, 1972)

Doris takes a leave of absence from *Today's World* to work as a press secretary to a Congressional candidate (and former lover) Jonathan Rusk. She then finds herself fending off the advances of her new boss and the unethical demands of her old one.

Featuring: Patrick O'Neal as Jonathan Rusk, Julie Adams as Louise Rusk; *Writer:* Laurence Marks; *Director:* Richard Kinon.

Peeping Tom (October 9, 1972)

Mr. Bennett is arrested in an attempt to help Doris catch a Peeping Tom. Mr. Bennett loses the Citizen of the Year award, but is given a citation for helping solve the case.

Featuring: Larry Hovis as Larry Madison, John Stephenson as Sgt. Murdock, Joseph Perry as Sam; *Writer:* Arthur Julian; *Director:* Marc Daniels.

Forgive and Forget (October 16, 1972)

Doris writes an article about forgiveness after some of her married friends are divorcing. But several married women are angered at the single Doris since she cannot relate to a married woman. When Peter makes an all-night house call to an attractive woman's home, Doris erroneously believes he slept with the woman.

Featuring: Peter Lawford as Dr. Peter Lawrence, Ginny Golden as Toni Rolfe, Noah Keen as Dr. Jerry Kruger, Murray Pollack as Walter Mercer, Jo De Winter as Marcia Kruger, Alene Towne as Louise Mercer, John Kroger as Herb Franklin; *Writer:* Laurence Marks; *Director:* William Wiard.

Debt of Honor (October 23, 1972)

When Doris learns she owes $1100 on a note she co-signed for a friend, she tries to collect old debts from other friends, including one from the man she had sold her car but never paid her.

Featuring: Richard Schaal as Greg Mitchell, Sid Melton as Al, Ed Begley, Jr., as Wally, Luis de Cordova as Maitre D'; *Writer:* Phil Sharp; *Director:* Peter Lawford.

Jimmy the Gent (November 6, 1972)

Doris goes undercover in a hospital to interview patient Jimmy the Gent, a notorious safecracker. Dr. Lawrence discovers Doris' scheme and orders her to stop. She leaves to apologize to Jimmy, then discovers that Jimmy and his brother switched places so the former could commit burglaries.

Featuring: Peter Lawford as Dr. Peter Lawrence, Elvia Allman as Nurse Howard, Walter Burke as Jimmy, Charles Wagenheim as Jenkins, Florida Friebus as Miss Peabody; *Writers:* Laurie Samara, Courtney Andrews; *Director:* Marc Daniels.

The Music Man (November 13, 1972)

Doris becomes involved with Johnny Reb, a rising, younger rock star. Johnny announces their engagement without first telling Doris. She breaks off the romance, telling him she loves him, but is not in love with him.

Featuring: Paul Hampton as Johnny Reb, Eldon Wuick as Mr. Barton, Melissa Whittaker as Mrs. Barton, Anne Randall as Nancy, Ed Garner as Charlie; *Writer:* Laurence Marks; *Director:* William Wiard.

Detective Story (November 20, 1972)

Mr. Bennett is offered a scoop on a story that an Eastern European general is secretly planning to defect to the west. Doris doesn't believe it is true, but when the general actually defects, Mr. Bennett blames Doris for robbing him of the biggest story of the year.

Featuring: Roger C. Carmel as Gen. Nikoli Smaltzoff, Alan Oppenheimer as Marvin, Dave Morick as Guard #1, Joseph Perry as Guard #2, Lidia Kristen as Zelinka, Ford Lile as Reporter; *Writer:* Charlotte Brown; *Director:* Richard Kinon.

The Co-Op (November 27, 1972)

After the landlord dies, Doris attempts to get the building's tenants to purchase the building themselves and form a co-op. Mr. Jarvis purchases the building and automatically raises the rent. The tenants retaliate by calling him to repair things at inconvenient times. He lowers the rent in the end.

Featuring: Billy De Wolfe as Mr. Jarvis, Alan DeWitt as Lester Hansen, Henry Corden as Mr. Lohman, Lester Fletcher as Lance Baker, Paula Victor as Mrs. Lohman, Dan Keough as Mr. Sinclair, Misty Rowe as Mrs. Sinclair; *Writer:* Arthur Julian; *Director:* Roger Duchowny.

The Anniversary Gift (December 11, 1972)

Peter gives Doris an antique car to mark their one-year anniversary of their first date. "Clara" continually breaks down so Doris asks a mechanic if she should sell it. He tells Doris to talk to the car as she would a person or an animal. She does so and the car works well.

Featuring: Peter Lawford as Dr. Peter Lawrence, Richard Hurst as Herbie, Kay Stewart as Mrs. Winston, William Tregoe as Mr. Winston, Dick Van Patten as Sam; *Writer:* Arthur Julian; *Director:* Roger Duchowny.

The New Boss (December 18, 1972)

Doris replaces Mr. Bennett as editor-in-chief of *Today's World* when Col. Fairburn decides to give the magazine a fresh look. Col. Fairburn suggests Doris may be an ideal permanent editor, but she tells him Mr. Bennett is the only person for the job.

Featuring: Edward Andrews as Col. Fairburn, Jack Wells as Fred, Joe Hoover as Jim, John Myhers as Mr. Grainger, Ben Wrigley as Charlie; *Writer:* Laurence Marks; *Director:* Marc Daniels.

Follow That Dog (January 1, 1973)

A gangster hires Doris to watch his terrier dog for two weeks in exchange for a $10,000 donation to an animal clinic. Unknown to Doris, inside the terrier's collar there is a hidden key to a locker which contains a list of other gangsters. Another mobster, as well as the police, each plot to acquire the key by switching the terrier with look-alike dogs.

Featuring: Bruce Gordon as Benedict, Joe Ruskin as Harry, Paul Stewart as Cantrell, Jack Griffin as Adams, with James B. Sikking, Dave Morick and John Stephenson; *Writers:* William Raynor, Myles Wilder; *Director:* William Wiard.

The Hoax (January 8, 1973)

A talent scout offers Doris a job with his talent agency. She accepts the offer to investigate the matter for an article. When the scout learns that Doris is a magazine reporter, he arranges for a screen test and gets her a contract as a shampoo spokesperson. He confesses he is a scam artist, but has Doris bound to her contract to do the commercial.

Featuring: Andy Griffith as Mitch Folger, David Frank as Ozzie, Ryan MacDonald as James Waterhouse, Ceil Cabot as Woman, Alan Dewitt as Man, Read Morgan as George; *Writer:* Laurence Marks; *Director:* Lee Philips.

The Last Huzzah (January 15, 1973)

Today's World employee Sam Johnson turns 65 and is forced into mandatory retirement. Doris looks into the days Mr. Bennett missed over the past year due to health problems and threatens to turn him in to the board. Mr. Bennett decides to give Sam a consultant job with the magazine.

Featuring: Henry Jones as Sam Johnson, Dan Keough as Mike; *Writers:* Arthur Julian, Rick Mittleman; *Director:* Richard Kinon.

Hospital Benefit (January 22, 1973)

Doris offers to produce a fashion show fundraiser for the new hospital wing. Doris meets nurse Lois Frazer and believes she is having an affair with Dr. Lawrence. The fashion show is a hit and Doris learns not only is Lois Dr. Lawrence's former wife, but that there is no affair going on between them.

Featuring: Peter Lawford as Dr. Peter Lawrence, Lee Meriwether as Lois Frazer, Noah Keen as Dr. Robertson, Peggy Rea as Mrs. Dawson, Betty McGuire as Nurse, Jeffrey Mannix as Mannequin; *Writer:* Laurence Marks; *Director:* Roger Duchowny.

It's a Dog's Life (January 29, 1973)

Doris rescues a couple of stray dogs, but Mr. Jarvis won't allow her to keep them. After he learns that the animals sent to the shelter will be exterminated, Mr. Jarvis changes his mind and adopts one of the dogs.

Featuring: Billy De Wolfe as Mr. Jarvis, Henry Corden as Mr. Lohman, Ford Lile as the Policeman, Cliff Norton as the Animal Control Man, Biggest and Myra Muffin as the canines (actually two of Doris Day's dogs); *Writer:* Arthur Julian; *Director:* Roger Duchowny.

Family Magazine (February 5, 1973)

When Mr. Bennett discovers that Sir Robert Kingsley has written a new book, he schemes to obtain the magazine rights by rekindling the romance between Doris and Sir Robert. The couple decide to get back at Mr. Bennett by announcing their engagement and that Doris is leaving the magazine.

Featuring: Jon Cypher as Sir Robert Kingsley, Martin Ashe as Willoughby, Dick Wilson as Motel Manager, John Kroger as Jack; *Writers:* Don Genson, Laurence Marks; *Director:* Lee Philips.

A Small Cure for Big Alimony (February 12, 1973)

Mr. Bennett's ex-wife Donna announces she is about to remarry, which relieves Mr. Bennett of alimony payments. Mr. Bennett loans her and her fiancé $10,000 to open a restaurant. But when Donna learns he is a fraud and has made passes at Doris, the engagement is broken off.

Featuring: Norma Crane as Donna Bennett, Lee Bergere as Jeff O'Neal, Marcel Hillaire as George Moreau, Buddy Lewis as Artie; *Writer:* Arthur Julian; *Director:* Lee Philips.

The Magnificent Fraud (February 19, 1973)

Doris' Uncle August returns and tells Doris he hid an expensive, original painting in her suitcase. She and Mr. Bennett return the original and steal the forgery. The two then believe they had actually stolen the original painting. Uncle August admits to the plot, then Doris and Mr. Bennett replace the forgery with the original they took.

Featuring: Bernie Kopell as Uncle August, Dan Tobin as Vincent Bissel, Kay Kuter as Prof. Druten, Betty McGuire as Woman, Towyna Thomas as Maid, Martin Ashe as Butler; *Writers:* William Raynor, Myles Wilder; *Director:* Marc Daniels.

Meant for Each Other (February 26, 1973)

Jonathan Rusk returns from New York and proposes marriage to Doris, who accepts. When she sees Jonathan with another woman, she becomes jealous, but then later learns the woman was an interview. The couple decide to resolve the handling of their bi-coastal careers before marrying.

Featuring: Patrick O'Neal as Jonathan Rusk, Peter Hobbs as Roberts, Joe Ross as Mr. Wilson, Jack Wells as Announcer, Louise Lane as Nurse, Sharyn Wynters as Madame Singh; *Writers:* Courtney Andrews, Laurie Samara; *Director:* Roger Duchowny.

Welcome to Big Sur, Sir (March 5, 1973)

Doris and Jonathan plan a romantic weekend at Big Sur, and offers Jackie and her boyfriend Sid a ride. All the rooms are booked at Big Sur so Jackie bunks with Doris, and Sid with Jonathan. Mr. Bennett arrives, asking Doris for help with an article. When everyone leaves, Doris and Jonathan learn they have an extra day alone as a storm is bringing everything to a halt.

Featuring: Patrick O'Neal as Jonathan Rusk, Sid Melton as Sid, Paul Vaughn as Clerk; *Writers:* William Raynor, Myles Wilder; *Director:* William Wiard.

Byline ... Alias Doris (March 12, 1973)

Scotty, a fellow *Today's World* reporter, asks Doris for help on an article he's written. She rewrites it, and he is rewarded with a big assignment. When Doris helps Scotty again, she secures an exclusive. Mr. Bennett learns the truth and reprimands Doris for her actions.

Featuring: Joey Forman as Scotty, Paul Fix as Senator Bergson, Ceil Cabot as Melissa Murphy, Louise Fitch as Louise Bergson; *Writer:* Laurence Marks; *Director:* William Wiard.

Notes

—Buck Webb's address in the country where Doris Martin lived the first two seasons was 32 Mill Valley Road near the town of Cotina.

—The telephone number on the farm: 534-0711

—Doris Martin's Social Security number: 371-40-8208

—Doris Martin's bank account number: 232-949-642-026-559

—The address of Doris' apartment above Pallucci's Italian Restaurant was 965 North Parkway #207, San Francisco—on the corner of Jefferson.

—Doris' rent at the apartment: $140 a month since the apartment was above a restaurant and needed much fixing up when she moved in. Two stewardesses had lived there previously.

—Doris' beginning salary at *Today's World*: $85 a week.

—*Today's World* reporter Ron Harvey's real name was Rudolph Valentino Harvey—his mother had just seen the film *The Sheik* before his birth and was a Valentino fan.

—Number of *The Doris Day Show* episodes: 128.

—Number of episodes directed by co-star Denver Pyle before following with his popular role in TV's *the Dukes of Hazzard*: 10.

Some of Day's film co-stars also appeared in *The Doris Day Show*. Among them include:

—John McGiver (*The Glass Bottom Boat*) in "Doris the Spy"

—Mary Wickes (*On Moonlight Bay, By the Light of the Silvery Moon, I'll See You in My Dreams*) in "The Buddy"

—John Gavin (*Midnight Lace*) in "Skiing, Anyone?"

—Alan Hale, Jr. (*The West Point Story, Young at Heart*) in "Have I Got a Fellow for You"

—Edward Andrews (*Send Me No Flowers, The Glass Bottom Boat*) played Col. Fairburn, owner of *Today's World*, in several episodes

—Billy De Wolfe (*Tea for Two, Lullaby of Broadway*) was the uptight Mr. Jarvis, and also played Mr. Jarvis' Uncle Randy, and then himself in a cameo in "The Great Talent Raid"

—Patrick O'Neal (*Where Were You When the Lights Went Out?*) was Doris Martin's fiancé Jonathan Rusk

—John Astin (*That Touch of Mink*) guested on "The Father-Son Weekend," and Richard Steele (*With Six You Get Eggroll*) played his son in the same episode

—Lord Nelson (*Please Don't Eat the Daisies, With Six You Get Eggroll*) played the Martin's dog, Nelson

A few actors occasionally played the same role on *The Doris Day Show* including:

—Johnny Haymer as fashion designer Montagne in two episodes

—Jon Cypher was Sir Robert Kingsley in two episodes

—Larry Storch as kind-hearted fighter Duke Farentino in "The Prizefighter and the Lady," "The Duke Returns," "Duke the Performer" and "Duke's Girlfriend"

—Strother Martin as Tyrone Lovey in a pair of season one shows

—Isaa Arnal played Helen the receptionist in six episodes (one unbilled)

Several other actors played different roles throughout the course of *The Doris Day Show*, with a handful given a recurring character:

—Kaye Ballard was best remembered on the show as Angie Pallucci, starting in season three. Ballard first appeared in "Kidnapped."

—Bernie Kopell played Angie Pallucci's husband Louie in several episodes, but Kopell also played other characters in the episodes "A Woman's Intuition" and "The Magnificent Fraud."

—Paul Smith was known as the skirt-chasing Ron Harvey, but portrayed a husband and father of four with one on the way in "The Baby Sitter."

—Carol Worthington appeared in "Singles Only," "Doris Gets a Job," "A Woman's Intuition" and "Doris Finds an Apartment" before playing the recurring role of Ethel.

—Luis de Cordova played Jules in both "No More Advice ... Please" and "The Great Talent Raid," and other characters in "Debt of Honor," "Doris Meets a Prince" and "The Woman Hater."

—Hal Smith was different drunks in "Let Them Out of the Nest" and "The Baby Sitter" before becoming Buck Webb's friend Merle in "Buck's Portrait" and "You're as Old as You Feel."

—Cesare Danova, known to fans as Carlo Benadetti in both "When in Rome, Don't" and "Cover Girl," was first a royal in "Doris Meets a Prince."

—Gordon Jump went onto to fame in the late 1970s with *WKRP in Cincinnati*, but was seen in several non-recurring roles on *The Doris Day Show*: "Doris Strikes Out," "A Woman's Intuition," "Doris Finds an Apartment," "The Forward Pass" and "A Fine Romance."

—Ceil Cabot was comic relief in "Billy's First Date," "There's a Horse Thief in Every Family Tree," "The Hoax" and "Byline ... Alias Doris."

—Lisa Gerritsen portrayed Jackie in "The Black Eye" and "The Friend," then later played in "Billy's First Date."

—Walter Sande was Doc Carpenter in two episodes, a different doctor in "*Today's World* Catches the Measles," then Santa Claus in "Whodunit, Doris."

—Joey Forman was in "Doris Goes to Hollywood," "Charity Begins in the Office" and "Byline ... Alias Doris."

—Peggy Rea appeared in "The Friend," "The Clock," "The Baby Sitter" and "Hospital Benefit."

—Elvia Allman was in "The Feminist," "Charity Begins in the Office" and "Jimmy the Gent."

—Estelle Winwood played in "The Antique," "Doris the Spy" and "Charity Begins in the Office."

—De De Young was seen in "The Great Talent Raid," "Col. Fairburn Takes Over" and "Lassoin' LeRoy."

—Lavina Dawson appeared in "The Feminist," "Charity Begins in the Office" and "The Health King."

—Scott Perry acted in "Kidnapped," "Col. Fairburn Takes Over" and "Skiing, Anyone?"

—Winifred Coffin was seen in "Charity Begins in the Office" and as Clara Bixby (Doris Day's real-life nickname among friends) in "Lassoin' LeRoy."

—Woodrow Parfey played in "The Uniform," "Buck's Portrait," "The Black Eye" and "The Friend."

And there are other stars Day never worked with in films who appeared in the series including Tony Bennett who played himself in "Tony Bennett Is Eating Here," Andy Griffith in "The Great Hoax," Ricardo Montalban in "Billy's First Date," Rory Calhoun in "Cover Girl," Jodie Foster in "The Baby Sitter" and Peter Lawford as the recurring love interest Dr. Peter Lawrence. A longtime favorite of Day's was Lew Ayres, who played multi-millionaire William Tyler in two two-part episodes ("Doris Hires a Millionaire" and "Doris Leaves *Today's World*"). Another favorite of Day's, Van Johnson was Charlie Webb ("Cousin Charlie" and "The Albatross").

DORIS DAY'S BEST FRIENDS

Christian Broadcast Network (The Family Channel;
U.S.A Cable Television) / 1985-86 / 30 minutes

TELEVISED:
Premiered July 16, 1985 Sundays 7:00 P.M. (EST)

CREDITS:
Executive Producers: David Freyss, Terry Melcher; *Producer:* Dan Evans; *Director:* Joe Coleman; *Writers:* Terry Melcher, Dan Evans; *Music Directors:* Terry Melcher, Bill House; *Director of Photography/Post Production Supervisor:* Randy Franken; *Features Producer/Production Coordinator:* George Atkinson; *Features Pro-*

ducer/Reporter: Steve Reid; *Videotape Editors:* John Rossi, Steve Childress, Dennis Gross, Brad Rothberg, Lisa Byrne, Roger Vater, Mike Malpass; *Unit Production Manager:* Jerry Cardwell; *Make up:* Michelle Rede; *Wardrobe:* Connie Edney; *Hairstylists:* Barbara Lampson, Jon Thanos; *Assistant Directors:* Dick Broder, Greg Quant; *Researchers:* John Jenney, Carol-Ann Touchberry; *Executive in Charge of Production:* Tim Robertson; *Theme Song "Best Friend" written by* Terry Melcher, Bill House; *Performed by:* Doris Day.

EPISODES:

1   Guest: Rock Hudson

Suffering from AIDS, Hudson made his last public appearance on this show where he reminisced with Day. There was a segment on the Lambs Program, which combines the mentally retarded and animals into a fruitful enterprise. This was followed by instructions on how to choose the right pet for your family. The show ended with a montage of Hudson-Day stills and Doris singing "My Buddy."

2   Guest: Les Brown and His Band of Renown

Les Brown and his Band paid Day a visit while on a concert tour. Brown asked Day to talk about her Pet Foundation and why she got involved with animals. Dr. Tom Kendall talked about the importance of spaying and neutering, and said that nine out of ten animals taken to animal shelters are put to sleep. Day concluded the show with a lip-synched version of "Sentimental Journey" with the band.

3   Guest: Robbie Benson

On a Carmel road, Benson encountered a stray dog and Day helped him save it. They took it to the veterinarian to be checked for illness. The vet told them that they are required by law to put the animals to sleep "after about three days" if they are not claimed or adopted. Benson suggested a friend of his may want to adopt the dog, which Day called "Barney." A story on the caring of the animals at the San Diego Zoo was shown.

4   Guest: Denver Pyle

Visiting Day in this episode was Pyle, who had played her father on *The Doris Day Show* while directing many of the series' episodes. Day spoke about the dangers of having dogs ride in the open back of the truck, and said they should travel in the cab. A segment followed on how to give first aid to an injured animal. A short on a day in the life of a show horse was followed by a visit to Joan Embry's home, where she showed her Toucan bird.

5   Guest: Earl Holliman

Holliman captured and delivered a stray dog to Day; it happened to belong to Day's neighbor. He and Day spoke about the importance of identification tags on animals, and Holliman talked about the Actors and Others for Animals celebrity fair. A segment on pet care concentrating on ticks and fleas was shown.

6   Guest: Dr. Kendall

Dr. Kendall spoke about pet health insurance. There was a feature on the Leader Dogs for the Blind and the people canines help. Day told how she found Biggest, her favorite canine companion.

7   Guest: Joan Fontaine

Joan Fontaine had just acquired a new Labrador retriever. Day convinced the actress to have the dog professionally trained rather than doing it herself because dogs learn by association. A segment on Sandy, the dog from the musical *Annie,* followed. The way to take your pet with you on an airline was shown, as was a story on feline leukemia virus.

8   Guest: Cleveland Amory

Day introduced her grandson Ryan Paul Melcher while looking at the horses in the stable. Day spoke with Cleveland Amory about his group's fight in rescuing wild horses, goats, burros and other animals. The pair talked about the different animal leagues working together and getting legislation to stop testing on animals. A segment on Amory's Black Beauty Ranch was included, as was animal poisoning.

9   Guest: Gretchen Wyler

A segment on the Monterey Bay Aquarium was shown, followed by a visit to Sea World. Day interviewed Gretchen Wyler, who spearheaded making public the tactics of laboratory testing on animals and the push to make changes in legislation.

10   Guest: Mickey Gilley

While conversing, Gilley admitted to Day that he didn't have a dog and showed interest in Barney, one of Day's dogs. But she declined to give him up because Barney has "two wives. He's a Mormon." She suggested he go to the local SPCA and adopt a couple of dogs or cats. Day talked about her Pet Foundation and a segment was shown on the headquarters with Judy Ruby. Following was a segment on the seriousness of and how to care for epilepsy in dogs.

11   Guest: Danny Cooksey

Child star Danny Cooksey played a bank president in a skit in which Day asked him for a loan to build a vet clinic. The pair went to Day's ranch to view her animals. The pros and cons on giving pets as gifts, especially during Christmas, was discussed. A story on George Bennett followed. Bennett was in a car accident with his dog, and the animal experienced multiple back fractures and the loss of its hind legs. Against the vet's opinions, Bennett decided to keep the dog and care for it.

12 Guest: CARDA

The California Rescue Dog Association (CARDA) was featured in this episode. Several CARDA dogs were used to save lives in the Mexico City earthquake, and the organization used dogs to locate missing people, from backpackers to avalanche victims. It was explained how the dogs were trained to find people. A segment on back problems dogs experience followed.

13 Guest: Alan Shepard

A rocket lands in Day's backyard containing Alan Shepard and a stray dog. Shepard spoke about space travel and the use of animals in the space program. There was a segment on Rockin' Hoskins and the K9 Comets, a group of performing dogs who retrieve Frisbees. The importance of vaccinations and yearly exams of pets was discussed.

14 Guest: Howard Keel

In a spoof of *Calamity Jane*, Day's stagecoach was held up with the robber mistaking her for Dinah Shore and then Patti Page. She was reunited with Wild Bill Hickok (Keel) when he arrived to rescue her. Keel talked about acting on *Dallas* and recording a recent album. A segment on the reptile garden at the San Diego Zoo and the preparation of meals for the animals was shown.

15 Guest: Kaye Ballard

Ballard visited Day (whom she calls Clara; Ballard had played Day's landlady on *The Doris Day Show*). Dr. Kendall told about the importance of dog's diets and the dangers of generic dog foods. A segment on Universal Studio's animal actors training program followed.

16 Guest: Monterey County SPCA

Day introduced members of the Monterey County SPCA chapter who spoke about the ways to adopt an animal, as well as caring for animals already placed in homes and the free spay and neuter day. A segment on the North Shore Animal League in Port Washington, New York, followed. Dr. Kendall discussed heartworms in dogs and how to treat them.

17 Guest: Angie Dickinson

Day met Dickinson for lunch, where Day asks her for help by joining her pet organization. When the pair discover neither have any money on them, the manager of the restaurant telephones the sheriff. But the officer recognizes Day and sings "Secret Love" to her, thinking it may be his lucky break. A story on Chicago's police horse patrol unit followed. A segment on "Tom Cats" and neutering cats concluded the episode.

18 Guest: Robert Wagner

Day and guest Robert Wagner rode horses then talked about his show *Hart to Hart* and about his racehorse. There was a segment on the Animal Care and

Education Center in Rancho Sante Fe, California, where there is a program on therapeutic horseback riding for the handicap. A story on influenza and cats followed.

19 Guests: Tony Randall, Ryan Melcher

Tony Randall (who co-starred in the three Hudson-Day films) was supposed to visit Day, but a stray he found just had puppies and he had to stay in New York. Day and her grandson Ryan introduced a new addition to the family, a puppy named Aggie. Dr. Kendall spoke about home remedies for pets, and a segment on hearing dogs for the deaf was featured.

20 Guest: Loni Anderson

Day goes whale-watching with Anderson. A segment on the Cannery Road Foundation in Monterey was shown. The importance of spaying and neutering in cats and a story on cat's reproductive cycles followed.

21 Guest: Jill St. John

Day and St. John go on a hayride driven by Robert Wagner. St. John talks about her home in Aspen and of her culinary skills for humans and animals. There was a story on a wildlife preserve called Wildlife Way Station in Rancho Santa Fe, California, which provides homes for wild animals who were either abused, injured or homeless. The importance of pet travel was discussed.

22 Guest: Gary Collins

On her way back from the vet, Day's truck tire had a blowout and she was offered a ride by Gary Collins. At Day's home, the two talked about their pets and Collins' animal experiences in Kenya while making *Born Free*. Day's daughter-in-law, Jacqueline, hosted a segment on animal training for films. A story on internal parasites in pets followed.

23 Guest: Gwen May

Day introduced Gwen May in this episode. May and her family had an organization which found homes for lost animals and cared for young abandoned animals in and around Carmel Valley. Day divulged that she purchased her property through May's husband. Dr. Kendall spoke about canine heart disease, and a story about the San Francisco SPCA's use of animals in human therapy was shown.

24 Guest: Tony Bennett

Day welcomed Bennett, who was in Carmel showing his paintings. A feature on a friendship between a cheetah and a golden retriever was shown. Day introduced Dr. Edward Jarvis, a chiropractor who treated Day. He spoke about chiropractic treatments for animals.

25 Guest: Connie Edney

Day introduced her family of dogs, then Day's friend and the series wardrobe person Connie Edney was featured in a story about her and her dog Lulu, who Day placed with during *The Doris Day Show*. There was a segment on Sue Stron, a quadriplegic who was cared for by a monkey named Henrietta. Dr. Kendall introduced a segment on hip displasia (displacement) in dogs.

26   Guest: Leslie Nielsen

Nielsen spoke to Day about the series *The Blue Frontier* which he hosted. A segment on great whale sharks and penguins from the series was shown. Day introduced her dog Honey, who survived cancer, and a segment on cancer research and treatment in dogs and cats was shown. Steve Reed spoke about the white arctic wolf, an endangered species.

VARIETY SHOWS

The Doris Mary Anne Kapplehoff Special
CBS / Sunday, March 14, 1971 10:00 P.M. EST / 60 minutes

Featuring: Doris Day, Perry Como, Rock Hudson
Executive Producers: Don Genson, Terry Melcher; Producers: Saul Ilson, Ernest Chambers; Director: Bill Foster; Writers: Saul Ilson, Ernest Chambers, Gary Belkin, Alex Barris; Music Director: Jimmie Haskell

SONGS:
Doris Day: "Both Sides Now"; "Gypsy in My Soul"; "Hurry! It's Lovely Up Here"; "It's Magic" / "Sentimental Journey" (medley); "Secret Love" / "Who Will Buy?" / "The 59th Street Song (Feelin' Groovy)" / "Ob-la-di, Ob-la-da" (medley); "Them Was the Good Old Days"; "You Must've Been a Beautiful Baby"
Doris Day and Perry Como: "Everybody Loves a Lover" / "Meditation" / "Quiet Nights of Quiet Stars" (medley); "In the Summertime" / "You Don't Want My Love" / "If I Had to Live My Life Over" / "Let Me Call You Sweetheart" (medley); "When You Were Sweet Sixteen"
Perry Como: "Didn't We?"

The special opens with a filmed outdoor sequence in which Day rides a bicycle. The soundtrack plays Day singing "Secret Love" and a medley of songs from the musical *Oliver!*, Simon & Garfunkel and the Beatles. On a garden set inside, Day introduces her dogs and presents guest star Perry Como, who solos with "Didn't We?"

Day introduces and comments over a montage of current fashions she models, intercut by two song-and-dance skits. She and Como then do an extended medley of songs. The hostess teases herself about "crying buckets of tears" in her films, which is followed with film clips illustrating the fact. Rock Hudson makes a surprise appearance at the end of the clips. Day concludes the special with versions of "Both Sides Now," "It's Magic" and "Sentimental Journey."

The title is Doris Day's real, full name—although "Kapplehoff" is misspelled.

REVIEW:

"As a first special effort, it was canny showcasing for Miss Day in a format comfortable to her, and informal warmth was enough despite a tendency for the content to be more looking-back than forward. One could have hoped for a demonstration of her ample comedy-playing capabilities, but as it was, all that charm and lilting melody was quite satisfactory."—*Variety*

EMMY NOMINATION:

Outstanding Writing Achievement in Comedy, Variety or Music for a Special Program

Doris day toDay

CBS / Wednesday, February 19, 1975 9:00 P.M. EST / 60 minutes

Featuring: Tim Conway, Rich Little, John Denver, The Locker Dancers
Producer: George Schlatter; Director: Tony Charmoli; Writers: Digby Wolfe, George Schlatter; Music Director: Tommy Oliver

SONGS:

Doris Day: "Day by Day"; "Midnight at the Oasis"; "The Way We Were"
Doris Day and Tim Conway: "My Baby Makes Me Proud"
Doris Day and John Denver: "Exactly Like You"; "Follow Me"; "Sing a Sunshine Song" / "You Are the Sunshine of My Life" / "Sunshine and Lollipops" / "You Are My Sunshine" / "Sunshine on My Shoulders" / "Sing a Sunshine Song" (medley) / "Tea for Two" / "Did You Ever See a Dream Walking?" / "Give Me a Little Kiss" / "On the Atchison, Topeka and Santa Fe" / "Put on a Happy Face" / (medley–changed lyrics)
Doris Day and Rich Little: "Everybody Loves a Lover" / "Young at Heart" / "Teacher's Pet" / "There Are Such Things" / "Love Me or Leave Me" / "Secret Love" / "With a Song in My Heart" / "Whatever Will Be, Will Be" / "Everybody Loves a Lover" (medley)
Doris Day, John Denver, Rich Little and Tim Conway: "Anything Goes"

Doris Day's second special is in the same variety format as her first, but this outing includes more guest stars and comedy than the first.

Day opens the special with "Anything Goes" and introduces her guest stars, who join her in the song. She then sings "Day by Day" (from *Godspell*), accompanied by casually and formally dressed musicians.

Day and John Denver sing "Exactly Like You" and a medley of songs with the lyrics changed. The pair also duet on a medley of "Sunshine" songs.

In a comedy sketch, Tim Conway and Day play honeymooners in a mobile home park, and in another Conway is her over-eager husband. Rich Little provides imitations of several of Day's film co-stars including Clark Gable, Cary Grant, James Stewart, Kirk Douglas, Frank Sinatra, Jack Lemmon and James Cagney, while Day sings parts of songs from her films co-starring the actors.

The special ends with a reprise of "Day by Day."

REVIEW:

"*Doris day toDay* was an entertaining, fast-moving hour showing a radiant Doris Day who looked sensational both above and below the neck.... Particularly enjoyable was the rapport she had with Denver. They did more than one duet together and the Sunshine medley was terrific."—Sue Cameron, *the Hollywood Reporter*

EMMY NOMINATION:

Outstanding Continuing or Single Performance by a Supporting Actor in Variety or Music: John Denver

SPECIAL APPEARANCES

The John Denver Show
ABC / December 1, 1974 / 60 minutes

Featuring: Doris Day, George Gobel, Dick Van Dyke
Producers: Rich Eustis, Al Rogers; Director: Bill Davis; Writers: Ray Jessel, Harry Lee Scott, and Rich Eustis, Al Rogers; Musical Director: Milt Okun; Executive Producer: Jerry Weintraub

SONGS:

John Denver and Doris Day: "By the Light of the Silvery Moon" (with alternate lyrics); "(On) Moonlight Bay" (with alternate lyrics); "I'll See You in My Dreams" (with alternate lyrics)

John Denver's second special opens with Denver talking about his high school friends followed by a performance of "Thank God I'm a Country Boy." A Pinocchio skit and dance routine with Dick Van Dyke follows. Denver remarks and praises the fiftieth anniversary of the Wilderness System, then performs "Rocky Mountain Suite."

Denver introduces Doris Day. A skit recreates a rebellious teenaged Denver, with his father (George Gobel) telling him he should strive for a girl like Doris Day. The teenager daydreams of starring in films with and ultimately marrying Doris Day.

Denver sings "Sweet Surrender" then follows with a magic tricks performance with Van Dyke.

The American Film Institute Salute to James Cagney
CBS / March 18, 1974 / 90 minutes

Hosted by: Frank Sinatra; Introduced by: Charlton Heston
Featuring: Doris Day, Kirk Douglas, Frank Gorshin, Bob Hope, Jack Lemmon, Shirley MacLaine, Ronald Reagan, George C. Scott, George Segal, George Stevens, Jr., Cicely Tyson, John Wayne
Producer: Paul W. Keyes; Director: Bill Foster; Writers: Paul W. Keyes, Marc London, and David Panich; Executive Producer: George Stevens, Jr.

James Cagney retired from films in 1961 and had not made a formal public appearance until this tribute, the second AFI fete. The actual event occurred on March 13, attended by 1,360 people who paid $125 a ticket to attend. The event lasted five hours, but was condensed for televising a scant five days later.

Day's appearance at the American Film Institute fete to James Cagney was a rarity since she simply did not attend many industry events, let alone speak at one of them. She only consented to the televised event because she held Cagney in high regard—a compliment he returned to Day on many occasions.

Sinatra introduced Day, who remarked that working with Cagney was a joy, and added: "Anyone who ever worked with you knows you're more than just an actor. You don't play a character, you live the character. You breathe life into your own performance and make the rest of us look really good." A clip of Day singing "You Made Me Love You" from *Love Me or Leave Me* followed her speech.

OTHER TELEVISION APPEARANCES

Although Doris Day shied away from television early in her career, primarily because she was busy with films and music, she eventually made appearances which only became more frequent as the years passed. She used the medium to help discuss her television shows and her book, and later for her animal causes and to promote *The Love Album* CD. Day also consented to appear on a handful of later projects that told her life story.

Some of Day's television appearances were cameos, such as speaking a few seconds to the emcee at the world premiere showing of 1954's *A Star Is Born*, and in the 1952 documentary *Screen Snapshots: Hollywood Night Life*. Another rarity is the show "So You Want a Television Set" from 1953 with Phyllis Coates.

Day's television appearances include:

What's My Line, mystery guest June 20, 1954 (CBS, U.S.)

The Ed Sullivan Show 1956 (CBS, U.S.)

What's My Line, mystery guest September 8, 1957 (CBS, U.S.)

30th Annual Academy Awards, presenter Best Screenplay Oscars March 26, 1958 (NBC, U.S.)

31st Academy Awards, presenter Best Cinematography Oscar April 6, 1959 (NBC, U.S.)

32nd Academy Awards, nominee and presenter Best Song Oscar April 4, 1960 (ABC, U.S.)

The Tonight Show November 26, 1973 (NBC, U.S.)

The Tonight Show September 2, 1974 (NBC, U.S.)

The Merv Griffin Show 1975 (syndicated, U.S.)

Today 1975 (NBC, U.S.)

The Mike Douglas Show 1976 (syndicated, U.S.)

The Tonight Show January 16, 1976 (NBC, U.S.)

Good Morning America (five-part series) May 23 through 27, 1983 (ABC, U.S.)

Various news shows of press conference announcing *Doris Day's Best Friends* July 1985

Hour Magazine (three-part series) November 25 through 27, 1985 (syndicated, U.S.)

Entertainment Tonight (*Entertainment This Weekend*) "Hollywood's Wildest Stars" (three-part series, host) 1988 (syndicated, U.S.)

46th Annual Golden Globe Awards February 1989 (TBS, U.S.)

I Don't Even Like Apple Pie documentary March 1989 (BBC, U.K.)

Doris Day: A Sentimental Journey documentary 1991 (PBS, U.S.)

Good Morning America 1993 (ABC, U.S.)

Vicki! October 1993 (syndicated, U.S.)

Entertainment Tonight October 1993 (syndicated, U.S.)

Des O'Connor Tonight October 1994 (ITV, U.K.)

Don't Pave Main Street: Carmel's Heritage (Clint Eastwood, host, with special appearance by Doris Day) 1994 (U.S.)

Pebble Mill Show 1995 (BBC, U.K.)

TELEVISION SHOWS THAT MIGHT HAVE BEEN

Apart from a handful of interviews and documentaries, Doris Day has not appeared on television since 1985. As with films, Day has been given countless offers to act in television, especially in guest roles. A few of the major projects offered to her:

Variety reported in the late 1950s a TV series based on *Calamity Jane* to star Day after she completed filming *The Pajama Game*. It was to be a 39-episode, $2 million production with three directors—one each for comedy skits, musical sequences and dramatic scenes. The series was not realized after her box office clout increased and her concentration remained on films for the next ten years.

In 1982, Day admitted, "The people who did *McMillan and Wife* offered me a new series that I liked—about a woman who ran a column like Ann Landers." Day turned down the offer as she was busy building her house in Carmel.

She was allegedly offered the lead in *Murder, She Wrote* but declined. Angela Lansbury accepted the role and worked on the series, which lasted for more than decade on CBS.

Day declined a 1983 TV film, *West Side Waltz*, with Katharine Hepburn. The two would have played spinster sisters, one a violinist, the other a pianist. The pathos between the two characters may have re-established Day's talents as a dramatic actress in the public's view.

In 1990 it was announced that the ABC television network secured a multipicture deal with Doris Day. The agreement called for her to star in three TV films a year as a recurring character. The films were to be shot in and near Carmel, and to be televised during the 1991–92 TV season. Nothing resulted as it was simply a rumor and Day had not consented to the idea.

Selected Bibliography

Alpert, Hollis. "Enough! Enough!" *Saturday Review*, circa 1956, page 29.

Amory, Cleveland. "The Dog Catcher of Beverly Hills." *TV Guide*, June 3, 1972, page 34–40.

Armstrong, Lois. "Doris Day Has Her Day in Court—And Wins $22.8 Million." *People*, October 7, 1974, pages 36–37.

Braun, Eric. *Doris Day*. London: Orion Books Ltd, 1998.

Casper, Joseph Andrew. *Stanley Donen*. Metuchen, N.J.: Scarecrow, 1983.

Considine, Shaun. *Bette and Joan: The Divine Feud*. London: Century Hutchinson, 1989.

Counts, Kyle. "More 'Pillow Talk'?" Los Angeles *Times Calendar*, September 2, 1990, page 36.

Cowan, Ronnie. "Doris Day: 'My Most Costly Mistake as a Wife.'" *Ladies' Home Journal*, January 1973, page 87, 127–28.

Davidson, Bill. "The Change in Doris Day." *TV Guide*, February 20, 1971, page 30–33.

_____. "Doris Day—Her Fortunes, Her Fears, Her Failures, Her Faith." *Look*, June 20, 1961, page 36+.

Day, Doris. *Please Take Care of Your Best Friend*. Washington, D.C.: Doris Day Animal League, 1997.

"Day in Court." *Forbes*, October 15, 1974, page 102.

Decatur, Stephen. "Off-screen & off-guard Doris." *Ladies' Home Journal*, September 1975, page 86, 147.

"Did Sly Stone and Doris Day Have an Affair?" (www.slyfamstone.com/dorisday.html), September 1999.

Doan, Richard K. "Doris Day Takes the TV Plunge." *TV Guide*, May 13, 1967, page A-3.

The Doris Day Animal League. Website: www.ddal.org, October 1998+.

"Doris Day Cracks Rib in Film 'Fight,'" Los Angeles *Times*, July 12, 1963, part I page 2.

"The Doris Day Show." *Variety* reviews, September 24, 1969; September 23, 1970; September 22, 1971; September 20, 1972.

Bibliography

"Doris Day Is Honored by Home Town, Cincy." *The Hollywood Reporter*, March 20, 1951.

"Doris Day *OK!*" *Magazine* interview, January 1996.

"Doris Day Pictures Herself as Abandoned Bride, Gets Divorce." *Herald-Express*, May 31, 1949.

"Doris Day Today." Gossip Magazine.com (www.gossipmagazine.com/managearticle.asp), 2001.

"The Doris Mary Anne Kappelhoff Special." *Variety* review, March 17, 1971.

Durslag, Melvin. "She Goes Along." *TV Guide*, April 18, 1970, page 22–24.

Gilbert, Bob, and Garry Theroux. *The Top Ten 1956–Present*. New York: Fireside Books, Simon & Shuster, 1982.

Haddad-Garcia, George. "Doris Day—the Sunshine Girl." *Hollywood Studio Magazine*, April 1980, page 9–11.

Hallowell, John. "Will the Real Doris Day Sing Out." New York *Times*, October 27, 1968.

Haskell, Molly. "An Interview with Doris Day." *Ms.* (issue unknown), 1975, page 54–58, 112.

Heffernan, Harold. "Doris Day: Will She Have a New Career at 43?" (source unknown), May 21, 1967.

Holland, Jack. "Doris Day: 'I Say Movies Should Burst with Sex and Nudity.'" *TV Radio Mirror*, July 1970, pages 28–34, 95–96.

"Honeymoon Daze." *Movie Life*, July 1951, pages 16–18.

Hopper, Hedda. "British Press Lauds Doris Day's Comedy." Los Angeles *Times*, June 2, 1959, page 26.

_____. "Happy Day!" Chicago Sunday *Tribune* Magazine, July 6, 1958, page 18, 20.

_____, and James Brough. *The Whole Truth and Nothing But*. New York: Doubleday, 1962.

Hotchner, A. E. "Doris Day Today." *Ladies' Home Journal*, June 1982, page 75–77, 123–28.

_____, with Doris Day. *Doris Day: Her Own Story*. New York: William Morrow, 1975.

Hudson, Rock, with Sara Davidson. *His Story*. New York: William Morrow, 1986.

Jacobi, Ernest. "If You Like What You Love You're in Luck." *Photoplay*, February 1955, page 49, 103–04.

Kieslowski, Krzysztof. "Doris Day Interviewed." BBC Online (www.bbc.co.uk/movies/archive/day/interview), February 1999.

Laredo, Joseph F. *It's Magic: Doris Day 1947–1950*. Germany: Bear Family Records, 1993.

_____. *Move Over, Darling: Doris Day 1960–1967*. Germany: Bear Family Records, 1997.

_____. *Que Será: Doris Day 1956–1959*. Germany: Bear Family Records, 1996.

_____. *Secret Love: Doris Day 1951–1955*. Germany: Bear Family Records, 1995.

Logan, Ann. "The Happiness Doris Day Denies Her Son." *Silver Screen*, May 1969, page 39, 57–60.

"Melcher Dies; Music Ties to Stay the Same." *Billboard*, May 4, 1968.

"Morning Report: Que Será, Será." Los Angeles *Times*, October 3, 1990, page F2.

Morris, George. *Doris Day: A Pyramid Illustrated History of the Movies*. New York: Pyramid Communications, 1976.

"One Minute Interview: Doris Day." *Gossip*, July 1976, page 60.

Parsons, Louella. "The Bright Days of Doris Day." Los Angeles *Examiner* "Pictorial Living," March 23, 1958, page 31, 35.

Patrick, Pierre. "A Movie Star's Sitcom Surprise: 'The Doris Day Show.'" *Television Chronicles*, No. 6.

"Pierre Patrick Interviews Doris Day, *The Doris Day Show*." Discovering Doris website (www.geocities.com/SunsetStrip/Amphitheatre/6146/tvshow.htm) June 1999.

Rich, Hortense. "The Truth About Mother and Me" (source unknown), page 24–27, 54–55.

Rockwell, Ruth. "Doris Day Dragged into Scandal." *TV Radio Mirror*, December 1970, pages 40, 96, 98.

Rollin, Betty. "Doris Day: Miss Apple Pie Hits TV." *Look*, November 26, 1968, page 54–56, 60.

Ryon, Art. "Rift Separates Doris Day and Marty Melcher." Los Angeles *Times*, December 1, 1962, part II, page 9.

Schallert, Edwin. "Doris Day Needs No Song to Get Others to Listen." Los Angeles *Times*, April 25, 1954.

Scott, John L. "It's Magic How Doris Day Sings Way to Film Peaks." Los Angeles *Times*, February 27, 1949.

Shapiro, Nat. *An Encyclopedia of Quotations About Music*. New York: DaCapo.

Simon, George T. *The Big Bands*. New York: Schirmer Books, 1981.

Smith, Liz. New York *Post*, "tempy sez!" (www.geocities.com/tempzine/3.htm), February 2003.

Thomas, Bob. "An Intimate Talk with Doris Day." *Good Housekeeping*, September 1979, pages 52–55, 58, 60.

Thompson, Howard. "On a Dawn of a Bright, New Day." New York *Times*, April 24, 1955.

Van Doren, Mamie, with Art Aveilhe. *Playing the Field—My Story*. New York: G. P. Putnam's Sons, 1987.

Viktek, Jack, and Jerry Oppenheimer. *Idol*. New York: Villard Books, 1986.

Wasserman, John L. "'I Don't Even Like Apple Pie.'" *TV Guide*, December 6, 1969, page 31–35.

Whitney, Dwight. "All Sugar, No Spice." *TV Guide*, December 28, 1968, page 18–21.

Documentary—Media Interviews

"A&E Biography: Doris Day," A&E cable, 1998.

"Des O'Conner Tonight," ITV television (U.K.), 1994.

"Doris Day: A Sentimental Journey," PBS (U.S.), 1991.

"Doris Day: The E! True Hollywood Story," E! cable station, 2003.

"Good Morning America" with David Hartman, Joan Lunden, ABC (U.S.), 1983, 1993.

"Hour Magazine" with Gary Collins (syndicated), 1985.

"I Don't Even Like Apple Pie," BBC (U.K.) 1989.

"The Merv Griffin Show" (syndicated), 1975.

"The Mike Douglas Show" (syndicated), 1976.

"Pebble Mill" show special with Gloria Hunniford (U.K.), 1995.

"Today" with Barbara Walters, NBC (U.S.), 1975.

"Vicki!" with Vicki Lawrence (syndicated), 1993.

Index

281